ROMAN
MILITARY
DRESS

ROMAN MILITARY DRESS

GRAHAM SUMNER

To Thomas Robinson 1927–2008

*and to my dearest Elaine, who has not only had to put up with
'Roman Military Dress' for far too many months but who has also had to
endure watching grown men parade in short skirts!*

All drawings and paintings are copyright of the author unless otherwise stated.

Back cover image: The Didymoi Hat, Egypt. (© *Dominique Cardon*)
Didymoi textile **D99.2511.4**., dated *c.*AD 96, excavations funded by the French Ministry of Foreign
Affairs and the French Institute for Oriental Archaeology (IFAO) in Cairo, under the direction of Dr
Hélène Cuvigny (CNRS). Restored by Ms Danièle Nadal, Laboratory Materia Viva, Toulouse.

First published 2009

The History Press
The Mill, Brimscombe Port
Stroud, Gloucestershire, GL5 2QG
www.thehistorypress.co.uk

Reprinted 2009

British Library Cataloguing in Publication Data.
A catalogue record for this book is available from the British Library.

ISBN 978 07524 4576 2

Typesetting and origination by The History Press
Printed in Great Britain

CONTENTS

FOREWORD

By John Peter Wild

A Roman legionary soldier in full battle dress is one of the most familiar figures of the ancient world. It is a potent symbol of latter-day perceptions, both colonial and post-colonial, of the character of the Roman Empire and the moving forces within it. Visual representations of the 'Roman soldier', however, rarely stand up to close scrutiny, not least by those who would question the evidence on which each detail is based.

The predominance given to military affairs in the study of the history and archaeology of the Roman provinces is due in no small measure to the influence of the classically-educated officer classes of the leading European powers during the past century and a half. The minutiae of soldiers' equipment and dress were of less concern to them, however, than the structure and prosopography of the Roman army. Academic studies followed a similar path. More recently, the rise of re-enactment groups and their desire to reconstruct the life of the Roman soldier in three dimensions has given urgency to new enquiries, not just tapping the archaeological record, representational art and literary and documentary sources, but also evaluating the emerging hypotheses by repeated experiment. Today, it is the re-enactor who can quote chapter and verse on an issue!

Graham Sumner is a leading artist in the field of military reconstruction. Dress may until now have played second fiddle to armour and weapons in that area, but in his three earlier short publications on the topic he has sought to redress the balance. The present volume provides him with a broader canvas on which to exhibit his work, and to marshal the evidence on which his reconstructions are based.

INTRODUCTION

Dicantes ei duas statuas equestres, pedestres duas habitu militari, sedentes civili habitu duas, item Divo Severo duas triumphales.

We ourselves shall dedicate to him statues, two on horseback, two on foot clad in the garb of a soldier, and two seated in civil garb, and likewise to the Deified Severus, two clad in the robes of a triumphal general. (SHA Opellius Macrinus VI.8.)

Even at the beginning of the twenty-first century a Roman soldier is still an instantly recognisable figure. Ancient Roman troops are often portrayed as part of a brutal military machine, in scarlet tunics and cloaks with metal strip or leather armour. It is a powerful stereotype reinforced by countless pictures of Roman triumphal sculpture, Hollywood biblical epics, television and stage productions, children's picture books, cartoons and latterly by modern day 'living history' re-enactors. But at least two questions must be asked. How accurate is this image and what is the evidence, if any, for Roman military clothing?

Although the arms and armour of the Roman soldier have received a great deal of attention, by comparison the study of the basic clothing worn by the soldiers has been sadly neglected. A recent weighty volume on the Roman army devoted less than a paragraph to soldiers' clothing! In 1968 the eminent textile archaeologist John Peter Wild wrote 'the student of archaeology of the provinces rightly directs his attention to those aspects of Roman material culture which are likely to contribute most to the political history of the period.' Luckily fashions change in archaeology as they do in costume, and archaeologists nowadays do not concentrate exclusively on Roman political life.

For many military historians, textiles lack the glamour and excitement of armour and weapons. Perhaps this is not surprising as in Britain and Northern Europe most textile finds are little more than brown rags. Maybe with more than a passing nod to Plutarch who wrote 'when the Sabines after their war against the Romans were reconciled with them it was agreed that their women should perform no other tasks for their households than those which were connected with spinning' (Rom. XV), Gillian Eastwood wrote in 1982 that textiles are only of interest to women!

To further complicate matters the spectacular discoveries of complete garments from the Roman period have fallen into two broad categories. They are either found outside the boundaries of the former Roman Empire, chiefly in Denmark or Germany, or are discovered in the deserts of Egypt. In the first instance they are almost certainly classified either as 'Barbarian',

'Migration period' or at best 'Roman Iron Age' and subsequently are deemed of little relevance to the Roman army. On the other hand garments found in Egypt are labelled 'Coptic' or worse because of their late date, classed as 'Byzantine' or even 'early medieval'. Under any of these convenient but misleading headings they are for the most part neglected by scholars and students of the Roman army.

A similar fate seems to have befallen the wonderful painted portraits of the Roman era also found in Egypt. Painted on wax in a technique known as encaustic painting, these vivid portraits offer a unique insight into the ancient world and are of special interest to costume students. In particular several portraits have been identified as Roman soldiers and some of them could be Centurions. Yet even books on Roman art display an almost cheerful indifference to these works, preferring instead to cram their pages with pictures of the Colosseum and the Pantheon as if there is a dearth of artistic material to utilise. Imagine the reaction to a book on the Impressionists which showed pictures of the Eiffel Tower rather than the paintings of Monet! When compiling the catalogue of evidence for colour, it was disheartening to finally track down some rare sources only to discover that many publications showed these colourful works of art, in monochrome. Furthermore the frustration felt on such occassions was often compounded when the accompanying narrative also failed to provide any description of what the colour of the clothing illustrated in these works might be.

In spite of this it should not be forgotten that the average Roman soldier, like his modern counterpart, spent far more of his service life in everyday dress or 'fatigues' than he did in 'battledress'. Furthermore if we are to believe some Roman sculptures as accurate portrayals, then for some soldiers clothing was their only protection! Roman soldiers off duty and out of armour were instantly recognisable when compared to the civilian population at large and soldiers were keen to stress both their group identity and status. The emperor Avidius Cassius for instance inspected the clothes, shoes and leg wrappings of his soldiers once a week. And even on one occasion threatened that if any soldier was caught off limits in his military dress, he could return to camp without it! (SHA. *Avid. Cass.* VI 2).

Although armour, equipment and dress accessories such as brooches and belt fittings feature in both the text and illustrations, this is not primarily another study of those subjects which have been covered extensively elsewhere and for works of that nature the reader is advised to consult the Bibliography for specialist publications dealing with these topics. Primarily this publication will deal with the principal garments worn by Roman soldiers. However on very rare occasions we also know that Roman soldiers wore completely non-military items of dress, at times perhaps even when they were on active service. Probably the most obvious occasion when this would happen would be when soldiers carried out undercover duties in which case they would dress in civilian clothing. One little known but important occasion when this occurred was during the governorship of Pontius Pilate in Judaea. Pilate had been forewarned of a potential demonstration against the building of an aqueduct in Jerusalem. As a precaution he therefore ordered some of his soldiers to dress in local clothes and mingle with the crowd. On a given signal from Pilate they broke up the demonstration by using clubs called a *fustis* which they had concealed beneath their cloaks, inflicting many casualties (Josephus *Ant.*3.2.). The duty Roster *P. Gen lat. Verso V* also lists one soldier as being *pagano cultu* – in 'plain clothes'.

Some tombstones show soldiers off duty – or rather they actually represent the deceased at his own funerary banquet. Therefore men are shown reclining on dining couches being attended by a servant as in life. They wear a loose tunic and drape their cloak around their body. This is how they would have appeared at home, away from the camp, or perhaps in more formal attire for dining and special occasions. When officers conducted religious services they would dress in civilian clothes, usually the toga, as depicted on the Bridgeness distance slab from Scotland. Sacrificial attendants would also wear the type of costume that can be seen in official sculptures depicting the emperor at a sacrifice. The Vindolanda documents also record other items of clothing which might be relevant here although the exact nature of many must for the time being remain speculative. They include undertunics, *subuclae*, and undercloaks, *subpaenulae*.

1 C. Vetienius Urbiquus a *Tubicen*, from a tombstone found in Cologne, now in the museum at St. Germaine en-Laye, France, and Sibbaeus, an auxiliary *Tubicen* serving with Cohors I Ituraeorum from Mainz. Both musicians choose to be represented on their funeral monuments in civilian rather than military dress.

2 T. Claudius Halotus, shown on his tombstone from Cologne. He was commander of an auxiliary cohort of Dalmatians and is dressed in civilian attire and even appears to hold a pet rabbit!

3 An attendant at a sacrifice. Detail from a sculpture in
Rome dating from the reign of Marcus Aurelius. The man
wears a sarong-like garment tied at the waist by a fabric
belt. Attendants at military sacrifices are shown on Trajan's
Column dressed in a similar manner.

4 M. Aemillus Durises shown
at his funeral banquet on his
tombstone found in Cologne. He
wears civilian clothing consisting
of a tunic draped around a short-
sleeved tunic.

5 Ares – an appropriately named weapons keeper (*custos armorum*) – is shown dressed in both military and civil style on his tombstone, now in the British Museum. Dating from the third century his military dress is comprised of a long-sleeved tunic and a *sagum* cloak. On his legs are what appear to be leg wrappings and he wears integrally laced boots. His civilian dress is the classic toga. © *Ross Cowan.*

   Garments evidently had new uses even after they were worn out; for instance, cloaks frequently became burial shrouds. There was a thriving second-hand clothes industry which cut up old garments into squares and made new items from them. Cato advised that this should be done with old tunics after new had been issued to farm workers (*de Agri.*, LIX). Evidence for this practice includes a partially complete tunic, discovered at Mons Claudianus in Egypt. This had in fact been assembled from the remains of an old cloak, as distinctive 'gamma' patterns normally found in the corners of cloaks were positioned haphazardly on the tunic. Old clothes could also be cut up and put to practical uses, such as packing for pottery or other valuable items, which might explain the textile remains found within the Corbridge armour hoard discovered near Hadrian's Wall.

   Soldiers undoubtedly cleaned their armour and equipment with old rags, while other worn out clothing might have been recycled and used as items such as leg bindings. Even less glamorous, some clothing was cut up and used as toilet paper, but it is generally in all these fragmentary states that the textiles themselves are ultimately preserved to be discovered by archaeologists. The development of Roman re-enactment societies since 1972 has stimulated both a general interest in Roman clothing and textiles, and a greater appreciation amongst academics of the value of practical reconstructions. For many years the British society 'The Ermine Street Guard' was the only society dealing with the Roman army and due to a lack of readily available scholarly material their garments were based almost entirely on observations of Roman monuments, in particular Trajan's Column.

   This study owes much to Nick Fuentes, who was himself involved with re-enactment and whose article 'The Roman Military Tunic' published in the *JRMES*, was the first work of its kind available in English. However, Fuentes himself admitted that his investigation was not exhaustive but if nothing else it was certainly divisive, as it split the re-enactment community over what colour the military tunic should be, humorously labelled the 'Tunic Wars'.

Since the publication of the article many new discoveries have been made and reports published, in particular from the excavations at Masada in Israel, at Vindolanda and Carlisle in England, and at other sites including Antinoe in Egypt and Carnuntum in Austria. Old finds have also been re-examined and together with the latest research this is enlarging the corpus of known textile finds on an almost daily basis. Also further clues to the colour of military clothing and the terminology that was originally used to describe them have been uncovered. It is hoped that this publication will raise awareness of this neglected subject and perhaps encourage others to study it further. Even with the limited space available it will hopefully illustrate how vast this subject really is and that a great deal of evidence is both already available and awaiting future discovery. At the very least it should provide answers to the two questions posed at the very beginning.

PART ONE

TUNICS AND CLOAKS

1

TUNICS

Tunica ab tuendo corpore, tunica ut (tu) endica

Tunica from tuendo 'protecting' the body: tunica as though it were tuendica. (Varro. *DLL*, V. 114)

REPUBLICAN TUNICS

Miles non timendus si vestitus, armatus, calciatus, et satur et habens aliquid in zonula

A soldier need not be feared if he is clothed, armed, shod, sated and has something in his money belt. (SHA, Severus Alexander, LII.3)

There is no physical evidence for the type of tunic used by the Roman army during the Republic, and reconstruction therefore relies on a combination of literary and artistic evidence. Well-known sculptures such as the Altar of Domitius Ahenobarbus and the Aemilius Paulus monument, while clearly influential on modern interpretations of Republican armour and equipment, actually reveal very little of the tunics themselves. This in itself can be deemed significant, as it confirms what the Roman writer Gellius said about early Roman tunics (*Noct. Act.*, VI, xii, 1–3) – that they were sleeveless and that the Romans considered long-sleeved tunics ridiculous (see also Virgil, *Aen*. IX, 616). Even worse accusations could be levelled at those who wore long-sleeved tunics, for moreover he states that one Publius Sulpicius Gallus was 'an effeminate man … who wore tunics which covered his whole hands.' (*Noct. Act.*VI. xii. 4.)

Another famous example of long sleeves being frowned upon was when Julius Caesar as a youth was openly criticised by the dictator Sulla. When Caesar appeared before the great man,

his dress was it seems unusual: he had added wrist-length sleeves with fringes to his purple striped senatorial tunic, and the belt which he wore over it was never tightly fastened … beware of that boy with the loose clothes! (Suet., *Caes*., XLV).

Situated between the Etruscan lands to the north and the Greek colonies to the south, the early Romans were clearly influenced in many ways by both cultures and this naturally extended to their clothing. However the first Roman tunics appear to have followed the types worn by the Iron Age Villanovan culture from central Italy. These early tunics were quite simple and decorated with coloured lines or dots. From the seventh century BC they became more elaborate and influenced by Etruscan fashion, including a very short tunic which only reached to the upper thigh and left the genitals exposed!

While the Greeks wore nothing beneath their tunics, a fact which can be observed in several artistic sources, the more austere Romans took to wearing a loin cloth. This was called called either a *subligaculum* or *campestre* (Ovid., *Fasti*, V.101). In the murals of the François Tomb at Vulci there is a white tunic trimmed with purple worn by Larth Ulthes. Other colours visible in Etruscan paintings indicate a wide spectrum of coloured tunics and include white, red, sand, ochre, brown, green, black and light blue. It is possible that these common colours were worn by the Roman plebs too, while the better equipped armoured hoplites and senior officers shown on the frieze of Praeneste are already wearing the purple clothing that became associated with later senior officers and emperors. The François tomb also shows a Roman warrior clad in a red tunic, but on special occasions and religious parades it seems the soldiers wore a white tunic (*candida vestis*), which was a symbol of purity. An example of one of these events was when soldiers transported the statue of Juno Regina from Veii to Rome in 396 BC (Livy, V, 22, 4). Livy says that 'after performing their ablutions and arraying themselves in white vestments [*candida vestis*] reverently entered the temple and in a spirit of holy dread placed their hands on the statue.' The Romans were not alone in this practice as Livy also tells us that a division of the Samnite army wore bleached linen clothes because they had consecrated themselves to the gods (Livy IX, 40, 2–3 and 40, 9).

Patricians and equestrians wore characteristic stripes of purple called *clavi*, a name which derived from the Latin word *clavus* meaning nail. These decorations were on the front and back of their white tunics. One of the Tribunes held senatorial rank and so was entitled to wear the wide *clavus* and so be *laticlavius*; the other Tribunes belonged to the middle-equestrian class so their tunics were decorated by narrower purple stripes – *angusticlavi*.

6 Esquiline tomb painting from Rome, which shows the surrender of the Samnite General Marcus Fannius to Consul Quintus Fabius. Behind Fabius on the extreme right are what appears to be his *cohors praetoria*, bodyguard who are dressed in white tunics. *After Revue Archéologique 1907, p.234. (See Col. Cat. (3))*.

7a South Italian warriors, possibly Sabellians, as depicted on local pottery dating to the fourth and third centuries BC. One warrior (top left) carries a belt and tunic over his shoulder, trophies of war. *Courtesy of Ross Cowan. (See colour plate 1 for a reconstruction.)*

7b Two Republican period cavalrymen from a relief in Mantua, Italy. They both wear short-sleeved tunics beneath their mail and scale armour.

Statuettes from Telamon and in the Villa Giulia, Rome, suggest that Republican tunics may have been slightly narrower than the subsequent early Imperial styles of tunic, but otherwise there does not appear to have been a great deal of difference. The early tunics were fastened at the waist by a simple leather belt, illustrated by a *Cornicen* or horn player on a relief from Osuna in Spain. Quintilian stated that centurions wore their tunics above the knee as can be seen on the tombstone of Minucius of Legio Martia from Padova (*Inst. Orat.*, XI, 138). Nevertheless the sculptural evidence suggests that this style was also worn by the other ranks too.

Officers of course continued to have even more elaborate styles. Durius, one of the officers in the army of Scipio, is recorded by Silius Italicus as having a garment (*vestis*) fringed or decorated with gold (*aurata*), probably of Punic or Iberian origin, '... tearing the gold embroidered garment from his breast!' (*Sil. It.*, XVI, 436).

EARLY IMPERIAL TUNICS

Metellus Pius in Hispania interrogatus, quid postera die facturus esset, 'tunicam meam, si eloqui posset,' inquit, 'comburerem'.

When Metellus Pius was in Spain and was asked what he was going to do the next day, he replied, 'if my tunic could tell, I would burn it!' (Frontinus., Strat, I. 1. 12)

Both Roman civilians and the military utilised a simple tunic which during the early Imperial period was normally very wide and sleeveless. It appears that tunics were scaled up or down proportionally from this very basic design to fit the individual. Roman tunic manufacture was rather basic. Two rectangular pieces of material were simply sewn together and closed with seams beneath the arms and down both sides. The neck and lower openings were therefore just selvedges,

8 Republican period warriors from Chieti, Telamon and the Villa Giulia in Italy. They all wear very short, short-sleeved tunics.

9 Tombstone of Minutius Lorarius centurion with *Legio Martia* found in Patavium, now in Padova, Italy. Lorarius wears a tunic and cloak with enclosed boots. © *Luca Bonacina Romanhideout.com. (See colour plate 5 for a reconstruction.)*

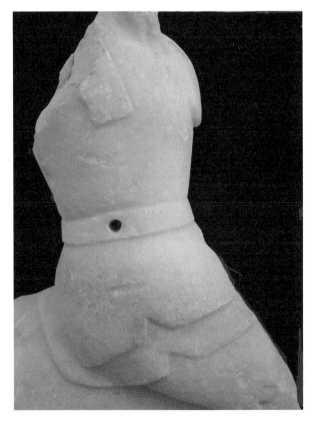

10 Roman soldiers from the Aemilius Paulus monument in Delphi, Greece. Two at least apparently wear mail shirts over short tunics. One cavalryman's tunic and mail shirt are both split at the lower side to allow freedom of movement. There is often no indication at this date that Roman cavalry had adopted the use of either trousers or *bracae*.

11 Fragment of a glass vessel from Vindolanda showing a gladiatorial combat. The referee wears a standard buff coloured Roman sleeveless tunic of the first century AD decorated with *clavi*. © *Vindolanda Museum*.

which made hemming unnecessary. A selvedge is a side border on both sides of the cloth which is formed automatically during the weaving process. The selvedge helped prevent some of the natural wear and tear to the edge of the garment, but it could also be reinforced. Two methods could be employed to do this. One was with the addition of a tablet woven border during the weaving process. The other method was a refinement of the selvedge technique known as a tubular selvedge. The latter was a popular skill employed by Roman and Gallo-Roman weavers, introduced into the empire from the North.

Fuentes stated that the Roman tunic of the early empire was narrow but the examples of complete tunics which survive from Israel and Egypt suggest otherwise. Even as late as the seventh century AD, Maurice (Maurikios) was still describing military tunics as broad and full (*Strat* 1.2). Pictorial evidence show workers in the clothing industry holding up tunics which are as wide as the person with their arms extended.

The only specific evidence discovered so far for the sizes of military tunics is *BGU VII* 1564, a papyrus copy from Egypt of an order for clothing and a blanket to be provided for the army in Cappadocia by the weavers of Philadelphia. This document dates from around AD 138. One tunic is specified in the document and this is 3½ cubits long (1.55m) and 3 cubits and 4 fingers wide (1.40m) weighing 3¾ minae (1.6kg), and costing 24 drachmae. Its size is roughly comparable with one of the largest tunic specimens found at Nahal Hever, Israel, and it is the same width as a tunic from Nubia. Still it is also interesting to note that it is much bigger in length than any of the Nahal Hever examples and in overall size larger than most other tunic remains found elsewhere. The measurements for *BGU VII* 1564 for example would dwarf the tunic sizes recommended by Cato for farm workers (*de Agri*, LIX), who states that they should be P.III S (1.07m) long.

Papyrus *BGU VII* 1564 specifies that all the garments should be made 'from fine soft white wool without dirt', and be 'well edged, pleasing and undamaged.' It is hard to imagine military uniforms being described that way today! The fact that most military garments would have been made from wool is supported by sculptural representations of tunics which in some cases are detailed enough to show the edging methods that were employed for wool garments rather than those for linen ones.

12 The Arch of Orange in southern France dating to the Augustan period shows at least three soldiers apparently in battle wearing only a tunic. The man on the right is even shown wearing a tunic that is tied into a knot behind the neck, a detail shown in several examples elsewhere. Apart from this curious fact the other details – such as the helmets and shields – appear to be quite accurately depicted.

13 A late Republican *Cornicen* depicted in a sculpture from Osuna near Seville in Spain.

14 Tunic plans.

A

B

Child's linen tunic from Nahal Hever, Israel, 0.38m long × 0.45m wide. *After Yadin.*

Military tunic after description from *BGU VII* 1564. 1.55m long x 1.40m wide.

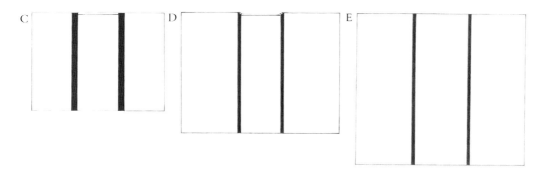

C

D

E

Nahal Hever, Tunic no. 6–210. 0.65m long × 0.90m wide. *After Yadin.*

Mons Claudianus, Egypt. Tunic A. 0.80m long × 1.07m wide. *After Mannering.*

Nahal Hever, Tunic 22–8–4. 1.0 long × 1.15m wide. *After Yadin.*

F

G

Nubia, Egypt Grave Q150. 1.27m long × 1.40m wide. *After Thurman and Williams.*

Khirbet Qazone, Jordan. 1.17m long × 1.42m wide. *After H. Granger-Taylor.*

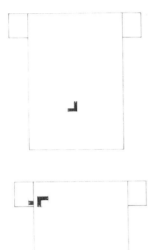

15 An example of a recycled tunic found at Mons Claudianus in Egypt's eastern desert. This tunic measured 1.0m long × 0.72m wide. It may have been worn by one of the poorer workers at the site.

16 Surviving tunic with *clavi* from Egypt. © *The British Museum.*

17 A–F: First century AD tunics on
tombstones from Germany.

A: Unknown,
Bingen-Bingerbrück.

B: Firmus,
Cohors Raetorum,
Andernach.

D: One of the finest depictions of the draped tunic in sculpture is this example from Nickenich in Germany. The character has been described as being a slave trader or even Hercules. Whoever he is he also seems to be wearing a fabric waistband. © *Rheinisches LandesMuseum Bonn.*

C: Unknown soldier, Bonn.

E: Unknown soldier, Bingen–Bingenbrück.   F: Unknown soldier, Bonn.

Because of the large size of tunics many surviving examples like those from Egypt and the woman's tunic from Les Martres-de-Veyre in France, have been shortened by tucks around the waist. It is conceivable therefore that when the military tunic from Philadelphia arrived at its destination it would have been altered in this manner by its owner or a military tailor. A humorous observation is provided by the writer Tertullian who comments that tunics should have been made shorter in the first place to avoid the need to gather up all the loose material (*de Pallio*, V). Furthermore it was possibly considered unsightly to show these tucks around the waist, and one method of concealing them could have been with a sash-like waistband called a *fascia ventralis*.

As yet the available evidence does not make it clear if military garments were produced and distributed in a wide variety of sizes. Egyptian documents such as *Columbia Papyrus IX* have the ambiguous Greek adjectives *teleios* and *paratelios* associated with tunics, which could conceivably relate to different types, sizes, qualities or finish.

Sculptural Evidence
Some first century tombstones show a quite elaborate style of tunic, in particular a group from the Rhineland at Andernach, Bonn, Bingen-Bingerbruck, Cologne and Mainz. A few others are known from London and Cherchel in Algeria. A figure – possibly a slave trader – from Nickenich in Germany clearly wears one too. The numerous folds that the sculptors have gone to great lengths to replicate would seem to suggest that these tunics were made from a fine material like linen, although this is not supported by archaeological finds. The linen might have been stiffened and offered some degree of protection. On the Mainz Column base one of the fighting legionaries – perhaps a marine from one of the Adiutrix legions – even appears to be wearing one of these tunics over another tunic rather than armour. A wide waist belt or waistband is also associated with these tunics. The band or belt may have helped to form the curved drapes which are a distinctive feature of these tunics.

Modern attempts to recreate this effect have not been entirely successful, leading to a number of conclusions. Firstly, the sculptures themselves may simply illustrate an artistic convention, but other details such as the side-arms and belts appear to be corroborated by archaeological finds. Secondly, the material may have been pleated and ironed, perhaps copying a tradition practised in ancient Egypt and which may also be discerned in Palmyrene art. It is interesting that some of the soldiers whose tunics are shown this way – such as Pantera and Hyperanor from Bingen – originated from the East. Pleating and ironing tunics would obviously be difficult on campaign but not too far-fetched for a tunic prepared for a parade. Another method might have used starched linen, a practice known by the ancient Egyptians and still used in parts of Italy today where it is called musolina.

Alternatively, the tunic may not have been made from one piece but rather two. Illustrations of the short kilt worn by gladiators also reveal the same curved draped effect, although not as extreme as those seen on the Rhineland tombstones. As gladiators generally wear no upper garment it is possible to see how the draped effect is created: by pulling up surplus material into bunches which are then held in place by a wide waist belt. If soldiers also wore this arrangement it would mean that they would have to wear a short tunic more like a modern t-shirt, under or over a separate kilt. What may confirm this theory is that on many of the Rhineland tombstones the drapery on the upper body does not correspond to that on the lower part of the tunic. A final possibility is that before the military belts were put on, a waistband (*fascia ventralis*) was worn to flatten the bunching around the waist, thus concealing how the drapes had been produced. These interpretations are purely speculative and, as with any interpretation based purely on sculptural evidence, are always fraught with difficulties.

As a large proportion of the available evidence from this period comes from the Rhineland area it is not known to what extent this type of tunic was worn elsewhere within the empire. To judge from the little evidence there is, this style of tunic was only popular from around the

22 A–E: Legionaries and auxiliaries on first century AD tombstones from Germany. Note the ridge on some of the feet which is an indication that the men were wearing *caligae*.

A: C. Petillius Secundus, Legio XV Primigenia, Bonn.

B: Annaius Daverzus, Cohors IIII Delmatarum, Bingen-Bingerbrück.

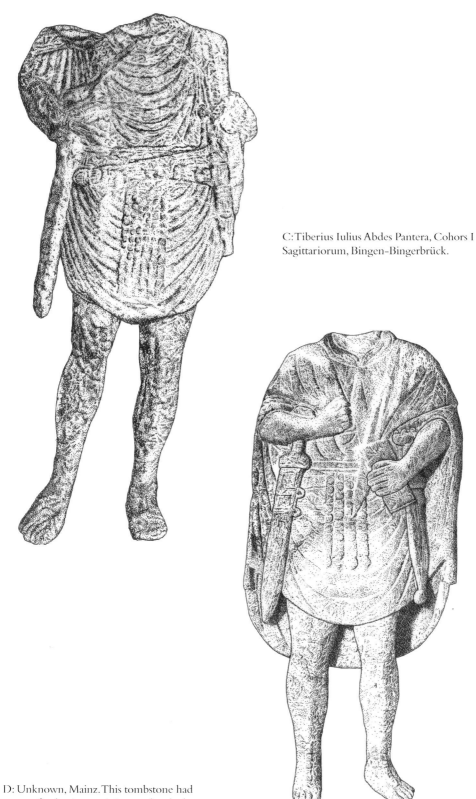

C: Tiberius Iulius Abdes Pantera, Cohors I
Sagittariorum, Bingen-Bingerbrück.

D: Unknown, Mainz. This tombstone had
traces of red paint surviving on the cloak
when first discovered.

E: Publius Flavoleius, Cordus Legio XIIII
Gemina, Mainz.

beginning to the latter half of the first century, when it disappears entirely. It is then superseded by a simpler, perhaps more utilitarian version. This practical form of tunic clearly existed before the Rhineland examples, as it can be seen on the Arch of Orange dating from the reign of Augustus, and on early Principate tombstones from Caesarea in Algeria. It is also the tunic made familiar by its depiction on Trajan's Column, and the Chatsworth relief of Hadrianic date and is clearly the style worn by the Camomile Street soldier from London. This tunic has a straight lower hem and very few folds at all.

Decoration

An instantly recognisable feature of many illustrated and surviving tunics from the Roman period are the two contrasting bands of colour known as *clavi* which run from the shoulders to the bottom edges. Although senatorial officers would be entitled to wide purple *clavi* on their tunics and Equestrian officers were supposed to have narrow bands, it is not known for certain if ordinary soldiers were allowed to display them. The use of purple *clavi* by soldiers from the third century onwards, however, is well evidenced both in the *Scriptores Historiae Augustae* (SHA, *Claudius*, XVII, 6) and on wall paintings from Dura Europos.

23 Detail of a column base from Mainz, showing two legionaries fighting. The foreground soldier
appears to be wearing a draped tunic over another short-sleeved tunic rather than any type of
recognisable armour. However this might actually illustrate a cover worn over the armour. The ancient
artist clearly knew how to depict armour as a soldier wearing the segmented type is shown elsewhere on
the same relief.

The *clavi* were woven horizontally on the loom because it was technically easier to do it
that way than weave them vertically. Tunics could be woven in one piece and it was quite
common to make them this way in Egypt, but the large nature of Roman garments meant that
producing them like this would require a very wide loom, impractical for most households or
one individual weaver. Therefore most tunics were made up of two tunic sheets produced on a
narrow width upright loom. One obvious advantage to making tunics this way was that if one
part of the tunic was damaged it could be replaced by a single tunic sheet rather than by an
entirely new tunic.

Tunic sheets were made using a typical weaving technique, with weft threads going
horizontally from left to right and warp threads going vertically. By weaving this way a selvedge
is produced on both left- and right-hand sides of the sheet, while the sheet width itself was
determined by the loom width. The *clavi* had to be centrally placed on each tunic sheet with
an equal width between them. This was important because when the sheets were both finished
each one was turned so the selvedge edges were now at the top and bottom. The top two
selvedge edges were then sewn together, forming the shoulders of the tunic, while a gap was
left between the *clavi* to form the neck opening. The side borders of the tunic were then sewn
together, again leaving a gap at the top of each side to allow the arms to pass through.

24 Auxiliary soldiers on tombstones from North Africa.

A: Unknown from Cohors IIII Milliaria Tungrorum, Rabat.

B: Civilis Balaterus, Cohors VI Delmatarum, Cherchel, Algeria.

Matching the two *clavi* required a degree of skill as Varro points out:

Non, si quis tunicam in usu ita consuit, ut altera plagula sit angustis clavis, altera latis, utraque pars in suo genere caret analogia.

if anyone were to sew together a tunic so that one sheet of the *clavi* were narrow and on the other wide, each would lack analogy, in its nature. (*Ling Lat.* IX. 79)

Evidently it was the sign of a good clothes maker if they could sew the two sheets together so that the *clavi* on both sides matched!

Fuentes believed that some musicians in a gladiatorial scene depicted on a mosaic from Zliten in North Africa may represent members of a military band; the men wear military style yellow-brown cloaks and have short white tunics with black *clavi*. However, this identification is in spite of the presence of a female member of the band who plays a water-powered organ, casting some doubt on the military status of the others. A couple of the portrait paintings from Egypt (discussed below) may also show common soldiers, who have tunics which are decorated with either red or black *clavi*.

Originally the width of the *clavi* on a person's tunic was particularly important, especially to distinguish those of senatorial class. However human nature being what it is, many people wore wider *clavi* than what they were entitled to. At Mons Claudianus, Egypt, the majority of *clavi* on textile fragments were between 1cm and 4cm in width, but there were also a number of fragments that had two and even three stripes. The *clavi* themselves are sometimes decorated and some of these examples can be around 7cm wide. One of the virtues of the Emperor Augustus according to Suetonius was that he wore ordinary clothes with *clavi* that were neither wide nor broad (*Augustus* LXXIII).

The Dropped Shoulder and Neck Knot

Soldiers were expected to work in the field in full armour if necessary and indeed are shown doing this on Trajan's Column. However the column also shows a few legionaries involved in construction duties wearing a tunic that is let down from their right shoulder. A similar appearance is found in contemporary representations of civilian workers, for example representations of blacksmiths and later depictions of Christ as the Good Shepherd. The tunics on the column with the side let down are clearly the standard wide sleeveless tunic. On the other hand some tunics shown this way appear to have a small sleeve, such as one worn by a small boy on the Ara Pacis in Rome.

It seems that under normal circumstances the wide neck opening of the tunic was gathered and fastened together in a small bunch of surplus material at the rear of the neck. This practice can be observed in a number of scenes on Trajan's Column, and also on the mid- to late second century Belvedere Sarcophagus, now in the Vatican. Here the detail survives clearly enough to show that the bunch was tied with a thong rather than pinned together by *fibulae* (brooches). An almost identical arrangement can still be observed today worn by nomadic tribesmen in Mauretania.

There are two obvious disadvantages to wearing a tunic tied into a bunch at the back of the neck. Firstly it might require the assistance of another in holding and tying, but was this was probably a skill learnt at an early age. Secondly it would appear an unnecessary encumbrance when worn beneath armour or under armour padding. Nevertheless, the existence of this peculiar fashion is confirmed by its appearance in more than one source, and when reconstructed the bunching at the rear produces all the types of folds observed in many sculptural renditions of military tunics. The narrower tunics introduced later did not have enough material to allow tying behind in this manner and the knot at the rear disappears from the pictorial record. However tunics with the right side lowered continue to be seen in Roman art, although not always in a purely military context like those on Trajan's Column.

Although there are many textile fragments from military sites, as yet no complete examples of positively identified military tunics exist. If they were similar in design and manufacture to other surviving tunics from this period, like those from Nahal Hever, then another problem presents

25 *Left*: Examples of legionary soldiers
on Trajan's Column engaged in manual
duties. Some of them wear their tunics
off one shoulder. In other cases the tied
knot behind the neck is clearly visible.

26 *Oppostie bottom and left:* Details of the Chatsworth sculpture commemorating the burning of tax records under the Emperor Hadrian. The figures are possibly Praetorians and they are wearing loose fitting tunics and in one case a paenula cloak. Other points of interest are the tunic knot behind the neck of one soldier and the belts crossing over the left shoulder which do not appear to be sword baldrics but keep the tunic clear away from the sword.

27 A–E: The most influential depiction of archers' clothing are those depicted on Trajan's Column which show them wearing long flowing eastern-style robes. However most other monuments illustrate them wearing clothing similar to other regular auxiliary troops.

A: Monimus, Cohors I Ituraeorum, Tahlbach near Mainz.

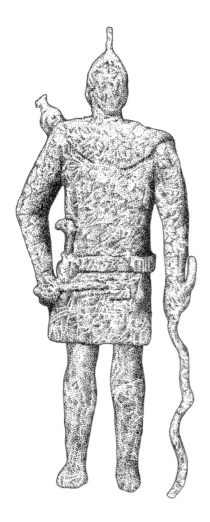

B: Housesteads, Hadrian's Wall.

C: Trajan's Column.

D: Trajan's Column.

E: Column of
Marcus Aurelius.

itself. As the surviving tunics are broader than they are long, this leaves a lot of surplus material underneath the wearer's arms. This phenomenon can be observed on the Chatsworth relief where the soldiers are shown in their undress uniform of tunic and belts. This surplus of material would appear to be an inconvenience, especially when the soldier was wearing any form of body armour.

More by accident than by design modern re-enactors have tendeed to favour a narrow 'T' shaped tunic. This was based on observations of sculpture rather than copying any surviving specimens which are generally published in less accessible works. The 'T' shape may therefore be incorrect for this early date, but it does at least fit comfortably underneath recreated armour. However one 'T' shaped tunic was discovered during the excavations at the imperial quarry site at Mons Claudianus in Egypt. Dating from the Trajanic period, it had been made up from old pieces of clothing, including what seems to have been a cloak which had been decorated with gamma patterns. Unless the soldiers at this site were desperately short of clothing it is unlikely to have belonged to a soldier, but it does show that the 'T' shape existed at this date.

If soldiers did indeed wear 'T' shaped tunics under armour it might lend support to the idea that Roman soldiers not only wore a special tunic when they went into action, but one that was a different design to those they wore out of armour. Recent experiments carried out by numerous re-enactors have demonstrated that the wide tunics can be worn comfortably beneath armour; indeed, they actually provide an extra layer of padding!

Fuentes detected another feature which can be seen on the Chatsworth relief. This is what appears to be a narrow strap that is decorated with studs which passes from under the right arm and crosses over the left shoulder. Fuentes used an anachronistic term for these belts and called them a 'pouch belt' like those used by eighteenth- and nineteenth-century cavalrymen. However his observation that their function was to restrict any blousing of the material – which would interfere with drawing a sword – deserves some merit. Even when off duty and not wearing armour, soldiers were still equipped with their side-arms, usually a sword and dagger. An example of this practice was brought to light when the body of what may well have been a soldier was discovered during the excavations at Herculaneum. When this individual was killed by the eruption of Vesuvius he had been carrying a bag of carpentry tools and was armed with a sword, dagger and had been wearing two belts.

Shoulder belts decorated with alternate bronze and silver discs are also seen on the encaustic portraits from Egypt. Usually these are identified as sword baldrics, but the high angle of the belts shown on the Chatsworth relief would rule out this function. Therefore the theory proposed by Fuentes that these belts are simply to prevent blousing may well be correct. The need to combat the effects of the surplus of material on large tunics left under the arm getting in the way may also answer why some soldiers let down the right side of their tunics when engaged in manual work.

Legionaries and Auxiliaries

Tombstones of the early empire show both legionaries and auxiliaries wearing identical tunics, but sculptural evidence seems to suggest that this may have changed towards the end of the first century. Trajan's Column, in particular, shows armoured auxiliaries wearing a tunic that is clearly much shorter than those worn by citizen soldiers. Nevertheless, the un-armoured auxiliaries depicted on the column such as the slingers are wearing the same type of tunic as the legionaries. The shorter tunic worn with very tight-fitting trouser-like *bracae* may be a device used by the sculptors to highlight the ethnic character of these soldiers for the benefit of the Roman viewers.

A similar emphasis is placed on some of the auxiliary archers, many of whom wear ankle-length flowing robes. These are generally assumed by modern commentators to represent Middle Eastern costume. Nonetheless, tombstones of eastern archers found in the frontier regions, such as that belonging to Hyperanor who wears one of the draped tunics and a Hamian archer based at Housesteads on Hadrian's Wall in the second century AD, suggest that bowmen were perhaps more frequently dressed in the same manner as any other soldier.

Mounted auxiliaries appear to have worn a short tunic from at least the early Principate, a practice which can also be detected in sculptures of cavalrymen during the Republic. This was probably because a short tunic would be more practical for riding, especially when worn in

28 Detail of Trajan's Column showing regular and irregular Roman auxiliaries fighting with Dacian warriors wearing long-sleeved tunics, cloaks and trousers. In a few years Roman sculptures would show their soldiers wearing similar dress.

combination with trousers, and this practice is likely to have originated with the Celts or the Germans. The small tunic found at Mons Claudianus would appear indecently short for an adult when compared with those from Nahal Hever, but it would make an ideal tunic for an auxiliary wearing *bracae*, as illustrated on Trajan's Column. It is interesting that the garrison at Mons Claudianus was indeed an auxiliary one, but the tunic could equally have belonged to a child.

LATE IMPERIAL TUNICS

> He [Caracalla] took off his Roman cloak and put on German dress, and showed himself in the silver decorated cape they wear; he also put on a blonde wig, neatly done in the German hairstyle. The barbarians, delighted with this, loved him greatly. (Herodian, 4.7.3)

The third century was a period of political, military and financial turmoil for the empire. In the fifty years from the murder of Alexander Severus in AD 235 to the accession of Diocletian in 284 there were nearly thirty emperors and only three of them died by natural causes. Fortunately the empire was saved by the rise of a succession of tough soldier emperors. Many of these men rose up through the ranks but they came not from Rome or even from Italy, but from the frontier, especially the Balkan provinces. Their direct, no-nonsense approach was reflected in the military equipment of this period, which for the first time in Roman history almost achieved a measure of uniformity.

Although the Arch of Severus which was dedicated in AD 203 still shows Roman soldiers wearing a style of tunic that would not appear out of place in the late Republic or early Empire, the third century saw the widespread introduction of long-sleeved tunics into mainstream fashion, which is reflected in the art of the period. One reason for this fashion was undoubtedly the increasing influence of Germanic troops and mercenaries serving with the Roman army. Another reason would be that the commanders of armies and even emperors were adopting the costume that was familiar on the frontiers. As early as the first century AD this fashion *faux pas* was observed and criticised by traditional Roman historians like Tacitus (*Hist.*, 2.30) who berated Aulus Caecina – a senior army commander and pretender to the throne – for adopting what he considered as 'barbarian dress'. On this occasion Tacitus only refers to a brightly coloured cape and trousers but we might expect that a long-sleeved garment would also have completed Caecina's garb.

Many emperors and high-ranking officers adopted barbarian bodyguards. One obvious method of winning and maintaining their favour was to adopt their style of dress. For example, Cicero verbally attacked Mark Antony because he wore both 'Gallic boots and cloak' after returning from the campaigns against the Gauls. Furthermore, the *Scriptores Historiae Augustae* tells us how the defeated Gallic separatist, the Emperor Tetricus (r.AD 270–273), was led in Aurelian's triumphal parade '*inter haec fuit Tetricus chalmyde coccea tunica galbina, bracis Gallicis ornatus*' – 'in the procession was Tetricus also arrayed in scarlet cloak, a yellow tunic, and Gallic trousers.' (*SHA, Aurelian, XXXIV*, 2). This fashion for wearing foreign garb was taken to its extreme by the Emperor Marcus Aurelius Antoninus Bassianus, more commonly known as Caracalla (r.AD211–217) after the 'Gallic cape', *caracallus*, that he frequently wore and helped popularise.

We are told Caracalla frequently went about dressed in Germanic costume, and as seen from the quotation previously cited, went even further on occasion by sporting a German wig! This approach may seem to us as exactly the type of eccentricity expected of dissolute emperors, but it was based on a serious appreciation of the need to maintain the favour of the troops in an age of very uncertain loyalties. Caracalla furthermore not only granted his soldiers generous increases in pay, but shared in their hardships endured on campaign. Dio records that he

> marched on foot with the soldiers and ran with them, did not wash nor change his clothes, joined in every task with them, and chose exactly the same kind of rations as they had. (*Epit.*, LXXVIII, 13.1)

Caracalla clearly understood that in order to survive he needed to be seen as a fellow soldier.

29 Quintus Statius Rufus was a praetorian serving with the fleet based at Misenum in Italy. His tombstone found in Athens shows him wearing a *sagum* cloak that was decorated with at least one small tassel on one corner. He also sports knee-length *bracae* and wears enclosed boots.

30 Trajanic period marching soldiers from a detail of the Adamklissi Monument in Romania and from a sculpture in Rome. Sculptures of this period still show soldiers wearing *caligae*.

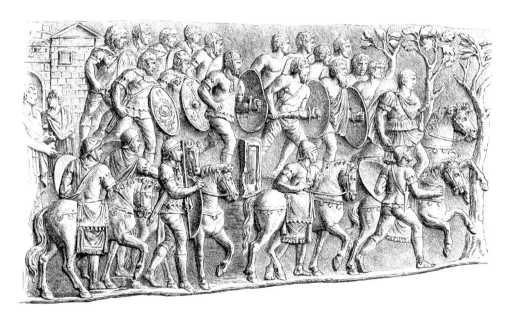

31 A scene from Trajan's Column showing Trajan himself (far right) surrounded by auxiliary troops wearing a variety of uniforms. *Courtesy Ross Cowan.*

The Thorsberg Finds

In the context of Roman military equipment and clothing the importance of the finds from Thorsberg in Schleswig Holstein, Germany, is often overlooked. Yet that site revealed a complete costume of tunic, cloak and trousers, dating no later than the third century AD. The remains were found in a peat bog and together they represent the stereotypical image of Celtic and Germanic clothing. In common with other textile finds from Germany and Scandinavia they were found with items of Roman military weapons and equipment. Nevertheless it has generally been assumed that while the Roman items are the result of trade or loot, the textiles themselves must have been Germanic in origin.

Lise Bender Jorgensen and other Scandinavian textile scholars have put forward an opposing view. They believe that the Thorsberg finds and others like them are Gallo-Roman in origin, and may actually represent the clothing of Roman auxiliaries. This hypothesis is based on the fact that the Thorsberg tunic and trousers are made from a type of cloth known as the Virring type which is also found on Roman military sites from around the empire. Although it is commonly found in German and Scandinavian sites many of these finds especially those from Scandinavia only date from the Roman period. Like the Thorsberg garments many of these other items of clothing can be associated with Roman goods and so while the identity of their final owners may never be proven either way, it is entirely plausible that these garments originated within the boundaries of the Roman Empire. In any event one other point cannot be dismissed and that is from the third century onwards a new Roman uniform appears in the iconographic record. This consists of a tunic with long, tight-fitting sleeves, a cloak and trousers. All of these garments, even if not identical in manufacture or materials, are to all intents and purposes similar to the Thorsberg finds.

The Thorsberg tunic is made from wool and measures 86cm in length and 52cm in width. The sleeves were sewn on separately and had tablet-woven borders. The tunic itself was made from a narrow piece of 2/2 diamond twill with tablet woven selvedges. An unusual feature is that the selvedges on the tunic sides are laced together down to the hips rather than stitched. The top edges of the tunic are also laced together and to the shoulders, which were separate pieces cut across the fabric in rectangles so that the selvedges would be at the cuffs and shoulder.

The story of the Thorsberg tunic trousers and cloak since their discovery is also a history of the technology used to analyse dyes and dyeing. When first discovered the initial researchers proclaimed that the tunic was red, the trousers beige and the cloak green. Later Karl Schlabow determined that the cloak was two shades of blue and the tunic like the trousers was also beige.

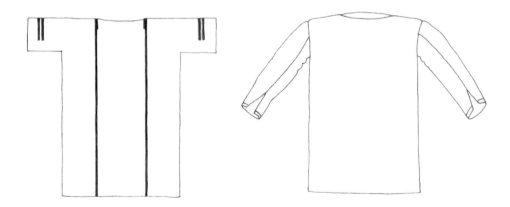

32 Late Roman period tunic plans.
Left: Dura Europos. 0.92m long × 0.63m wide. *Charles W. Evans-Gunther.*
Right: Thorsberg. 0.88m long × 0.54m wide. *After Wild.*

Now after more recent research by Fischer that found traces of madder and a purple lichen dye in the tunic, it has become red again!

Other tunics have been found in Germany. A slightly later example from Bernuthsfeld had been repeatedly repaired and patched together with square pieces in the manner of the Roman second-hand clothes makers. It was longer than the Thorsberg tunic, being 1.15m in length and 550m wide. A tunic from Reepsholt exhibits many features of Roman garments and may indeed be one. It was woven to shape and is 1.15m wide – the same as the length of the Bernuthsfeld tunic. Wild has identified this particular garment as a Gallic coat, the classic garment of the North west Roman provinces.

It is probably safe to conclude that clothing styles from Northern Europe were introduced into the Roman army, firstly by the auxiliaries both regular and irregular that were recruited both within the Northern provinces and from beyond the empire. Later this process was advanced by Germans serving as Imperial bodyguards and then finally by the legionaries based on the northern frontier who adopted the fashions themselves. Ultimately this fashion was then made mainstream by emperors like Caracalla, who is recorded as always wearing German clothing even when he was in Syria and Mesopotamia (Dio, *Epit.*, LXXIX, 2–3).

Barbarians or Romans?

This study concentrates on the clothing worn by the regular soldiers of the Imperial armies. However, the Romans increasingly made use of irregular soldiers formed up into small detachments called the *numeri* and *cunei*. Later on came the *foederati*, Germanic settlers who were given land within the empire on the condition that they provided troops for the army when required. All of these types of troops, probably commanded by their own chieftains, would have worn their own clothing which might be both traditional and a hybrid mixture of Romano-Germanic fashion, providing many more diverse styles and influences within the army. When the army led by Septimius Severus marched from the Danube frontier on Rome, the civilian population, doubtless accustomed like ourselves to images of Roman troops on the Columns of Trajan and Marcus Aurelius, were shocked to see what their frontier soldiers actually looked like (Dio, LXXV; 2.6).

What probably horrified them most was undoubtedly the soldiers' 'barbarian' appearance. This is presumably because they were wearing long-sleeved tunics and trousers or *bracae*. These garments had for generations been considered unacceptable and un-Roman by conservatives, and amongst the faults of disgraced emperors like Elagabalus and Commodus were included

33 Aurelius Iustinus, a soldier with Legio II Italica, who died in the wars against the Dacians. He is wearing a rare example of a tunic with loose-fitting cuffs. His tombstone is now in the Regional Museum at Celje in Slovenia.

34 An unknown soldier on a tombstone in Augsburg Germany. He is wearing a ring buckle belt which was a major feature of Roman military dress in the third century AD. © *Florian Himmler.*

35 Tombstone of Aurelius Bitus, *cornicen* with Legio I Adiutrix showing a belt with a large ring buckle. © *Florian Himmler.*

36 Tombstone of an unknown cavalry trooper with the Equites Singulares Augusti, the imperial horse guards based in Rome. His ring buckle belt has an elaborate loop which extends on his right side and which splits into two strips with metal terminals. In this and other cases there could even be perhaps a return of the hanging 'apron' of earlier times. He wears a fringed sagum cloak and a long-sleeved tunic. As with many monuments of this period, it is not always clear if the soldiers are wearing tight-fitting trousers or are bare-legged.

their fondness for long-sleeved tunics considered effeminate by the more puritanical writers. Even today both academics and the public at large are not likely to associate long-sleeved tunics and trousers with the Roman army and archaeological reconstruction paintings and re-enactors are unlikely to depict Roman soldiers of the early Imperial period wearing either of these garments.

It was not only the Germans and Gauls who wore long-sleeved tunics: the Romans were practically surrounded by peoples who had always favoured them. At least one auxiliary cavalryman from the first century AD, Flavius Bassus (almost certainly of Thracian origin), chose to be remembered on his tombstone wearing such a tunic. His sleeves also have distinctive turned-back cuffs, reminiscent of those seen on a famous Romano-Celtic sculpture depicting a warrior which is now in the Calvert Museum in Avignon, France. Since large numbers of Celts and Germans were recruited into the army – especially the cavalry – it is not surprising to find cavalrymen wearing similar garments to what would have been worn in everyday life.

Documents from Egypt written in Greek – the principal language of the Eastern Empire – refer to a number of different tunics. The military tunic is known as the *sticharion*, which probably originated from the Greek word for 'striped', and which might be a reference to the *clavi*. The army also requisitioned another garment called a *dalmatica*, although, judging by the documents, in smaller numbers than the *sticharion*. The *dalmatica* is documented as being amongst the ostentatious types of garment worn by the profligate Emperor Elagabalus, so therefore not seen initially in a favourable light. However, his successor Alexander Severus wore a plain version and the fact that it had long sleeves seems to have been overlooked on this occasion. The *dalmatica*, as its name suggests, had probably originated in the province of Dalmatia and had doubtless been popular with the third century soldier-emperors.

Another type of long-sleeved garment was the *camisia*, generally understood as a tight-fitting linen shirt. It has been argued that the term derives from a Germanic loan word which came into Latin usage via the Celts. The *camisia* was later popular with priests, but it has been suggested that they themselves had adopted it from the army. Palladius (*Hist. Laus.*, LXV, 4) speaks of an inner tunic of linen, called the *linea*, and we are told that the Emperor Alexander Severus loved pure white linen garments, even preferring them to purple ones (SHA, Al. Sev., XL, 10).

37 A–D: Examples of third-century soldiers of various ranks showing the uniformity of equipment styles at this period, even between private soldiers of the lowest rank such as Lecterus, and the highest such as Lucianus and Valerinus.

A: Aurelius Mucianus, *Lanciarius* with Legio II Parthica, Apamea. *(See colour plate 12 for a reconstruction.)*

B: M. Aurelius Lucianus, praetorian with Cohors VI Praetoria Rome.

C: Unknown *Signifer*,
Budapest.

D: Left: Aprillius Lecterus, serving with the Numerus Divitesium, Istanbul.
    Right: L. Septimius Valerinus, Cohors IX Pretoria, Rome.

38 Tombstone of Insus, a cavalryman with the
Ala Augusta. Found in Lancaster, England. *(See
colour plate 18 for a reconstruction.) Photograph by
Stephen Bull © Lancashire Museums.*

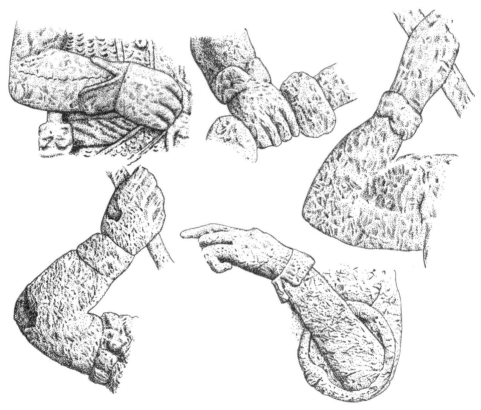

39 Details of cavalry tombstones showing possible tunic cuffs.
Clockwise from top left: Avignon, Lancaster, Cologne, Arlon, Bertrange

40 A tombstone of Aurelius Sabius a legionary with
Legio II Traiana Fortis, in the Graeco-Roman Museum
in Alexandria, Egypt. © *Jenny Cline.*

41 A *dipinto* from Dura Europos, Syria, showing a Roman soldier (left), possibly a centurion, sacrificing
before the god Iarhibol (right). Note the fringe to the long-sleeved tunic and the early form of
decoration in the form of a small cross. *After S. James.*

In the east long-sleeved tunics were also commonplace, and it is from the eastern half of the empire that the best evidence comes for the very widespread use of such garments in the Roman army of the third century AD. A remarkable series of tombstones has been discovered, re-used in the defences at Apamea, Syria, dating from between 214 and 252. They show a wide range of junior officers, specialists and ordinary soldiers, all of whom wear long-sleeved tunics. Indeed, at a short distance it is quite impossible to tell them apart. Contemporary praetorian guards and even emperors too look little different from the Apamea soldiers. Based on their tombstones one could almost say the Romans of the third century had achieved a uniform appearance, an effect heightened by the popular military fashion of wearing a close cropped hairstyle and stubbly beard. Doubtless colour and quality of material would have picked out the more important individuals were we able to see them in all their true glory.

Decoration: From Clavi to Orbiculi

One other fashion that probably spread from the eastern frontiers was the taste for elaborately decorated clothes, sometimes including decoration made from silver or gold thread. Early Imperial biographers listed amongst the chief excesses of the worst emperors, such as Nero and Elagabalus, their taste for highly decorated clothing (SHA. *Ant. Ela.* XXIII. 3). Therefore, while originally scorned by the Romans as hopelessly barbarian and even effeminate, ironically this manner of dress was ultimately to become the attire not only of all the later emperors, but of their courts and their bodyguards too.

42 Detail from an ivory lipsanotheca in the Museo Civico dell Età Cristiana, Brescia. It shows scenes from the Passion, including a number of Roman guards.

43 A–C: Soldiers from fourth-century AD
Italian frescoes.

A:Via Latina catacomb. Rome.

B:Via Maria, Syracuse, Sicily. (*See colour
plate 33.*)

C:Via Latina catacomb, Rome.

44 Decoration from a tunic. © *British Museum.*

45 A–C: Tunic
decorations found in
Egypt. Photographs
by Russell Hartman
© *California Academy
of Sciences, San
Francisco.*

A

B

C

As early as the reign of Hadrian we know this practice had already begun, because Hadrian tried to stop it. Although the *Scriptores Historiae Augustae* say he improved the soldiers' arms and equipment, they say he banished many of the luxuries that were beginning to creep into military life and to set an example wore common clothing without gold ornaments (SHA. *Had.* X. 5). Marcus Aurelius is also said to have informed a Prefect that another officer, in fact the future pretender Clodius Albinus, should be provided with a plain uniform, *vestem militarem simplicem*, although one still suitable for his rank (SHA. *Clod. Alb.* X.8.).

After the excesses of the reign of Elagabalus, his successor Alexander Severus was praised for removing the jewels from Imperial garments and footwear, and for dressing himself in a plain white tunic, without any gold, and plain rough cloaks and togas (SHA *Sev. Alex.* IV.2.). It is implied that Alexander furthermore removed some of the lavish garments that Elagabalus had provided for some of his soldiers, possibly guards, who were now accordingly dressed in bright, elegant but inexpensive uniforms (SHA. *Sev. Alex.* XXXIII. 3.). He declared that the power of Rome should be based on valour, not on outward show.

When the pretender Procopius was proclaimed emperor in AD 365 no purple cloak was available, so in order to look the part he wore a gold embroidered tunic, purple trousers and shoes, and held a small piece of purple cloth (Amm. Mar., XXVI, 6.15). Ironically, while many third-century emperors felt it necessary to court the company and copy the dress of ordinary soldiers, later emperors adopted a completely opposite approach and preferred that of splendid isolation and oriental magnificence. Periodically the more disciplinarian and austere emperors tried to stem the tide of these non-Roman influences, but with little success. The Emperor Tacitus (r.AD 275–276), for example, was another emperor who was recorded as dressing like his men, and he too attempted to ban the wearing of silk tunics and gold *clavi* (SHA, *Aurelian* XLV. 5, *Tacitus* XI.6).

It is possible that these prohibitions were aimed not just at the population as a whole but at the army in particular. Even early Church historians such as Asterius, Bishop of Amaseia in

46 Just two of the many figures from the Great Hunting Mosaic in Piazza Armerina, Sicily dating to the late fourth century AD. The many bands on the tunic cuffs support the description of them in the *Scriptores Historia Augustae*.

Pontus, chastised their contemporaries for 'wearing pictured garments, looking like painted walls.' An idea of how lavish these garments could be can be gleaned from the ivory diptych often believed to represent the early fifth-century Roman general Stilicho, who was himself of Germanic origin, being the son of a Vandal. Stilicho's tunic is wrought with architectural arcades and statues proving that the observations of Asterius were correct. The *clavi* and *tablia* on the tunic of Stilicho are decorated with an interlaced swastika pattern, while his cloak is covered with circles with portraits – probably of the Imperial family.

Actual cloaks with similar designs to those depicted on this carving have been found at Antinoe in Egypt, which confirms that garments like those represented in ancient art really did exist. At the same time we can easily imagine that the simple wool and linen decorations on the clothing of ordinary people were replaced with silver and gold thread for the garments of the Imperial guards and officers. And yet even these ostentatious costumes were simply a foretaste of the grandeur that was later seen as an essential element of Byzantine court ritual.

At the beginning of the third century, soldiers such as Aurelius Gennaius – horseman of I Legio Adiutrix Severiana – wore a tunic with simple purple *clavi*, but this was soon replaced by more elaborate styles, even for humble soldiers. In its simplest form this decoration was comprised of patterned purple roundels – known as *orbiculi* – on the shoulders and skirts of tunics; later small rectangular patches also appeared. Some scholars believe that they were placed over vulnerable areas of the body as a form of protection. These decorations were woven into the fabric but were frequently removed and attached to new clothes when older ones wore out.

The patterns continued to develop over time. First a yoke at the neck joined the two vertical *clavi*, which themselves became wider and shorter, ending just above the waist. The terminals of the shorter *clavi* were often decorated with leaf or tassel ends or sometimes with arrowheads. This latter style is confirmed by Apuleius who describes 'off-white tunics decorated with purple stripes shaped as small spears' (*Metamorph.*, VIII, 27.). There were further changes. Unlike earlier times, the tunic was no longer pulled up and bloused over the belt, but simply belted snugly at the waist, and was usually worn modestly just over the knees rather than above them as before.

47 Late Roman tunic plans from Egypt. *Charles W. Evans-Gunther, after Gervers.*

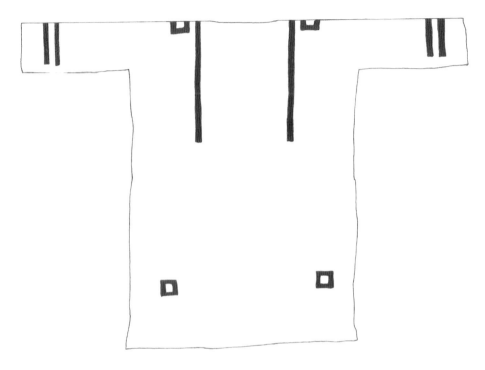

1.37m long × 0.97m wide *After Gervers..*

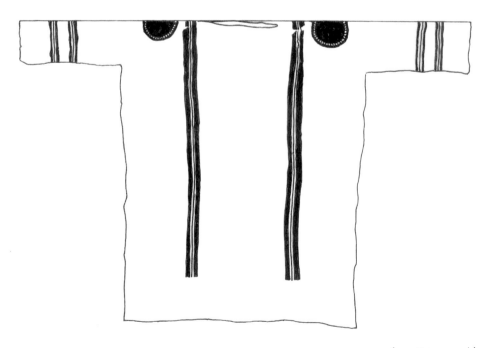

1.0m long × 0.95m wide.

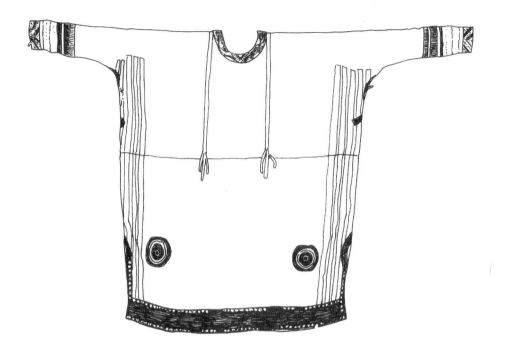

1.41m long × 1.14m wide.

At other times soldiers wore a shorter tunic perhaps when engaged in heavy duties, such as hunting fugitives or executing prisoners. This style may h ave followed the earlier practice of wearing the tunic dropped off one shoulder. It is frequently seen in early Christian art perhaps because many Christians had first hand experience of Roman soldiers engaged in these duties.

However, the physical remains of purely military tunics remain difficult to identify even from supposedly military sites, most obviously, because of the large numbers of civilians who would be present in and around forts, especially in the late Roman period. Furthermore, the fashion for wearing military-style garments was extremely popular with minor officials, civic dignitaries and civil servants. An example of this trend can be observed on a tapestry found in Egypt, which apparently shows a priest whose appearance could easily be mistaken for that of a soldier. This is not surprising, considering the important role the army played in Roman society, and at a more practical level military clothing was always suitable for outdoor wear just like modern 'combat'-style trousers are popular today.

The results of excavations at the isolated desert forts of Egypt, which should contain a higher proportion of textiles for military use, should ultimately provide us with a better understanding of military clothing. It is only recently that we have come to appreciate that some military garments could clearly be very ornate. For example, Claudius Herculanus, an Imperial horse guard of the Emperor Aurelian is depicted on his tombstone clothed in either a tunic or a cloak decorated with a large sunburst design; this would be particularly appropriate given Aurelian's association with worship of the sun god. A motif like this would have looked especially impressive if it had been picked out with gold thread, and was probably worn by all of Aurelian's guards, to whom doubtless presented them himself. Even so, Aurelian is said to have remarked '*Absit ut auro fila pensentur*', 'God forbid that a fabric should be worth its weight in gold' (SHA. *Aurelian* XLV.5.).

An extravagance such as this would not have been unusual; expensive clothing was often given out as gifts by the emperors to their troops, to emphasise their own and their regime's magnificence. The Emperor Maximinus Daia 'spent money everywhere indiscriminately and without limit', and to the further disgust of the Church historian Lactantius he awarded 'costly dress and gold coins to his guardsmen' (*De Mort.*, 37.5s). This luxurious dress was not just an extravagance, as it was instrumental in impressing the local population, overawing foreign dignitaries or potential enemies and boosting the soldiers' morale.

Later Tunics

The long-sleeved 'T' shaped tunic continued to be the main garment worn by soldiers. The *tunica manicata* or in Greek *chiton cheiridotos* was frequently mentioned by Procopius. (*BP*, II, 21, 6; *BV*, II, 23, 22; 26, 26; 28,10). Wool and linen in summer were still the chief materials used, although silk and Egyptian cotton garments are also known. The 'T' shaped tunics were woven on a very large loom in one giant cross-shaped piece. When completed it was folded in half, sewn up the sides, and a slit was cut out for the neck. Another feature on many late tunics which is also repeatedly illustrated in the pictorial sources is the very long tight-fitting sleeves.

Soldiers still wore a second inner tunic called *linea* or *camisia* as confirmed by St Jerome, who tells us that 'the soldiers usually wear inner tunics, *lineae*, which they call '*camisia*', fitted to the limbs and very tight to the body.' (*Ep.*, LXIV, 11, 2). Judging by archaeological specimens, the average size for a tunic in the fifth century was 1.12m in length by 0.90m wide, increasing in the sixth century to an average size of 1.16m long x 0.92m wide.

The Byzantine historian Lydus has left us an interesting observation on Roman magistrates, in which he gave a description of the patrician tunic in white wool (*alba*), trimmed with purple (*paragauda*) (Lydus, *De Mag.* 1,17). The average for tunics – judging from both written sources and actual specimens – was a length of 1.12m and a width (open sleeves) of 0.90m in the fifth century, increasing to a length of 1.16m and a width of 0.92m (open sleeves) in the sixth to seventh centuries, but this should not be taken as rule. There is no obvious evidence that late military tunics were much smaller than in earlier periods to accommodate the reduced height requirements attested by Vegetius (*Epit.*, 1.5). Differences among various types of tunics are seen

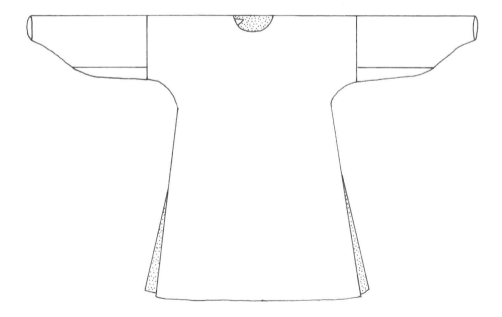

48 Bleached linen tunic, possibly an under-tunic, probably from Antinoe, Egypt dating from the sixth to seventh century AD. 1.05m long × 0.62m wide. *Charles W. Evans-Gunther, after Gervers.*

in the existing specimens and by the evidence in the pictorial and artistic sources, especially for clothing worn by the Imperial Guardsmen.

While the bulk of the artistic evidence comes from frescoes, mosaics, manuscript miniatures, statues and coins found all over the Roman world, in contrast the archaeological evidence comes almost exclusively from Egypt. Thanks to the dryness of the climate, discoveries at the necropoleis of Akhmim, Assiout and Antinoe have revealed the dead intact, dressed in their own clothing; the rigid folds of the drapery, the appearance of the capes of the garments, the heavy ornaments and the embroidery decorated with gems all dramatically confirm the pictorial sources. However this association with Egypt has led to a tendency for people not to connect these finds with the Romans at all, certainly not with the army.

The manufacture of textiles in the late eastern Greek style continued in the fifth and even the sixth century in Alexandria and at many other centres in the east. In addition many magnificent tunics that were imported from beyond the eastern frontier and used by both the Romans and their Persian enemies have been found in Egyptian graves of the late Roman period. In the excavations at Antinoe by A. Gayet, from 1896 in the so-called 'horsemen's graves', he found hundreds of complete and fragmented clothing specimens and parts of tunic decoration. Some of these items can be assigned to senior army officers, many of whom were also Christians, as attested by the presence of small crucifixes and inscriptions with figures of saints. The Hellenised names of some owners (Pamios, for instance) also attest to their Romano-Egyptian origin.

The best remaining tunics are dated between the fifth and the eighth centuries. One of the tunics was made of linen constructed of several pieces of material sewn together and with the neck opening of triangular shape, extending down to the upper breast with a vent. The sleeves have tightly closed cuffs with silk bands sewn on the cuff trimmings, which is also present around the vent and neck opening, and is carried on down the shoulders. A fragment of neck decoration from a similar tunic has a wool embroidered band. This kind of tunic decoration is visible on soldiers and cavalrymen represented on the frescoes at Bawit, shown in paintings representing infantry and cavalrymen and also on the soldiers depicted in the pyxis of St Menas – now in the British Museum. This confirms that these tunics were used in a military context.

49 Detail of a silver plate from Kertch, showing the Emperor Constantius II with one of his guards.

50 Aphrodisius and his retainers
as depicted in a mosaic scene
from the church of St Maria
Maggiore in Rome. *Elaine
Norbury.*

New Tunic Designs

Other new tunic patterns began to appear in the fifth and sixth centuries. The *Strategikon* of
the Emperor Maurice mentions two types, either *zostaria*, or *armelausia,* 'the infantry soldiers
should wear either Gothic tunics coming down to their knees or short ones split up the
sides.'(XII, B, 1). Maurice speaks of tunics worn by soldiers both over and under their armour.
The first type, *zostaria* – meaning 'closed by belts' – were of Germanic origin, and are visible
for the first time on the fragments of Theodosian columns. The Carrand Diptych in Florence
shows an eastern soldier of Germanic origin wearing a *zostarion* together with wide trousers
and a shaggy cloak with hanging sleeves like a nineteenth century Hussar!

Later during the sixth century tunics were characterised by tablet-woven decoration, often with
lozenge-shaped patterns. These were worn together with trousers which were similarly decorated.
These styles were adopted from the Goths and Iranians. Examples of them are represented in the
Barberini Diptych in the Louvre, and on the Cathedra of Maximianus. A central, vertical band of
embroidery extended down the front from the decoration of the neck vent to the waist or below,
and a second band extended in a T-shape along the top of the shoulders, sometimes to the elbow.

The *Strategikon* uses the word *himation* to describe a specific type of cavalry tunic also
belonging to the category of belt-closed *zostaria*. This was a barbarian fashion that had evolved
in Byzantium into a new garment called the *skaramangion*, a variation of the steppes kaftan
that came directly from Sassanian Iran and from the steppe peoples (Theophanes, 319). The
Strategikon gives us a description of the tunics which should be used by the cavalry:

> The men's clothing, especially their tunics, whether made of linen, goats hair, or rough wool should
> be broad and full, cut according to the Avar pattern, so they can be fastened to cover the knees
> while riding and give a neat appearance (I, 2, 46 fl.).

It was secured by a belt of flax, goatskin or smooth leather, sometimes covered with silk, *himatia
olosirika,*(Theophanes 322). In later times this became the distinctive dress of the emperor and
senior officers.

51 A late Roman Consul and his bodyguard shown on a
diptych originally from Constantinople dating to the late
fifth century AD. The elaborate costumes of this period are
well illustrated, including the detail of the *orbiculi* on the
tunic of the guard. *Elaine Norbury.*

2881 S. 47

52 Late Roman tunic from
Egypt. *Photograph courtesy of
Raffaele D'Amato.*

53 A figure from a mosaic in Kissoufim, Israel. The 'T'-shaped decorative trim on the tunic was quite common in the fifth and sixth centuries AD. *Elaine Norbury.*

54 Part of the Legend of Achilles Mosaic now in the National Museum of Antiquities, Algiers. It shows a fifth-century *tubator* in a white tunic decorated with swastikas and an orange red sagum. The other soldier looks very similar to those on the much earlier Piazza Armerina Mosaic, highlighting the continuity of Roman military dress. *Elaine Norbury.*

55 A *kamision* or *himation* from a seventh-century grave at Antinoe in Egypt. It is made from fine linen with tightly closed cuffs. It is decorated with bands of silk. *Photograph courtesy of Raffaele D'Amato.*

The Latin term *scaramangium* may originally have meant cover or protection, and have passed into Roman use together with the actual garment itself from the sixth and seventh century Gothic *foederati*. We may therefore suppose that originally this garment was worn over other clothing for warmth. Horsemen from Dura Europos and Palmyra were already using garments like this as early as the second and third centuries AD.

The contemporary Isidorus of Seville describes a second kind of tunic called an *armelausion* (*Origines*, X IX, xxii). This was so-called because it was cut and open at the front and back and closed only on the arms, i.e. *armiclausa*. The word may well have come from a tunic worn in the Roman army by Germanic infantry, that was actually seen by Isidorus himself. However, the *armilausion* is also described as a kind of military surcoat that extended over the lower abdomen. It was sleeveless and had wide armholes. Isidores also believed its origin to be Germanic and the etymology could indeed mean a 'garment without arms', or perhaps 'short-sleeved', more appropriately.

There existed two main types of *armilausion*. The first was also called *epomis* or *scapulare* and covered the shoulders down to the elbows. *Epomis* meant a cloak or garment that covered the whole body and was also large enough to conceal a sword (BV, IV, 28). It was sometimes worn over armour, and was then called *epilorikon* – literally '*over the armour*' –*lorica* being the old traditional Roman name for armour. The other *armilausion* was a sleeveless version, worn over an under-tunic but under the cuirass. The first of these garments can be compared to a military cloak and, like them, was often red in colour (Martyrium of St Bonifatius, 14: 'wearing a red armelausion'; Paulinus, *Ep.* 17: 'the armelausion was of shining red').

The dress and equipment of Guardsmen and the Imperial retinues was always more splendid and costly than those of the other soldiers. Being the Imperial court and the Imperial *Comitatus* the earthly representation of the court of heaven, the dress and the pomp was resplendent in all its magnificence both in peacetime as well as war. White dress was the favourite of the Guardsmen in close attendance to the emperor, because white was one of the Imperial colours. As for instance in the case of the 40 *Candidati* who were taken from the sixth *Schola Palatina* and who always guarded the emperor. They wore white uniforms of silk with a gold *maniakis* around their neck (*De Cer.*, I, 86, pp.391–392). Writing at the beginning of the fifth century about the martyrdom of the 40 Martyrs of Sebaste, St Gaudentius mentions '*clarae vestae*' or 'splendid clothing' given by the angels to the military martyrs. It is a clear reference to angels' uniforms – said to be both white and shining – worn by their terrestrial counterparts the 'angels' of the Imperial bodyguard.

This representation fits very well with the description of angels given by John of Ephesus, who speaks about 'a white tunic with very beautiful woven decoration' (John Heph., HE, II,6). The word *plumia* is used to indicate the decoration of such a tunic, and in the following passages John mentions that a tunic was 'beautifully woven in its fringes, on which were roundels of figures [*rotae figurarum*] both up and down'. This is a precise reference to the highly decorated *orbiculi* of the garment, positioned, as confirmed by actual surviving specimens, on the upper body and shoulders and down on the lower skirts of the tunic.

Furthermore the superior tunics of the soldiers in the *Scholae Palatinae* were of pure white linen (*candidus*) according to Jerome (*Ep.* LX, 9, 2). It was a further distinctive element from the other soldiers, who wore red or red-brown tunics (Isid, *Orig.*, XIX, 22, 10). *Palatini* officers also wore red or red purple tunics, because when Jerome writes about Ausonius – a young officer ready to leave for war – he says that he was 'clothed in a scarlet tunic as befitted his rank' (*Ep.* 118–1).

Imperial Guardsmen are also described by ancient authors as wearing golden or other splendid uniforms. The ancient sources always represent them wearing these clothes in combination with *anaxyrides* and black *campagi*. The members of the *Scholae* are often referred to as *chlamidati* or *palliati*. This point underlines the particular importance held by white garments as a distinctive sign of their rank.

Late Tunic Decoration

Aurelian is said to have been the first emperor to present to soldiers the kind of tunics known as *paragaudae*, which were decorated with purple silk and interwoven with gold thread. The passage in the *Scriptores Historiae Augustae* is important because it allows us to visualise the red tunic decorated with two vertical *clavi* and a number of bands around the sleeves.

> He, too, was the first to give to his soldiers the Paragaudae, whereas previously they had received only straight-woven tunics of purple [*recti purpurei*] – and to some he presented tunics with one band; to others those having two bands or three bands and even up to five bands [*lores*], as are today's linen tunic.

The *paragaudae* were at first cloth stripes sewn on the dress or garment, then the name itself came to designate a type of tunic or dress. They could even be a kind of silk tunic, ornamented with gold or purple stripes worked with Phrygian or barbarian decoration. The wrists and borders were of gold cloth or sewn with gold thread (*plumia*). The image that immediately comes to mind is that of the Dura Europos tunics and of the Piazza Armerina and Tellaro mosaics, where the cuffs and the shoulders of the soldiers' tunics are decorated by a different number of stripes. This corresponds well to the *monolores* (one band), *dilores, trilores* and *pentelores* tunics described in the *Scriptores Historiae Augustae*. It is probable that the numbers of the *lores* did determine the rank of the warriors. If so it is possible that two purple stripes on the cuffs might indicate the rank of an auxiliary tribune, as shown on the third century fresco of Dura-Europos. The same pattern is also visible worn by soldiers in the fifth century mosaic at Santa Maria Maggiore in Rome or in the frescoes at Santa Maria Stella in Verona. Unfortunately, almost all sleeved tunics including those for women and children found in Egypt have two cuff bands and not everyone could have been a tribune!

Other patterns, symbols and colour combinations may have had equally important meanings, perhaps suggesting different grades of soldiers which were as subtle as some of the modern methods used to indicate rank. The combination of green, blue and yellow on the uniforms is typical of the Tetrarchic age for instance, as seen in the Felix Romuliana mosaics. If this was the case, then unfortunately these meanings have been lost over the course of time.

Typical tunic decoration therefore consisted of narrow shoulder-to-hem bands, and square, oval or round tapestry inserts, many fragments of which have survived, chiefly from Egypt. Some tunics had a slit opening from the neck down to the breast, trimmed on both edges by repeated chevrons. From the neck opening extended two separate shoulder pieces, about 10–12cm long, giving the whole decoration a 'T' shaped appearance. The *clavi* were either cloth strips applied to the garment, or tapestry woven into the fabric during manufacture. Sometimes the vertical stripe was filled by foliage designs or pots with emerging stalks, then arabesques of the same pattern as that around the neck (brown or violet in Achmim). Other *clavi* were reused from old garments and applied to a new tunic. *Clavi* were present on both parts of the garment and ended at the edge of the tunica or terminated mid-garment with a roundel or square element called *orbiculi*, *calliculae* or *segmenta*. Throughout this period round *orbiculi* frequently decorated the shoulders and the lower part of tunics and *kamisia*.

The cuffs which closed the wrists of both tunic and *kamision* were also embellished with silk or wool chevrons, silk in multicoloured arabesques, or trimmed with delicate ornaments. Often we find that the pattern of the cuffs repeated the pattern found on the collar. On the wrists these *segmenta* or *patagi* were worn in different numbers, and as suggested previously were probably an indication of rank. During this era Egyptian weavers produced incredibly intricate works of textile art. They featured traditional classical designs and delicate interlaced motifs. The main wool colour used in most of the early pieces was a dark brownish purple (the 'royal purple' of antiquity), which was set in contrast with the natural cream-coloured linen.

All the preserved examples of *tunicae* are ornamented, some quite simply, others much more elaborately. Usually the silk or wool decoration was distributed around the neck opening, on the wrists and around the hems. The skirts of the tunic were decorated with patches or inserts of various shapes, including ovals, stars, and squares. Typical tunic decoration of the early 'Coptic' period consisted of narrow vertical bands from the shoulders, and squared, oval or round 'loom tapestry' inserts. The neck opening was trimmed on both edges, the trim carried down onto the breast. Two stripes ran straight down both front and back.

Applied *clavi* could even be re-used from another piece or possibly purchased as commercially-made trim. *Clavi* might extend to the hem, or terminate part-way in roundels or squared elements. Similar patches or inserts were seen at thigh height on the skirts. Frescoes and mosaics of the sixth and seventh centuries show military tunics with this typical decoration that is also confirmed by actual surviving specimens. Silk appliqué at the cuffs, neck and borders characterised the many finds from Antinoopolis, and a pictorial example of one of these tunics is worn by the executioner of St Menas, as depicted on a British ivory casket.

Often this kind of trim featured tablet-woven lozenges. They are visible on the garments of soldiers which probably illustrated troops from *Legio Quinta Macedonica* serving in Egypt, and the Germanic Buccellarii depicted on the ivory Cathedra of Maximianus in Ravenna. This style of trim was typical for soldiers based in Egypt and can be seen in sixth-century coptic paintings of David and Goliath. By the end of the Roman era the decoration was gradually reduced to a chevron-shaped trim around the edges of the neck opening, and narrow stripes on the edges and the breast. The ornamentation of the trim itself was reduced to simple interlaced foliage patterns that were usually in blue and violet.

Patterns and Symbols

On late Roman military clothing, brightly multicoloured decoration offered a riot of infinitely varied images which characterised the latter days of Roman domination in the Middle East and Africa. This art form still by and large followed the old Hellenistic traditions and geometric designs, and was filled with fantastic creatures, religious images or elaborate repetitive floral motifs. The usual features were flowers and plants, produced in monochrome designs or sometimes multicoloured like those on the sixth–seventh century *kamisia* found at Deir el Keyr. In that instance even the *clavi* are multicoloured, and filled with patterns of embrasures, medallions, foliage, flowers, fishes, birds and figures of children. The whole classical pagan repertory was also drawn upon to illustrate these bands and panels, so we find gods and goddesses, exotic dancers, lions, dolphins, seahorses, figures personifying royal power, and armed warriors. Dolphins in particular symbolised speed and strength and had featured in decorations of military equipment before, such as on scabbards of the third century.

56 Details of the frescoes in the chapels at Bawit representing various saints dressed as military officers in contemporary style. St Sisinnios above wears the clothing of a cavalry officer, including an off-white tunic and what may be a short *armelausion* with elbow-length sleeves, trimmed with the typical 'T'-shaped decoration. Just visible on his white cloak is a reddish-purple *tablion*. He has linen trousers in Persian style that are decorated above the ankles. Below: representation of Saul wearing a white tunic decorated with purple cuff bands, *clavi* and roundels at the shoulders. He has a purple cloak and a yellow waist sash. *Elaine Norbury.*

57 Part of a sixth-century painting on a wood panel from Egypt, depicting a cavalryman leading his horse. The man has a white tunic decorated with 'T'-shaped trim in purple with white spots. *Elaine Norbury.*

58 Imperial guardsmen from the time of Heraclius, illustrated on silver plates. Some of them wear decorative chest and shoulder bands which perhaps imitates the armour of earlier times. One of them has elaborately decorated trousers. *Elaine Norbury.*

Christian subjects for decoration would also have been suitable motifs for officers, guardsmen and emperors, or just devout Christian soldiers. In particular figures of St George and St Michael are represented as armoured horsemen. Other garments continue to be decorated with the less obviously Pagan classical motifs such as vines, palms, birds, fishes, baskets with bread and archways which were also open to interpretation and had been adopted and adapted as Christian symbolism. One of the most common subjects was the horseman, in particular a victorious emperor which from the seventh century onwards had the addition of a nimbus. Interaction with Sassanid Persia gradually led to these patterns and motifs becoming more and more stylised and gradually classical naturalism was discarded in favour of the intricately worked abstract motifs. In places like Egypt and the Middle East this can be seen as a metaphor for the gradual change from the Roman world to that of Islam.

2

CLOAKS

REPUBLICAN CLOAKS

Paluda a paludamentis. Haec insignia atque ornamenta militaria: ideo ad bellum cum exit imperator ac lictores mutarunt vestem et signa incinuerunt, paludatus dicitur proficisci; quae propter quod conspiciunter qui ea habent ac fiunt palam, paludamenta dicta.

Paluda is from Paludamenta which are distinguishing garments and adornments in the army; therefore when the general goes forth to war and the lictors have changed their garb and have sounded the signals, he is said to set forth paludatus 'wearing the paludamentum'. The reason why these garments are called paludamenta is that those who wear them are on account of them conspicuous and are made palam 'plainly' visible. (Varro. *DLL*, VII, 37.)

Togas

According to the Roman writer Propertius, the first Senate House was not full of the 'hem frocked Senators' of his own day but 'a rustic company of fathers clad in skins!', and for this reason they received the nickname of *pelliti* (*El.* IV,1,12). It may also be a surprise to learn that the most famous Roman garment of all, the toga, was initially worn into battle, a fashion said to derive from the Latin town of Gabii. Furthermore Gellius adds that initially the toga was worn without a tunic! (*Noct. Attic.*,VII,12.)

Illustrated scenes in the Etruscan grave known as the Francois Tomb — although painted around 340 BC — are said to represent events taking place in the seventh century BC and show Romans dressed only in white togas with red edging. If the toga was made of fairly thick wool then it might have offered a limited degree of protection. To hold it in place but to allow some movement it appears to have been drawn tightly around the body like a girdle (*cinctus*) and tied with a knot at the front then fastened with a brooch. Servius describes a whole army about to fight and wearing the *Cinctus Gabinius* (*Ad.Aen.*VII,612).

Ancient writers, including Dionysius of Halicarnassus (*Roman Antiquities* III, 61) and Servius (*Ad. Aen.* II, 781) ascribe an Etruscan origin to the toga, saying it evolved from a garment of theirs called the *Tebenna*. These early togas were apparently made from very course wool and Pliny the Elder relates how the Roman historian Varro actually saw the original toga believed to have been worn by the hero Servius Tullius and which by Varro's day was already 300 years old! (*HN.*IX, 63, 136.)

The use of the toga in battle continued for some time, in particular for military commanders. In the Francois Tomb a Roman leader is shown dressed in a purple-trimmed toga or *praetexta*. The famous Coriolanus is described taking his shield and putting on his toga to go into battle

(Plutarch, *Cor.* IX, 2). Plutarch furthermore says 'it was a custom with the Romans of that time when they were going into action and were about to gird up their cloaks and take up their bucklers, to make at the same time an unwritten will.'

The drapery around the sides always followed the *cinctus Gabinus* method, which was also preserved in sacred ceremonies. The most famous episode associating the military use of the *cinctus Gabinus* with sacred rituals is mentioned by Livy on the occasion of the sacrifice of the Consul Decius during the battle against the Latins (Liv.VIII, 9). It was customary when the tide of battle had turned against the Romans that a picked warrior would perform an almost suicidal mission and sacrifice his life (*devotus*) for the final victory. On this celebrated occasion it was Decius who dressed in the toga *Praetexta* and performed the rite of the *devotion*. With his head veiled and one hand thrust out from the toga, standing upon a javelin that lay at his feet he proclaimed the ritual formula. Then after rolling up his toga in the Gabinian fashion he charged the enemy single-handed on horseback. The Latins were not only taken aback by this action but were equally impressed by his imposing mantle!

A white toga was worn by the Consul Q. Fabius Rullianus, together with the *hasta summa imperii*, in the famous Esquiline fresco which possibly illustrates events from the Samnite war of 326 BC. Elsewhere in the fresco the toga appears to have been made from off-white, grey or brown wool. Around the main group of figures other warriors are dressed in short white tunics and kilts, but it is not clear if they are Romans or Samnites. In the triumph awarded after a victorious battle the commander wore the dress of the Etruscan kings or *vestis triumphalis* called by Livy 'the august robe of one that drives the chariots of the gods', otherwise known as the *toga picta* or the *tunica palmata*, the tunic embroidered with palms – the symbols of victory (Prop *El.*, IV, 4, 53).

Paludamentum

According to Lydus, early Roman officers wore the *Paludamentum* which he says was like the Greek mantle called a *Chlamys* (Lydus. *De Mag.*, I, 17, 1). It is also possible that most early Roman soldiers also wore the Etruscan *tebennos* already mentioned.

The *paludamentum* was the cloak of senior officers such as the consul. Although somewhat stylised, the Veii statuette shows two edges of the cloak on the breast decorated by a couple of sphere-like objects which could be pinned brooches or *fibulae*. The characteristic *paludamentum* of the Tribunes was usually in a purple shade, but alternatively could be in white. The dark cloak or *pullus atratus* was synonymous with the plebs. The nickname *Atratinus* given to the tribune Aulus Sempronius would therefore indicate his dark *paludamentum*.

Sagum

According to Livy (VII, 34.15), there was clearly a visible difference between the cloaks worn by officers and their men. He describes how the Tribune Publius Decius and some of his centurions wrapped themselves in common soldiers' cloaks to disguise their rank when they went out on reconnaissance. The origin of the *sagum* appears to have been Celtic and it became the typical military garment as opposed to the civilian toga. The Roman historian Varro (*DLL*, V, 167) claimed that the *sagum* was of Gallic origin and had been adopted by the Romans during the Celtic wars of the fourth century BC. There is little evidence to dispute this, but *sagum*-style cloaks are also present in German and Spanish contexts. The *sagum* was therefore an early example of the Romans borrowing what was originally a barbarian form of dress and making it their own. It was normally forbidden to wear the *sagum* inside the sacred perimeter of Rome's walls (*pomoerium*).

Livy's *sagulum gregale* would literally mean 'small cloak for common soldiers'. It comprised a square piece of woollen cloth, similar to the Etruscan military cloak and to the Greek *chlamys*. The *sagulum* was mainly pinned on the right breast but sometimes in the middle of the upper body, with a fibula. The right arm was therefore left free to use weapons, as depicted on the Praeneste plaques. Inside the sacred perimeter of Rome's walls the lictores wore the *toga praetexta* – the same as the consul. If they went out on campaign they wore the *sagulum*. During combat only officers would wear the *paludamentum*, as the method of draping the cloak around the body and arms made it less practical to fight in than the *sagum*.

EARLY IMPERIAL CLOAKS

Paenula

To judge from early Imperial sculpture the common soldiers appear to have favoured either the *paenula* or the *sagum*, while officers of the rank of centurion and above continued to wear the more formal *paludamentum*. In the past it was only possible to reconstruct the design of the *paenula* by interpreting the available sculptural evidence. It is best described as a hooded cape and later original specimens would suggest that it was semi-circular with a hood that was attached separately. Some commentators have suggested that its design was circular with the hood attached behind a central opening for the head, but there is no corroboration for this other than the sculptural evidence previously mentioned. Recent work by Hero Granger-Taylor has confirmed the semi-circular shape and she has identified a cloak from Ballana in Egypt as being a *paenula*-type cloak of Italian origin.

The finest example of the evidence from a military context for a *paenula* cloak is the tombstone of an unknown soldier found in Camomile Street in London. The military version of the *paenula* appears to have had an opening at the front which was then fastened or in some cases sewn together. It is also possible that the *paenula* was fastened under the chin, and what might have been the remains of a cloak with a leather thong attached was found at Vindonissa.

Some types of *paenula* also appear to have been much shorter than others, and in many cases it is unclear from sculptures whether or not the *paenula* had a hood at all, although according to Pliny the *paenula* was fitted with a long-pointed hood, which when not in use hung down the wearer's back, shaped 'like a bindweed leaf' (*HN*, XXIV, 138). Cloaks with this type of hood can be seen on Trajan's Column and in a famous fresco of a bakery scene from Pompeii. Both

59 Tombstone of Quintus Sertorius Festus, a *centurio* serving with Legio XI Claudia Pia Fidelis. It shows him wearing the *paludamentum* cloak of an officer with what appears to be a ball shaped tassel hanging from one lower corner. It can be seen in this and subsequent examples how the cloak hangs on the left shoulder, often without a brooch, and is then draped over and around the left arm with the remainder left to hang at the side. *Photograph by Luca Bonacina © RomanHideout.com.*

60 The emperor Marcus Aurelius wears
a *paludamentum* in this statue, now in the
Baltimore Art Gallery.

61 A statue from Epidaurus, Greece,
apparently showing a *centurio* also with a
paludamentum that has a tassel on the visible
lower corner.

sources clearly illustrate that unless the hood is seen directly from the rear or from one side it is very difficult to see. Because of the wide neck opening of the *paenula* it was necessary to wear a scarf, shown by the Camomile Street sculpture now in the Museum of London and various other figures represented in sculpture including those on the Adamklissi Tropaeum in Romania.

The four frontal fastenings on the Camomile Street soldier's *paenula* are extremely well defined but nevertheless somewhat confusing since two distinct types are represented. The top two are circular and look like those classed by Wild as 'button-and-loop', Type IV or V. They were probably made of bronze, which in turn may have been silvered and filled with coloured enamel. Although the third fastener is damaged the bottom one is clearly of a different type. It resembles the wooden toggle on a modern duffel coat. A recent discovery of a bronze toggle means that this type did indeed exist. The closet parallel in Wild might be Type IX. The overall accuracy of the sculpture and its attention to detail would seem to rule out the possibility that the lower two fasteners were brooches of some sort.

A *paenula* on the Chatsworth relief is closed entirely with four of these 'toggle' fasteners which, if they were brooches, would be awkward to fasten and unfasten. It may not have been unusual that the Camomile Street soldier used two different types of fastener on his cloak and the ancient artist commissioned to produce his portrait clearly felt this fashion statement was worthy of recording for posterity. A more humble method of fastening seems to have been employed on a paenula worn by S. Ennius Fuscus from the Cohors VIII Voluntariorum depicted on his tombstone now in Split Museum. This is simply closed by laces in a criss-cross fashion.

One of the Vindolanda tablets (no.87.598) appears to be a list of household goods belonging to the Cohort commander Flavius Cerialis.

cubitor(a	for dining
lodicum.pa(r	pair(s) of blankets
paenulas. can(	*paenulae,* white (?)
de synthesi . (	from an outfit:
paenulas . e.(	*paenulae* …
et laenam . e(t	and a *laena* and a (?)
cenatoria(	for dining
sunthesi(	loose robe(s)
subpaenu(l	under-*paenula(e)* …
lia.(	vests …
subuclas . b(	
a Tranqu(illo	from Tranquillus
subpaenu(l	under-*paenula(e)*
((a Tranquill(o))	((from Tranquillus)
A Broccho (	from Brocchus
tunicas . im(	tunics …
simic.(	half-belted (?)
tunicas . cen(	tunics for dining (?)

(Trans. Bowman. & Thomas 2003)

The mention of dining tunics, loose robes and a white *paenula* would also seem to suggest that these are amongst the commander's best clothes.

According to the *Scriptores Historiae Augustae* the *paenula* was not always suitable attire for an emperor to appear in before a public audience. It relates how on one occasion Hadrian lost his *paenula* – which is described as a cloak always worn by tribunes of the plebs in rainy weather, but not by emperors. Hadrian apparently saw this as an omen of continuous tribunician power and so therefore it was said that emperors no longer wore the *paenula* in front of civilians (SHA *Hadrian* III. 5).

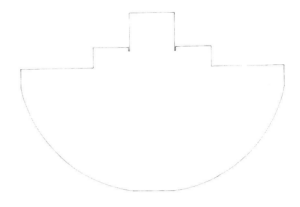

62 Restored cloak plans,. *Elaine Norbury, after J.M. Farrent and H. Granger-Taylor.*
Top: Cloak from Lahun, Egypt; now in the University Museum, University of Pennsylvania, Philadelphia. 1.98m long × 3.0m wide.
Bottom: Cloak from Ballana, Egypt. 1.66m long × 2.83m wide.

63 A sculpture now known as the Camomile Street soldier from London. The man was possibly attached to the governor's staff in London, and wears a *paenula* cloak fastened with at least two different types of fastener. © *Museum of London.*

64 A–D: Praetorian guards
from Italy wearing *paenula*
cloaks.

A: *Right and below:* Arch of Domitian, Puteoli.

B: Cancelleria Relief,
Rome.

C: Belgioloso.

D: A rear view of a *paenula* cloak, revealing the hood. Detail from Trajan's Column.

65 C. Valerius Valens, a legionary serving with Legio VIII Augusta, on a tombstone now in Corinth. Like the Camomile Street soldier, Valens carries a bundle of writing tablets to illustrate his administrative duties, but he also carries a *fustis* – a baton which could be used during policing duties and crowd control or even to execute sentries who fell asleep on duty! © *Florian Himmler.*

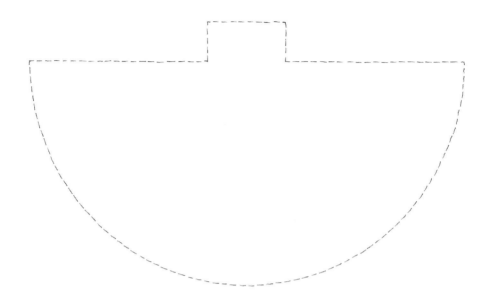

66 Restored plan of a cloak from Qasr Ibrim, Egypt, not to scale. *Elaine Norbury after J.M. Farrent & H. Granger-Taylor.*

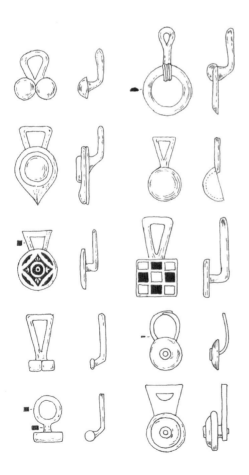

67 Button and loop fasteners as classified by Wild. *Charles W. Evans-Gunther after Wild.* From top row, left then right: Type I, Type II; Type III, Type IV; Type Vb, Type VI a; Type VII, Type VIIIa; Type IX, Type X.

Sagum

Both the *sagum* and its shorter derivative, the *sagulum*, were simply rectangular pieces of heavy wool material. The papyrus document *BGU VII* 1564 is an order for clothing and includes four cloaks that are each 6 cubits (2.66m) long x 4 cubits (1.77m) wide. These measurements can be compared with a surviving cloak from Nubia which was 1.75m long x 1.05m wide, another from Nahal Hever (no.43) which was 2.70m long x 1.40m wide, and a further example from Thorsberg in Schleswig-Holstein, Germany, that measured 2.50m long by 1.68m wide. In addition the document records that the cloaks should weigh 3¾ *minae* (1.6kg), and cost 24 drachmae (6 denarii) each.

The cloaks in *BGU VII* 1564 were identical in size to a blanket recorded in the same document that was destined for a military hospital, although the blanket was heavier and cost 28 drachmae (7 denarii). Cloaks of this nature were therefore very broad and could be wrapped easily around the body for extra warmth. Further proof of the size of cloaks is provided by the legend of St Martin (*c.*AD 371–397). When Martin was serving as a tribune at Amiens he came across a beggar outside the city gates. As it was bitterly cold Martin was moved by the man's plight. He therefore cut his own cloak up in to two parts and offered one half to the beggar.

In the first century AD the poet Martial made a humorous comment about a man called Artemidorus. He said that as Artemidorus always wore thick cloaks he should really have been named 'sagaris' (*Epig.* VIII, 58). In contrast to the large heavy cloaks there were also lighter versions of the *sagum* which could be worn during the summer or even indoors. The cloaks documented on the Rhineland tombstones have almost as many folds as the tunics, which might suggest that they too were made from a relatively light material. The *sagum* – in keeping with many other cloak types – was fastened at the right shoulder by means of a brooch, and this is one reason for the large numbers of brooches found on military sites.

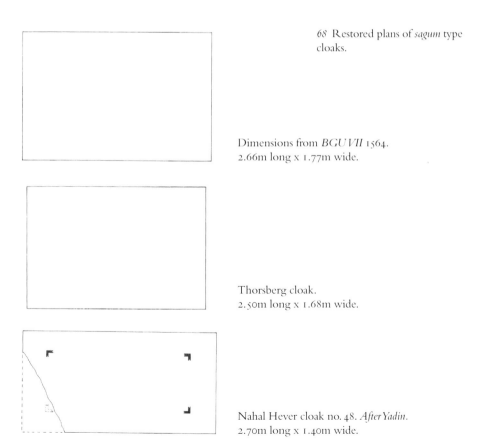

68 Restored plans of *sagum* type cloaks.

Dimensions from *BGU VII* 1564.
2.66m long x 1.77m wide.

Thorsberg cloak.
2.50m long x 1.68m wide.

Nahal Hever cloak no. 48. *After Yadin.*
2.70m long x 1.40m wide.

To judge from the available artistic evidence it seems that the *sagum* was especially popular with the military and was worn by all ranks from common soldier to emperor, and is by far the most common type of cloak represented on Trajan's Column. In fact the *sagum* became so associated with the army that the phrase 'putting on the military *sagum*' was synonymous with going to war. It was because of this militaristic association that the pacific Emperor Marcus Aurelius later tried unsuccessfully to ban its use (SHA, *Marc.Ant.* XXVII, 3). To reinforce this statement when Marcus Aurelius set off on his military campaign against the Victuali and Marcomanni with his co-emperor Lucius Verus, both men wore the *Paludamentum* to signal the beginning of the expedition (SHA. *Marc. Ant.* XIV. 1).

A wooden tablet document discovered recently in Carlisle, refers to ten *saga militaria* – military cloaks. This is not a unique reference by any means, as 'military cloaks' are also mentioned by both Appian (V, 100) and Caesar (*Civil War*, 1.5.6). Furthermore Dio Cassius says that Octavian's soldiers put on their military cloaks immediately after war had been declared against Cleopatra even though the enemy were of course nowhere near (*Epit.*, 50.4)! This association of the *sagum* with particular circumstances reinforces the impression that soldiers could wear different garments at different times.

The *sagum* would have been more practical in battle than the *paenula*, because the latter completely covered both arms, so it is perhaps not surprising that it is the *sagum* which is referred to specifically as the 'military cloak'. There were many other applications for the *sagum* apart from the obvious one of keeping the wearer warm, and it was probably used by soldiers on campaign as a groundsheet or blanket. According to Vegetius 'double thickness cloaks and goat's hair mats, are strung up along the battlements to absorb the impact of arrows. For darts do not easily pass through material which yields and swings.' (*Epit.* IV, 6.) Tacitus left a vivid account of how during the Batavian revolt, rebel soldiers broke into the Romans' camp, the latter being so taken by surprise that they had to wrap cloaks around their forearms to act as shields (*Hist.*,V, 22). Tacitus also tells us that the Batavians themselves had on one occasion even resorted to using their own cloaks as sails (*Hist.*,V, 23)!

69 First-century standard bearer on a column base from Mainz. The cloak is of the *sagum* variety but also appears to be decorated on the lower edge with tablet weaving and a fringe. This is very similar to the later Thorsberg cloak and might be evidence of a soldier wearing native-style dress even at this early date. It is also possible that he is wearing a long-sleeved tunic which again would be an early example of this fashion, but the bands around the wrist could be *armillae*, the bracelet-type military awards rather than the edge of sleeves.

70 Examples of *sagum*-style cloaks depicted on Trajan's Column, two of which have a fringe on at least one edge. These illustrations also emphasise the shortness of the auxiliary tunic at this date and the knee-length *bracae*.

It is a continuing matter of debate as to whether cloaks could be worn in battle. Julius Caesar certainly wore his into battle on at least two occasions which together with its bright colour was one way that he was instantly recognisable. This may imply that the rest of his men did not wear theirs. During Caesar's humiliating retreat from the battle for the Pharos at Alexandria, he suffered the further indignity of losing his cloak. This was subsequently carried off by the victorious Alexandrians as a highly prized battle trophy (Appian, II, 90).

On Trajan's Column Roman legionary and auxiliary soldiers engaged in battle are depicted fighting without cloaks. The exceptions are the slingers, who carry extra ammunition in a fold of their cloaks. For cavalrymen, not wearing a cloak into battle might seem a wise precaution, as to an enemy on foot a cloak might prove a tempting means of dragging someone off their horse. However there are plenty of other monuments which show riders wearing their cloaks into combat. The Roman soldiers killed when a countermine collapsed due to a fire during the siege of Dura Europos in *c.*AD 256 appeared to have been wearing their cloaks when this happened. This was deduced from the fact that their cloak brooches survived. Indeed Simon James suggested that the soldiers had been in the act of fanning the flames with their cloaks when the mine had suddenly collapsed.

A number of cloaks depicted both on Trajan's Column and elsewhere clearly have at least one edge that is fringed. It is not certain if this indicates any kind of status but it does appear to be associated with higher grade troops including cavalrymen, *beneficarii*, praetorians and senior officers such as tribunes. Other sculpture and artworks indicate that some cloaks could be further decorated with tassels at the bottom corners. Some paintings indicate that cloaks could be decorated with *clavi* like those seen on tunics.

Emperors, senior officers and centurions still wore the *paludamentum* but some officers were equally likely to be seen wearing the more functional *sagum*. After the death of the emperor Commodus the sale of his clothes included:

> clothes of silk woven with gold thread of remarkable workmanship; tunics, capes and cloaks; tunics made with long sleeves in the manner of the Dalmatians and fringed military cloaks; purple cloaks

71 Irregular auxiliaries shown on Trajan's Column. One is a slinger, the other a stone thrower. Both hold their supplies of missiles in the folds of their cloaks.

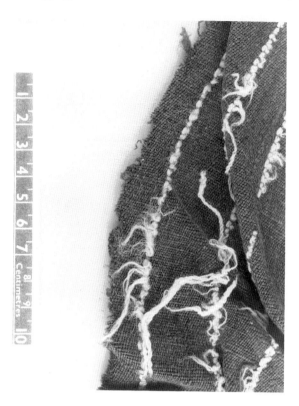

72 Detail of a cloak edge found in
Egypt. © *British Museum.*

made in the Greek fashion and purple cloaks made for service in the camp. Also Bardaean hooded
cloaks and a gladiator's toga and arms finished in gold and jewels. (SHA. *Pertinax*, 8.2–4)

Other cloaks are mentioned at this time, including the *lacerna*, in the above list of the clothes
of Commodus, and the *abolla*. The *lacerna* according to Propertius was part of a cavalryman's
equipment (El., III, 12, 7). Martial writes that the province of Baetica provided good quality
white wool for the making of *lacernae* (*Epig.* XIV., 133). The *abolla* simply seems to be a smaller
version of the *sagum*. Martial also mentions both *lacernae* and *abollae* in red, (*coccinus*) white,
(*albus*) and purple (*Epig.*,VIII, 10; 48; *Epig.*, XIV, 131, 136).

LATE IMPERIAL CLOAKS

The rectangular *sagum* cloak, which had been worn by soldiers for centuries, remains the most
popular cloak represented in Roman art in this period. Cloaks of this type were found in
excavations at Achmim-Panopolis in Egypt. They measure approximately 2m in length and 1m
wide. Similar sizes were recorded by excavators in the late nineteenth century.

Other types are known to exist, however, and some of them appear to have been adopted by
the army. The *paenula*, used in the early Roman period, seems temporarily to have lost its appeal,
although this is based mainly on lack of evidence from sculpture. The *paenula* does not appear
on surviving soldiers' tombstones from the late second century, although it clearly remained in
civilian use. However a *paenula* or something very like it is worn by soldiers depicted on the
wooden door of the fifth-century Santa Sabina in Rome. It is possible therefore that in the early
third century the *paenula* was associated with the Praetorian Guard, as it is frequently represented
on their tombstones and seems to have been retained by them longer than the frontier troops
who generally seem to wear the *sagum*. Its apparent temporary eclipse may therefore be associated

with the disbandment of the Guard by the Emperor Septimius Severus, who replaced them with a personal bodyguard drawn from amongst his own provincial legionaries.

The Emperor Marcus Aurelius Antoninus – the son of Severus – earned his famous nickname 'Caracalla' after his fondness for wearing a cloak known as the *caracalla*. Regrettably, it is not known for certain what the *caracalla* actually looked like, although the best guess is that it was a hooded, sleeveless cape. If that is the case it may have resembled the *paenula* or the long type of hooded cloaks seen on many Gallo-Roman and Romano-British sculptures. Pollux actually says that it was like the *paenula* (*Onom.*,7, 60) and Dio Cassius records that it was Caracalla himself who invented this peculiar garment (*Epit.*, LXXIX). According to Dio he did this by cutting up and sewing together in a barbarian fashion another form of cloak. This would be innovative, because with the exception of the hood, Roman capes were not normally sewn up.

Another author, Spartian also gives the credit for the design of the *caracalla* to the emperor, who in his biography of Caracalla also says that the emperor was responsible for its length, which reached the ankles (Anton. *Cara.*, 9, 7–8). It is likely that the *caracalla* was of heavy wool, as it needed to be suitable for outdoor wear on the northern frontier. There might have been a version used on the eastern front, because the price edict of Diocletian specifically states that there was a linen version of the *caracalla* as well. This linen version was apparently so cheap compared with the other cloaks that it cannot have been as large and probably only covered the head and shoulders. It might therefore conceivably be the *caracallus minor* that the price edict also records.

As Wild has observed, there is no known evidence for the *caracalla* outside of Gaul before the beginning of the third century, which corresponds with Caracalla's campaigns along the Rhine. Dio Cassius records that Caracalla liked to be seen by his troops as a comrade and he took to wearing the clothing of the ordinary soldier (*Epit.*, LXXIX). Further evidence of this is supplied by Herodian who states that Caracalla based his clothing on that worn by his personal German bodyguard (*Hist.*, IV, 7.3). Perhaps the Romans were reintroduced to

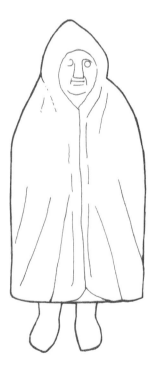 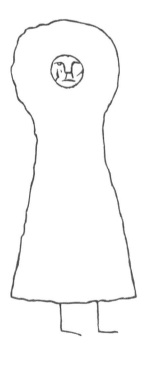

73 Representations of hooded cloaks from Provincial art. Their long length might indicate that they represent the *caracalla*. Left: Housesteads, England. *Charles W. Evans-Gunther.* Right: North Africa. *Charles W. Evans-Gunther after A. Wilson.*

74 Grotesque figure from Augst in Switzerland
wearing a long hooded cloak that might represent a
caracalla.

the idea of long ankle-length cloaks by German warriors serving in the Imperial armies, as
Germanic clothing could be made up from sewn pieces of material.

Other Roman writers refer to a hooded cloak called a *birrus.* The price edict of Diocletian
records a *birrus Britannicus*, which implies a British origin for these garments, although Wild
suggests a Gallic source. A letter from Terentianus – an Egyptian recruit to the fleet based at
Alexandria during the reign of Hadrian – mentions a *byrrus castalinus*, which may refer to a
cloak made of beaver skin. This would not be too unusual and indeed would make an ideal
waterproof garment for use on board ship.

The *birrus* was probably very similar to the *paenula* in shape but with perhaps the addition
of an extra flap-type fastening at the neck. This covered the 'V' shaped gap at the neck that
was a distinctive feature of the *paenula* which had required the additional use of a scarf. The
birrus was also apparently longer than the *paenula* and together this combination of factors
might explain why in written sources at least the *birrus* rapidly replaced the *paenula* as the
outdoor garment of choice. However, apart from the mention by Terentianus there does not
appear to be much evidence that it was used in the army, although telling a *birrus* apart from
a *paenula* in a sculpture or mosaic would be extremely difficult.

For officers the *chlamys* or *paludamentum* was still the principal cloak worn, and it remained
a symbol of the *militia armata* or military calling (*Cod. Theod.*VIII, 4, 30 = *Cod. Just.* XII, 33, 4).
The most common type was a semi-circular cloak that reached to the hips. From AD 382
this was limited to soldiers, officers, and officials charged with civil functions but formally
part of the military. It distinguished the *armati* from the *officiates* (*Cod. Theod.* XIV, 10, 1).
This was necessary because military garments were technically forbidden to civilians. The
cloaks of senior military officials were longer, ankle-length, and usually trapezoid in shape.

75 Drawing of part of the fresco that remained in the chapel of the standards at Luxor Temple in Egypt which was converted into a fort during the late third century AD. Remarkable as this discovery is, it is also sobering to think that virtually every Roman fort would have been decorated in this manner and that subsequently many thousands of similar images from all over the Roman world have been lost. The scene shows a variety of officers with highly decorated cloaks. *Charles W. Evans-Gunther after J. Deckers.*

They were ornamented on both sides with squared panels butting up against the vertical edges, called *tabula* or *tablion*, which were of two contrasting colours.

Even though the physical differences between the *sagum* and the *chlamys* were always negligible, the word *sagion* (Latin *sagum*) was consistently used to describe the rectangular campaign cloak. If it was worn by a *Magister Militum* it was a purple colour (*sagion alethinon*), while the smaller version for use by the cavalry was still called the *sagulum*. Another short military cloak that we hear about was called the *mantion* (*Chronicum Alexandrinum* p.102). This cloak was thrown back over both shoulders and fastened at the centre over the breast by a round brooch.

There seems less evidence in the later empire for the previously popular yellow-brown coloured cloaks with red or red-brown colours becoming more common, as clearly demonstrated in the mosaics at Sta Maria Maggiore. The materials were much the same as before with linen for summer and wool in winter. The wool cloaks apparently were sometimes coated with a waterproofing substance (*gausape*) perhaps because some of the natural lanolins had been lost in the dyeing process.

At the desert site of Achmim-Panopolis in Egypt squared trapezoidal shaped cloaks were found that had decorations in each corner. These could be either squared or round *segmenta* that were often woven in purple. The edges of the cloaks had in addition one, two or even three red or violet stripes. Their length varied from 1.98m to just over 2.44m, and the width from 1.02m to just under 1.50m. Another cloak still in use was the old *paenula*. At this date the *paenulae* were also ornamented like their earlier counterparts with *clavi*, although in keeping with later trends these were likely to be more ornamental than the previously plain versions. *Paenulae* decorated with the addition of a fringe are seen being worn by officers in the drawings of the lost Column of Theodosius. This feature is also discernable on the Sta Sabina door.

76 Another part of the Luxor fresco *(see also colour plate (13a))* depicting a number of soldiers and a standard bearer carrying the *vexillum*, a flag type standard. *Charles W. Evans-Gunther after J. Deckers.*

77 More officers from the Luxor fresco. The best preserved is wearing a yellow brown *sagum* cloak with a purple decorative band and a fringe on the lower edge. His staff of office indicates that he might be a centurion. Somewhat unusually this officer also wears a black short-sleeved tunic. *Charles W. Evans-Gunther after J. Deckers.*

78 Examples of *sagum* cloaks on provincial mosaics, both of which are yellow-brown in colour.
Left: Cologne, Germany. Right: Piazza Armerina, Sicily.

New Military Garments

The *Strategikon* (1, 2, 50) refers to an extra large cloak with a hood that was used by the cavalry called a *gounoberonikion*. It was made of felt or padded material (*kentouklon*). The origin of the word is clearly not from the Roman world but is Slavic – from *guna* meaning a hairy or fur garment. The Strategikon continues:

> Then, in case it should rain or be damp from the dew, by wearing this garment over the coat of mail and the bow they may protect their armament and still not find it awkward to use the bow or the lance. Such cloaks are also necessary in another way on patrol, for when the mail is covered by them, its brightness will not be seen at a distance by the enemy, and they should provide some protection against arrows. (1.2.)

A garment of this type could perhaps be identified with that of Iranian origin (*kandys*), worn with the long sleeves hanging down behind. Such coats, of fur or woven materials, are seen in late Roman monuments representing mercenaries, soldiers and senior officers of East Germanic or Iranian stock in Imperial service, e.g. on the Carrand Diptych and the St Menas pyx in Egypt; they are also clearly visible on relief carvings of Georgian and Armenian vassal princes. This type of garment, adapted from the Iranian lambskin coat with dangling sleeves, was probably introduced via the Goths and Slavs.

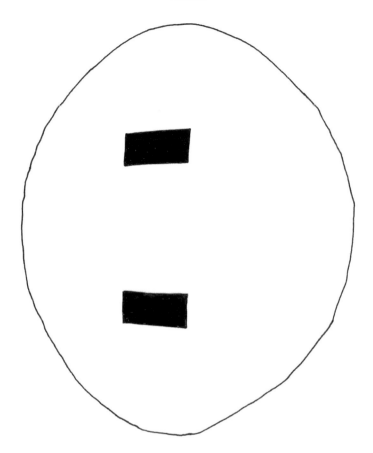

79 Plan of a late Roman cloak found in Egypt. 2.86 × 2.42m.

Asiatic influence on late Roman clothing, especially in Egypt, is explained by the long (sometimes even peaceful) co-existence of the Roman and Persian Empires in the Near East, and Rome's employment of Persian mercenaries (e.g. the Perso-Justiniani regiment stationed at Grado, north Italy, in the sixth–seventh centuries). Several beautiful specimens of riding coats were found in the Antinoopolis necropolis; these were sturdily made, but lighter types may have existed. One grave revealed a green-blue coat ornamented with red silk brocade, worn over a second linen garment with black and white patterns. The horse harness and whips found with the bodies indicated cavalrymen, although Gayet assigned these coats to high-ranking officers. Examples are preserved in the Berlin Museum, the Lyon Textile Museum, the Louvre and several other collections.

These riding coats are formed from sewn sections, with very long sleeves narrowing towards the cuff and then flaring out. All are made from a woollen cloth whose combed fibres give a napped appearance. The front is open, with the right side cut so that it overlaps to the left, and silk brocade bands decorate the edges, cuffs and neck. The very long sleeves are sometimes extended by a leather cuff; their ends are decorated with coloured wool embroidery or applied silk bands. Gayet mentions that in two graves he found 'Byzantine gauntlets' attached directly to the sleeve; fragments of silk sleeves associated with a leather background are still visible in the Louvre. The average length of the coats is 1.30m, and the sleeves often surpass 1m.

The problem of identifying such coats with the *gounoberonikion* described in the *Strategikon* is the absence of the wide sleeves mentioned there. However, one of the riding coat specimens preserved in Berlin (inv. 9965) has underarm openings. Many of the new military garments, tunics as well as coats, were characterised by these, which allowed the arm to pass through, leaving the sleeves hanging decoratively from the shoulders and allowing free movement. Such apertures are found with reinforcing braids or cords, and two specimens have openings approximately 23cm long – ample for the brawniest arm.

Decoration

In spite of the fact that early Roman writers regarded the wearing of brightly decorated clothing as both barbarian and effeminate, the practice of wearing decorative cloaks was yet another fashion that found its way into the ranks of the Roman army. The cloaks depicted on the temple frescos at Luxor, for instance, are decorated with large *orbiculi*. An indication of how elaborate some of these garments became is that in the late third century price edict of Diocletian a guardsman's cloak was more expensive than his horse…

80 Fragment of a stone relief found near Cordoba in Spain. It shows three men wearing the short cape with a hood called an *alicula*. One of the men is wearing a mail shirt so he at least is a soldier. The sculpture indicates the cape's shaggy texture and at least two different methods of fastening. The soldier's seems to be closed with a metal clasp.

81 A hunter shown on a stone sarcophagus also wears a short shoulder cape, this time with a hood.

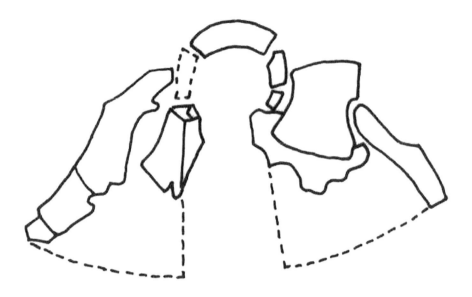

82 A skin shoulder cape from Krogens Mose, Denmark which was probably similar to the *alicula*. *After Wild*.

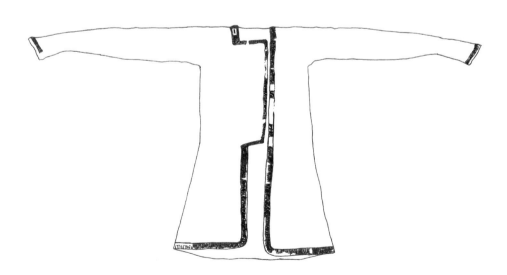

83 Plan of a riding coat from Antinoe (Antinoopolis) Egypt. *Charles W. Evans-Gunther after A. Voight in Fluck and Vogelsang-Eastwood*.

84 The Aghias Menas Pyxis – an ivory carving in the British Museum – which appears to show a riding coat draped over the shoulders. *Elaine Norbury.*

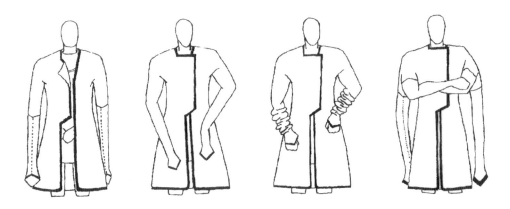

85 The various methods of wearing the Persian style riding coat. *Elaine Norbury after K. Mälck.*

86 Seventh-century riding coat from Antinoe (Antinoopolis) found during the nineteenth century excavations of Gayet. It is blue-green wool trimmed with tablet woven silk. *See colour plate 37 for a reconstruction. Photograph courtesy of Raffaele D'Amato.*

During a mock naval battle, Agrippina, wife of the Emperor Claudius, had worn a military cloak made entirely of gold cloth. Ornamented cloaks might be woven with gold and silver thread, frequently in the form of mythical beasts, deities, or flowers. The *Scriptores Historiae Augustae* relate that the Emperor Alexander Severus thought that inserting purple and gold threads into linen clothing was madness: he believed that this practice defeated the object of wearing finer materials in the first place, and that the gold thread made the garments heavier (SHA, *Sev. Alex.*, XLI, 11). The Emperor Aurelian was also opposed to garments made from silk or decorated with gold.

Nevertheless Aurelian himself was not averse to presenting his own soldiers with decorated clothing (SHA, *Aurelian*, XLVI, 6); his Imperial guards in particular had lavish golden clothing and armour (*Ammianus*, 31, 10.9). They were even referred to as *ostensionales* (SHA, *Sev. Alex.*, XXXIII, 3). In spite of periodic objections the practice of wearing decorated clothing caught on, and according to the writer Eusebius an embassy to the Emperor Constantine I (r.AD 306–337) brought cloaks that were bedecked in this manner. This group of decorated cloaks are known as *sagulum versicolor*, but Roman writers such as Eusebius also referred to them as *barbarica*, leaving us in no doubt as to their origins (*Vita Const.*, 4, 7).

Cloaks had other functions and could also be used for signalling, as demonstrated by the Emperor Aurelian (SHA, *Aurelian*, XXIV, 1). Two episodes in the Persian wars of the mid-fourth century, as recounted by the soldier–historian Ammianus Marcellinus also mention cloaks used for this purpose. When Ammianus was fleeing from the Persians he encountered a body of Roman cavalry whom he signalled by waving his cloak, which he adds was the usual way of indicating that the enemy were close at hand (Ammianus, 18, 6.11). Later in the war, Ammianus describes how a detachment of Persian archers captured a section of a city's defences and used a scarlet cloak to signal that it was safe for the rest of their comrades to attack (19, 5).

The *Scriptores Historiae Augustae* document the existence of varieties of cloaks worn on different occasions, and still refer to some as 'military'. For example, the soldiers of the usurper Saturninus wore heavy military cloaks in winter but very light cloaks in summer (SHA, *Sat*, XXIV, 10). Saturninus also insisted that his soldiers wear their cloaks when reclining at the dinner table, so they would not expose too much of their legs!

PART TWO

THE CLOTHING INDUSTRY AND THE COLOUR OF MILITARY CLOTHING

3

THE CLOTHING
INDUSTRY I

MATERIALS, CLOTHING COSTS AND SUPPLY

Eme, mi vir, lanam, unde tibi pallium malaeum et calidum conficiatur tunicaeque hibernae bonae, ne algeas hac hieme

Husband mine; do buy me some wool to make a soft warm cloak for you, and some nice heavy tunics so that you won't be cold this winter. (Plautus. Mil. Glor.)

The Roman lawyer Ulpian wrote that the materials used for clothing were wool (*lanea*), linen (*linea*) silk, (*serica*) and cotton (*bombucina*) (Ulp., Lib.44 *ad Sabinum, De Vestibus et Vestimentiis in Digestorum Lib* XXXIV, Tit.II).

Wool
The principal material for the production of Roman military clothing was wool. Wool has many properties which made it suitable for this role. The natural wave of the fibres forms air locks, giving good insulation. Furthermore it is not only water repellent but its elasticity allows it to retain its shape even after creasing.

By a combination of pressure, friction, heat and moisture, wool can also be made into felt (*coactile*) which had many practical military uses. Pliny for example says that if vinegar was added it could make felt garments withstand not only steel but fire as well! '*lanae et per se coactae vestem faciunt et, si addatur acetum, etiam ferro resistunt, immo vero etiam ignibus novissimo sui purgamento.*' (*Nat Hist* VIII 192.) This would make felt an ideal material for the garment worn under armour, helmet linings or indeed as a protective garment in its own right. Felt blankets could be used to fight fires and were probably a necessary item of equipment in forts and camps. Felt making is shown on a wall painting from Pompeii outside the workshop of Verecundus who was a felt maker or *coactiliarius*. The painting shows two workers standing either side of a small funnel-shaped boiler, kneading rolls of hot, wet, wool fibre in triangular-shaped draining boards raised on trestles. The surplus liquid would drain back into the boiler.

As sheep could be raised on every farmstead, the weaving of wool cloth could be done in virtually every early Roman home, and women were expected to provide clothing for the household and their menfolk when they went to war. Conservative Roman men such as the first Emperor Augustus still expected the ladies of the house to engage in this traditional activity long after professional weavers had taken over the production of clothing.

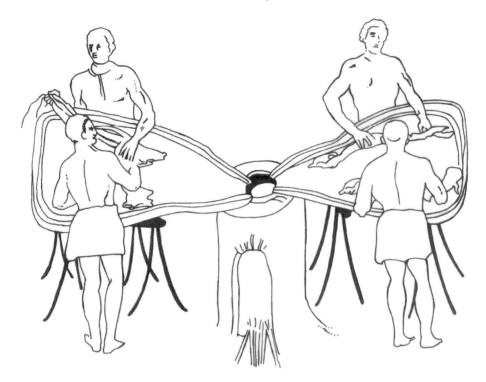

87 Felt makers at work from a wall painting outside the felt workshop of Verecundus in Pompeii. *Elaine Norbury after Wild.*

According to Columella, sheep producing pure white wool were raised in Northern Italy (VII.II.3–4, 6). Some sheep in Asia Minor were known for their dark red wool (Columella VII. 4). Pliny gives a lengthy description of the various types of sheep and wool known in Roman times. He states with some satisfaction that the best wool was from Apulia, which oddly he says was known in Italy as 'wool of the Greek breed', but everywhere else was called 'Italian wool' (*Nat. Hist.*VIII, 190–1).

Linen

The predominant fabric in the Eastern Empire was linen, from the spun fibre of the flax plant. Egypt was the main producer, and Alexandria manufactured and exported linen garments for centuries. The linen – especially that used for the *kamision* worn under the main tunic – appears to have been of high quality; some shirts found by Gayet at Antinoopolis are true transparent chiffons. Nevertheless, what may have been flax seeds have even been found on Roman sites in Britain, indicating that the linen industry was widely distributed throughout the empire.

Linen would have had many uses for the military. It is ideal for making sail-cloth and can be woven to make a very fine cloth so is perfect for underclothes and was almost certainly used for under-tunics. Furthermore it can be bleached white so would be suitable for parade wear and religious occasions when the purity associated with white was a requirement. Although linen can be dyed, flax fibres take dye less readily than wool. Ancient dye recipes rarely mention linen.

Cotton

Many people think of cotton as being a product of the modern age. This is certainly not the case and recent finds have even suggested its use was more widespread in Roman times than previously suspected. Cotton is soft and less rough than linen, and is also lighter – making it popular in hot climates. The cotton plant fortunately flourishes in hot temperatures, so it is not surprising to find that cotton garments are frequently mentioned in papyri from Egypt. In Roman times Egypt was also the centre of the cotton trade with India, where soldiers of Alexander the Great had seen it grown and even used it as padding for their saddles (Strabo XV.693). In spite of the fact that it must be considered a luxury product, nevertheless we find various Roman authors attesting to the use of cotton for sail-cloths, curtains, and awnings in the theatre! (Catul.LXIV, 227; Ovid, *Metam*.XI 477, *Fast*. 587; Val. Flac.IV, 422.)

Silk

Such was the value of silk to the Romans it can be only be compared to the value of oil today, in that its use had an effect on foreign, diplomatic and military policy. This was especially true in the late Empire but in earlier periods its rarity was regarded as something of a novelty and to the more conservative Romans, best avoided. Tacitus records how Tiberius for example passed a law forbidding men to wear silk garments (*Annals* II,33.1.) Naturally amongst the chief faults of the most depraved emperors like Nero and Elagabalus was their fondness for wearing silk clothes. Silk is a perfect material for garments worn next to the skin.

The biggest difference in later Roman clothing from the Classical period was the greater use of silk, much of which was purchased from the Persians (a state monopoly restricted its primary purchase to the *commerciarii* of the Praetorian Prefecture, reserving what was necessary for state manufacture and selling on the rest). In the time of Justinian the merchants were obliged to raise prices – due both to the high prices demanded by the Persians and the tariffs extracted by the Imperial bureaucracy. In AD 540 Justinian fixed the official price and proposed an agreement with the Ethiopians which would allow the purchase of silk directly from India (*BP, I, XX, HA, XXV*). This plan never reached fruition but, a little later Christian monks managed to smuggle silkworms directly from China; this must have been something of a revelation, as in earlier times even educated Romans like Pliny thought silk grew on trees!

The cultivation of silk was now diffused throughout the eastern Empire (*BG*, VIII, 17), though remaining a state monopoly. Silk was so expensive that it was often combined with other fibres to make more affordable fabrics. Byzantium began its own silk industry, the tapestry-woven brocades in various qualities being finished by needlework in multicoloured silk and or gold thread.

Clothing Supply

According to the Greek historian Polybius, in Republican times deductions were made from a soldier's pay: 'for the Romans, the Quaestor deducts from their pay a set price for food and clothing and any arms they need.'(6.39.15) Later, according to Plutarch, one of the popular reforms introduced by Tribune C. Gracchus was that soldiers were to be supplied with clothing at the public's expense. He therefore forced the Senate to pass a law by which the public treasury had to supply the army's clothes (*C. Gracchus*, V). Nevertheless, one well-known fact is that soldiers in the early Imperial era had money subtracted from their pay to provide their food, equipment and clothing. Surviving pay receipts indicate that up to 30 per cent of a soldier's earnings could be deducted for his clothing alone.

Clothing might also be supplied as a part of a levy, which Livy says the newly conquered territories of Spain, Sardinia and Sicily had to do for Scipio's army in Africa (Livy XXIX, 36; XXX, 3). Livy adds that 1,200 cloaks and 12,000 tunics were quickly dispatched. While it is accepted that soldiers usually wore wool tunics, it has become clear that they would own more than one of each item of clothing and that at least one other tunic might be made from a lightweight wool or even linen which would be available for off-duty wear. One occasion of this happening is briefly mentioned by Plutarch when he described the effect that billeting Roman troops commanded by Sulla had on the local population of Asia Minor, roughly where modern Turkey is today:

> Sulla now imposed on Asia as a whole an indemnity of 20,000 talents. At the same time private
> families were entirely ruined by the brutal behaviour and extortion of the troops quartered on

them. Orders were issued that every host should give his guest four tetradrachms a day and should provide for him an evening meal to which he might invite as many of his friends as he liked. An officer should receive fifty drachmas a day and two suits of clothes, one to wear at home and one to wear when he went out. (Sulla, XXV)

Writing towards the end of the first century AD, Tacitus has left us with a somewhat bleak image of what it was like to serve in the Roman army.

Military service was burdensome and unprofitable, mind and body were assessed at 10 asses per day: from this they had to buy clothing, weapons and tents, and also to pay off the cruel centurion and buy time off from [fatigue] duty (*Annals*, 1.17)

This often led soldiers to resort to acts of extortion to supplement their pay, a fact documented with outstanding clarity in the private business accounts of one individual in Egypt who regularly paid soldiers money on demand (*SB* 9207). Even the New Testament writers were fully aware of the problem, as Luke writes when soldiers asked John the Baptist 'what shall we do?' He replied 'do not extort money from anyone, do not use blackmail; be satisfied with your pay.' (Luke, 3.14)

The supply of clothing was now in the care of the state, but Propertius informs us that even at this late date certain soldiers received clothing woven by their wives (Prop., *El.*, IV, 3, 18) and mentions a woman called Arethusa who complains of the great distance between her and her husband, engaged in the war against the Parthians. She remembers the four *lacernae* she has made for him, and the fact that she was always dealing with his camp clothes (*pensa castrensia*). This document is not unique and together with other evidence, including a letter from Vindolanda, shows that soldiers were able to receive items of clothing from home.

Perhaps the clearest evidence of this is provided by the remarkable private letters discovered at Karanis in Egypt, written by one Terentianus serving with the fleet at Alexandria to one Tiberianus presumably his father. Terentianus writes (Inv. 5391)

Claudius Terentianus to Claudius Tiberianus, his lord and dearest father, very many greetings. Before all else, I pray that you be strong and cheerful and well, together with our entire family, and I am pleased whenever I have news from you. Know, father, that I have received … a cloak, a tunic, and the girdled clothes, and from Nepotianus … But you gave him rough ones. Do you come … You know very well how much he has lied to his comrades. Know that I am being sent off to Syria and am about to leave with a detachment. I asked him to give them to me, but he denied that he had the rough ones. He said to me: 'If you do not return … to me, I shall tell your father.' If I did not need to … I would have returned it to him gladly, so that you might recover from him our … Both Kalabel and Deipistus have enlisted in the Augustan fleet of Alexandria … no one has reckoned up the chances of his life … nor do I hate Marcellus on this account. Since they were nothing to me - (I say this) in the presence of the gods - but words, I conceived a hatred of no one. I went … by boat, and with their help I enlisted in the fleet lest I seem to you to wander like a fugitive, lured on by a bitter hope. I ask and beg you, father, for I have no one dear to me except you, after the gods, to send to me by Valerius a battle sword, a … a pickaxe, a grappling iron, two of the best lances obtainable, a … cloak, and a girdled tunic, together with my trousers, so that I may have them, since I wore out my tunic before I entered the service and my trousers were laid away new. And if you are going to send anything, put an address on everything and describe the seals to me by letter lest any exchange be made en route. And if you write me a letter, address it: 'on the liburnian of Neptune.' Know that everything is going well at home, through the beneficence of the gods. I sent you two jars of olives, one in brine and one black. These jars are the same as those … that I sent; from them you can identify these too. I ask and beg you, father, to go to the Delta on a trading boat, so that you may buy and send three breeders … My mother, my father Ptolemaeus, and all my brothers salute you … 'Salute Aphrodisia, Isityche' … Serenus the clerk, your colleague Marcellus, your colleague Terentius, and all your comrades. I pray that you enjoy good health for many years, together with your entire family. Farewell.

In a further letter Terentianus writes the following, adding even more revealing information about military life. (Inv.5390)

> Claudius Terentianus to Claudius Tiberianus, his father and lord, very many greetings. Before all else, I pray for your health, which is my especial wish. Know, father, that I have received the things that you sent me by ... the veteran and by Numesianus, the ... and the short cloak (palliolum), and I thank you because you considered me worthy and have made me free from care. I have sent you, father, by Martialis a bag sewn together, in which you have two mantles (amicla), two capes (amictoria), two linen towels, two sacks, a wooden bed. I had bought the last together with a mattress and a pillow, and while I was lying ill on the ship (liburna) they were stolen from me. You have also in the bag a cape of single thickness; my mother sent this to you. Receive also a chicken coop, in which you have sets of glassware, two bowls of quinarius size, a dozen goblets, two papyrus rolls for school use, ink inside the papyrus, five (?) pens, and twenty Alexandrian loaves. I beg you, father, to be content with that. If only I had not been ill, I was hoping to send you more, and again I hope so if I live. I beg you, father, if it meets with your approval, to send me from there low leathern boots (caligae) and a pair of felt socks (udones). Boots with buttons (?) are worthless; I provide myself with footgear twice a month.. And I beg you to send me a pickaxe. The Optio took from me the one that you sent me, but I am grateful to him for furnishing me ...
>
> Moreover, I ask and beg you, father, to reply to me immediately about your health, that you are well (?). I am worried about trouble at home (?) if you do not write back. And if god should be willing, I hope to live frugally and to be transferred to a cohort; but here nothing will be accomplished without money, and letters of recommendation will have no value unless a man help himself. I beg you, father, to send me a reply promptly. Know that Carpus came here in his wanderings and Dius was found (?) in the legion and I accepted 6 denarii on his behalf. My mother and my father and brothers salute you; and know that everything goes very well at home. Salute Aphrodisia and Isityche. Salute Arrius the centurion together with his family, Saturninus the clerk together with his family, Capito the centurion together with his family, Cassius the adjutant together with his family, Tyrannius the adjutant together with his family, Sallustius together with his family, Terentius the pilot, Fronto together with his family, Sempronius Italicus, Publicius, Severinus, your colleague Marcellus, and Lucius. Salute Serenus the clerk together with his family. Salute all our comrades. Farewell.

(Trans. Youtie & Winter 1951)

After reading the correspondence of Terentianus, one is often left wondering what in fact the army actually supplied its soldiers! Serving in particular theatres also demanded clothing to suit the local climate and once again we find a soldier resorting to asking privately for the items he needs. Apollinarius serving in the legion based at Bostra, Syria, wrote to Tasicharion his mother at Karanis in Egypt asking her to 'make an inquiry of a friend of mine at Alexandria, so that you may send to me through him coarse fibred linens. For there is none here, and the weather is very hot.' (*P.Mich* Inv.5888)

Clothing (*vestimenta*) could also be handed out as rewards or pay for the soldiers, and distinctive clothing, especially if belonging to famous enemies, was considered worthy war booty for the gods. Severus Alexander supplied his troops with leg wrappings, trousers and boots (SHA *Sev. Alex.* XL. 6), and others were more fortunate, receiving all of their military equipment, including clothing, directly from the emperor himself (SHA. *Hadrian* XVII. 2).

The cost of 25 drachmae (6.25 denarii) paid to the weavers of Philadelphia in AD 138 for the military tunic can be compared with the deductions on soldiers' pay receipts for clothing in P. Geneva Lat.l from Egypt from AD 81, and the receipt of C. Messius from Masada dated to AD 72. In the Geneva papyrus Q. Iulius Proclus had 205.5 drachmae deducted in one year towards clothing, while his comrade C. Valerius Germanus was docked 245.5 drachmae (61.375 denarii). In the last pay period they had 60 drachmae (15 denarii) and 100 drachmae (25 denarii) deducted respectively, which can be compared with the 7 denarii (equivalent to 28 drachmae) paid for a linen tunic by C. Messius.

The dramatic effects of the economic, military and political turmoil which befell the empire from the late second century onwards is graphically illustrated by the hugely inflated cost of clothing, as documented in the price edict issued in AD 301, during the reign of the Emperor Diocletian (AD 284–305). In this we find that the three grades of military tunic available cost 1,000, 1,250 and 1,500 denarii!

The most important evidence for both the purchase and supply of clothing comes from the numerous papyri found in Egypt. It transpires that orders for clothing were issued by the Prefect of Egypt and that they were divided equally amongst the districts so as to lessen the impact this would have had on individual communities.

P.Cair Isid. 54. January 15, AD 314

To Antoninus Sarapammon, strategos of the Arsinoite nome, from Aurelius Isidorus, son of Palenus and Aurelius Doulus, son of Timotheus, both Komarchs of the village of Karanis, and Aurelius Isidorus, tesserarius of the same village.

We have received from the bankers of public monies of the nome, in accordance with your warrant, as the price of tunics and cloaks which we supplied and delivered for the 7th and 5th year:

Delivered to Cyrillus and Demeas, receivers

Tunics 22 at 4000 dr. each	14 tal. 4000 dr.
Cloaks 8 at 5000 dr. each	6 tal. 4000 dr.
Total	21 tal. 8000 dr.
Deducted, 6½ per cent	1 tal. 2190 dr.
Total remainder	19 tal. 5810 dr.

Let the receipt be valid. In response to the formal question we have made acknowledgement.
The year after the 3rd consulship of our lords Constantine and Licinius Augusti, Tybi 20
[2nd hand] We Aurelius Iidorus, Aurelius Doulas, and Aurelius Isidorus have received the amount stated above. I Aurelius Ision, have written for them since they are illiterate.

(Trans Boak & Youtie 1960)

However, we also find that individual soldiers were themselves still able to requisition supplies. The production of clothing in Egypt was so well advanced that it seems villages in Egypt would also receive orders for military clothing from other provinces if necessity demanded.

By the reign of Diocletian (r.AD 284–305) the manufacture of uniforms was largely concentrated in state factories (*gynaecea* and *linyfia*) under the direct supervision of an officer called the *Comes Sacrarum Largitionum*. Even so, documents (e.g. *P.Oxy.* XII 1448) and (*P.Cair. Isid.* 54), show that clothing was still purchased directly by the army even after that date from small villages in Egypt.

The principal material for military tunics and cloaks in the later empire remained wool, although linen garments may have been equally popular in the east. State controlled workshops called *gynaecea* responsible for the production of wool garments were established – perhaps by Diocletian – and at least 15 *gynaecea* are known in the Western Empire. In contrast only two *linyfia* producing linen clothes are found in the records. In addition there were nine dyeing houses or *bafia* in the west. Unfortunately there is very little corresponding information concerning the production of garments in the east. This is perhaps because very little changed in the eastern provinces especially in Egypt, where textile manufacture had been well established for centuries.

The state factories provided the finishing and dyeing of cloth necessary for troops and court officials. In Italy they were based near the Imperial courts or in centres of established clothing industries such as Milan, Aquileia, Cissa, Ravenna, Rome, Canosa, Venosa, Taranto and Syracuse (*ND* Occ. XI, 49–52, 63, 65, 67–68). Each factory was commanded by a procurator

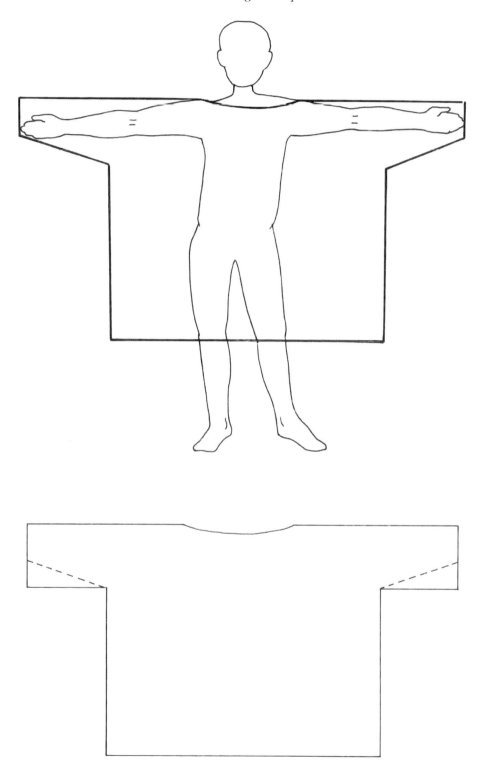

88 Plan and reconstruction of a tunic found at Reepsholt. This is probably similar to the type of garment termed by Wild 'the Gallic coat', a tunic commonly worn in the northern provinces by people of all ranks. It would have been used by soldiers off duty and is also a further indication of the wide width of garments in this period. *Charles W. Evans-Gunther after Malling.*

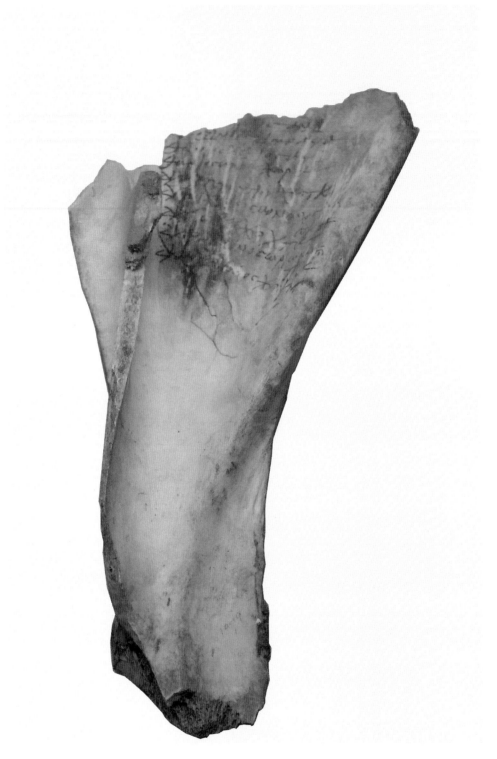

89 Not all documents were written on writing tablets or even papyrus. This animal bone from Egypt, now in the British Museum, appears to refer to the collection of military clothing. © *The author.*

and defended by a small garrison. According to Maurikios (*Strat.*, 1.2), soldiers in the Eastern army of the seventh century wore tunics made from either rough wool, linen or even goat hair. Linen especially would be a preferable alternative in hotter climates and also for more formal occasions. The army of the Eastern Empire always had at its disposal greater financial resources than that of the Western Empire, and military garments were produced in a variety of sizes. Specialised centres of textile manufacture such as Antinoe, Arsinoe, Panopolis and Alexandria in Egypt were involved in uniform production.

Procopius with his own eyes saw recruits (*tyrones*) arriving from the country to Constantinople with only a small tunic (*chitoniskon*) and a wallet (BV, IV,16,13). Recruits and soldiers received a uniform (*militaris vestis*) gratis, produced by the state industry *gynaecea*. Other *milites* received only a small allowance for clothing, and consequently they resorted to private as well as the state-manufactured clothes. A lex of 396 (Cod. Theod VII, 6,4 = Cod. Just XII, 39–3) mentions that the soldiers of Illyricum received a solidus for purchasing their mantle (*chlamis*). A lex of 423 records a tax collected in the provinces for the Comes Sacrarum Largitionum; five-sixths of the revenues raised by this was distributed among the soldiers specifically for the purchase of uniforms, and the remainder was sent to the *gynaecea* for state production (Cod. Theod V. 11,6,2–5 = Cod. Just.X 11,39,1–4).

The responsibility for the collection of military clothing moved away from the army and became the province of bureaucrats and officials. This process culminated in the *vestis militaris* or clothing tax. Local officials, town councillors, landowners and vast numbers of civil servants acted as middlemen between the weavers and the army. All that remains of the vast amount of paperwork this tax created are a few fragmentary scraps of papyri from Egypt. Modern scholars are of the opinion that although these documents seem to indicate that the tax was collected in kind, a cash equivalent was paid instead.

It is further presumed that all the money collected by the tax was then spent on the purpose for which it was intended – clothing the army. However it remains unclear why the documents themselves refer to clothing rather than to money. One reason proposed by historians was that given the known systematic corruption within the Roman bureaucracy, this was perhaps a way of explaining to taxpayers what their money was going to be spent on in a way they would understand, helping to sweeten the bitter pill of paying yet another unpopular tax. There is no archaeological corroboration for the clothing tax anywhere else within the empire; however, the Code of Theodosius states that it was collected throughout the Eastern Empire.

The Last References
During the collapse of the Western Empire, the attendants of clerics and local *duces* were equipped at the expense of the remaining leaders of Gallo-Roman society. One of them, the aristocratic bishop Sidonius Apollinaris (died *c.*480) pointed out to his retainers 'You are well supplied with horses, armour, clothing' (1, 6). Nevertheless, Roman traditions remained strong in the army almost to the last. In Gaul, at the end of the fifth century, local troops (*Laeti*), even though of Germanic origin, preserved their Roman identity, carried their own standards in battle, and retained Roman dress in every particular, 'even as regards their shoes' (Procopius,BG,V, 12).

The revenues of the Eastern Empire were practically double those of the Western Empire and an essential reason for its continuing survival. A considerable proportion of its budget was spent on the army, but it produced superior training, discipline, efficiency and especially equipment. Military garments were produced at textile centres such as Antinoopolis (Antinoe), Arsinoe. Panopolis and Alexandria in Egypt, while Laodicea was famous for the manufacture of luxurious fabrics (*Paragaudis Ladikhenou*).

In AD 594 the Emperor Maurice planned to reduce cash payments by offsetting the cost of state provision of clothing and equipment against wages, thereby cutting the yearly allowance of the Comitatensis troops (Theoph.Sim. 7,1,2; Theophanes p.274). This act however provoked a mutiny that was only settled when the emperor backed down and offered generous concessions to demobilised soldiers and war orphans. Local populations, governed by the Church, were expected to contribute goods in kind for the military. This occurred in AD 588 when the Bishop of Antioch organised the distribution of food, clothing and money to locally enrolled soldiers and to those who passed through the city (Evagrius, 6,11). Spare army clothing (*himatia*) was stored in the military baggage train, together with weapons and supplies (BG,VII, 11).

Allied Arab clans on the eastern borders were heavily subsidised by the Romans with clothing, weapons, food and money. The Emperor Tiberius II sent gifts for the Ghassanid Phylarcha Mondir, including weapons, gold, silver, silver horse furniture and 'splendid garments'. Both material and clothing could be very costly and so was frequently acquired as plunder. Theophanes describes a Roman victory over hostile Arabs: 'having occupied their camp they captured a large number of Saracens, men, women and children, and a lot of Roman prisoners … herds … silk and clothing.' The allied Ghassanians who sacked the town of Haurin, carried away vast quantities of linen and wool garments (John of Ephesus, III, 42). War booty might also account for the large number of Sassanian silk garments that are found in sixth and seventh century Egyptian graves. Clothing was also looted during internal conflicts. John of Ephesus mentions *Excubitores* Romans (i.e. soldiers) and *Scholastici* taking clothing and shoes from the general populace during ecclesiastical disputes.

Crime and Punishment

The Theodosian Code offers dire warnings against corruption in the clothing industry, including the fraudulent use of dyes in the dye works! This was a serious matter and any offenders that were caught were stripped of their citizenship and beheaded. The late Christian writer Lactantius gives an account of how large numbers of Christians were sent to do penal servitude in the *Gynaecea* and *Linyfia* in the east (*De Mort.Persecut.*, 21, 4). Further evidence of this practice is supplied by Johannes Chrysostomus (*Ad Viduan*, 4) who says that even the wife of a convicted government official was sent to work with the fiscal wool workers. Clearly therefore, work in these state run establishments was harsh and unpleasant and Eusebius says that during the reign of Constantine I workers in the Gynacea endured 'rough and miserable toil' (*Vita Constantini II*, 39).

4

THE CLOTHING INDUSTRY II

FULLING, DYES AND DYEING

> He [Nero] saw a matron in the audience at one of his recitals clad in the forbidden colour. He pointed her out to his agents who dragged her out and stripped her on the spot! (Suet. Nero VI. 3.)

Fulling

Detailed accounts of the fulling and dyeing processes during the Classical period have been carried out by various authors including Forbes, Moeller and Wild. Therefore only a brief introduction is provided here. Cleaning cloth and improving its quality by shrinking and stretching was carried out by a fuller in a building called a *fullonica*. Fabrics were placed in a tub or vat of cold water with an added cleaning agent. Roman detergents were generally types of alkali or 'fuller's earth' (hydrated aluminium silicate) or lye (vegetable ash) but one of the most effective was human urine. A pot was often placed outside a fulling establishment which customers and passers-by were invited to use. This practice was taxed by the Emperor Vespasian, leading to public latrines acquiring the nickname of *Vespasiani*. Pliny provides us with a typical old wives' tale pointing out that urine was not only good enough for removing ink blots but men's urine especially could also cure gout! Proof of this he says was that fullers who were constantly exposed to urine never suffered from the complaint (*Nat Hist*. XXVIII. 66). He also states elsewhere that in the east camel urine was highly prized by the fullers (*Nat Hist* XXVIII.91).

A Roman relief from Sens in France and a fresco from a *fullonica* at Pompeii show cloth in tubs being cleaned this way. The process is known as 'walking' as it involves someone standing on the cloth and pounding it with their feet. The relief from Sens shows an adult male doing this work but the Pompeii fresco strongly suggests that child labour was also widely used for this task.

The *fullonica* was also more than just a laundry, as the appearance of cloth could also be improved in a variety of ways. After washing the cloth was stretched and beaten and then rewashed and rinsed. The nap on a wool fabric could then be raised by hand with a board covered with hedgehog skin or wooden spikes called an *aena* and then trimmed closely with a large pair of shears. This is a technique now known as cropping and gave the material a soft blanket-like finish. White clothes and cloth were then taken outside to dry; in Pompeii this was done by placing the cloth over a domed wickerwork frame. We know this because one is shown on the same fresco which shows the 'walking' taking place.

90 The Clothing Industry. *Charles W. Evans-Gunther.*

A dyer from a funerary monument at Arlon in Belgium. *After Wild.*

Cleaning cloth in the fuller's workshop of Hypsaeus. A scene from a fresco in Pompeii. *After Moeller.*

Scenes from a
tombstone of a fuller
from Sens in France
showing treading the
cloth and cropping the
nap. *After Wild*.

Workers in the fuller's
workshop of Hypsaeus
at Pompeii. One worker
carries a drying frame
(*viminea cave* and a sulphur
pot while another brushes
cloth with an *aena*. After
Moeller.

The next step was to place sulphur in a bucket or pot underneath the frame and burn it, which in turn bleached the cloth. Pliny describes the process:

> There are four kinds [of sulphur] the second kind is called clod sulphur and is commonly found only in fullers workshops. The third kind is only employed for one purpose, for smoking woollens from beneath as it bestows whiteness and softness. This sort is called equla. (*Nat Hist.* XXV 175)

Linen in particular was treated in this way because natural linen had a grey colour.
   The practice was not without its difficulties and required a certain amount of skill.

> another use also made of Cimolus earth is in regard to cloth. The kind called Sarda, which is bought from Sardinia is only used for white fabrics and is no use for cloths of various colours. It is the cheapest of all the Cimolus kinds; more valuable are the Umbrian and the one called 'rock'. The peculiarity of the latter is that it increases in size when it is steeped in liquid; consequently it is sold by weight, whereas Umbrian is sold by measure. Umbrian earth is only employed for giving lustre to cloths. It will not be out of place to touch on this part of the subject also, as a Metilian law referring to fullers still stands, the law which Gaius Flaminius and Lucius Aemilius as censors put forward [220 BC]; so careful about everything were our ancestors. The process then is this the cloth is first washed with earth of Sardinia, and then it is fumigated with sulphur, and afterwards scoured with Cimolian earth provided that the dye is fast; if it is coloured with bad dye it is detected and turns black and its colour is spread by the action of the sulphur; whereas genuine and valuable colours are softened and brightened up with a sort of brilliance by Cimolian earth when they have been made sombre by the sulphur. The 'rock' kind is more serviceable for white garments, after the application of sulphur, but it is very detrimental to colour. In Greece they use Tymphaea gypsum instead of Cimolian earth. (*Nat. Hist*)

After the cleaning and drying process was completed cloth and clothing could then be pressed in a clothes press, an example of which actually survives from Herculaneum. Before pressing, the bleacher sprinkled water held in his mouth on the cloth (Seneca Q Nat.i.3.2). Linen could also be made smoother by rubbing it with rods or a wooden block. Alternatively smooth stones could be used for this purpose. The bleaching process was not permanent as wool re-oxidises to a yellowish shade, therefore requiring repeated visits to the fuller.

Dyes and Dyeing

The Romans inherited a range of dyeing techniques and traditions from across their empire. Initially this would have been in the form of goods supplied as part of a levy. Livy records that the newly conquered territories of Spain, Sardinia and Sicily had to supply clothing to the army of Scipio in Africa (XXIX, 36, & XXX, 3). As new provinces became more organised, specialist craftsmen – including dye workers – were exploited by the Romans; for instance, Pliny states that Gaul was famous for its extensive range of dyestuffs (*Nat.Hist*, XXII.2). All the same it is worth remembering that in early Anglo-Saxon England for example, evidence for dying large fabrics is rare and many large fabrics were possibly not dyed at all. This could explain the high proportion of yellow-brown cloaks seen in Roman art which were in all likelihood made from un-dyed wool.
   The Roman dye establishment was called either a *tinctorium* or an *infectorium* and there are a number of remains of such dye houses in Pompeii. Other specialist dyers called *offectores* renewed faded dyed clothes, restoring their brightness. The majority of dyes were vegetable in origin and some required a mordant to fix the dye to the fibre. Mordants were generally common minerals such as alum or iron salts, which could even be obtained by using rusty nails. One useful side effect of this process was that alum enhanced the brightness of the dye and iron extended the colour range. A range of other colours could be achieved by vat dyeing, which fermented and oxidised the fibres within the dye. The best known colour achieved by this method was the blue obtained from woad (*isatis tinctoria*).
   Wool was easier to dye than linen – which does not take dye so readily and therefore was invariably left its natural shade or bleached in sunlight. Wool was generally dyed while still in

1 Early Roman warrior, perhaps even Romulus, *c.*750–700 BC based on research by Raffaele D'Amato. His bronze crested helmet is based on a type found in Rome, as are the spear head and butt. The shield and bronze pectoral breast plate are copies of examples found on the Esquiline in Rome. At this date the toga was used as a form of protection. Its off-white colour with red border follows the version shown in the François tomb.

2 Based on wall paintings from Nola this painting shows a victorious warrior, possibly a Samnite of the late fourth century BC. Even at this early date red was a popular colour for the clothing used by Italian warriors. The warrior carries some spoils including a bronze belt and a decorated tunic, perhaps taken from a Roman, although there was probably little difference in the equipment and clothing of the various states at this time.

3 Legionary soldier at the Battle of Emporion during the Spanish campaign of Marcus Porcius Cato in 195 BC. He wears a helmet and has a shield boss based on ones found at Emporion itself. The rest of his equipment is based on Italian finds, including the padded *subarmalis* after a sculpture in Volterra, while the thick linen *pteryges* are alternatively coloured as shown on Etruscan sculptures that have surviving paint.

4 This sculpture from Volterra in Italy possibly shows a *subarmalis* worn as body armour in its own right.

5 Detail of re-used sculpture of Antonine date found on the Arch of Constantine. It shows an unusual form of armour, perhaps of either fabric or leather.

6 Detail of the 'armour' worn by the god Mars on a building inscription from High Rochester, England. Rather than a stylised form of muscled cuirass the armour appears to be padded fabric instead.

7 The 'armour' of Severius Acceptus of Legio VIII Augusta as shown on his tombstone from Istanbul.

8 Another Romano-British representation of Mars, this time on a votive tablet from Bisley, again showing what looks like fabric armour.

9 Detail of the torso of a soldier from a sarcophagus depicting Pharaoh's army crossing the Red Sea, now in Split Archaeological Museum. In a medieval context this would be recognised as a clear example of padded armour.

10 Late Republican legionary at the time of the reforms of Marius. He wears the 'terrible dress' of the god Mars – a red tunic – but has also made some amendments to his basic kit as a result of campaigning in the north against the German invaders, such as the short *bracae* and leg bindings.

11 Centurions of the time of Julius Caesar. The centurion in undress uniform is based on the tombstone of Minucius Lorarius. The colour of his clothing follows the later funeral portraits from Egypt, some of which appear to show centurions. The armoured centurion is based on the equipment shown on a triumphal relief from Aquileia. The body armour follows the colours shown in several paintings which show a white torso with red reinforcements at the waist and over the shoulders. Like his commanders Caesar and Antony – who are documented as wearing Gallic clothing on occasion – this officer has adopted a cloak of locally-made material. Both officers have enclosed boots like those from Qasr Ibrim and Mainz.

12 Reconstruction of M. Favonius
Facilis, centurion of Legio XX based
on his famous tombstone found
at Colchester dating to the mid
first century AD. Unlike previous
reconstructions which give Facilis
mail body armour, this version
utilises several sources which show
white linen or leather body armour
with reinforcements in red at the
shoulder and around the waist. The
waist defence on the tombstone of
Facilis clearly shows a continuous
design, not individual belt plates, with
raised floral motifs. These have been
interpreted here as gilded moulded
leather patterns. Once again the tunic
and cloak colours follow the Fayum
portraits.

13 A–E: What may be further examples
of decorated waist reinforcements appear
throughout the Roman period. Top to bottom:
A: From a fresco in the Orcus tomb, Italy.
B: Turin. From a drawing of a relief now lost.
C: Paris, Cluny Museum.
D: Colchester.

13 E: Pompeii. (*See also* (*22*) *in the colour catalogue.*)

14 Soldier in a *paenula* cloak from Pompeii. (*See* (*21*) *in the colour catalogue.*)

15 Figure in *sagum* cloak from Pompeii. (*See* (*23*) *in the colour catalogue.*)

16 Encaustic portrait of a soldier, Hawara, Egypt *c.*AD 160–180. (*See (43) in the colour catalogue*) © *Manchester Museum*

17 Legionary soldier from Legio VIII Augusta. The classic legionary with all the equipment including the shield design based on finds from the legionary fortress at Vindonissa in Switzerland. The red tunic with dark *clavi* is however based on one of the near contemporary tunics found at Nahal Hever in Israel.

18 Roman auxiliary cavalryman serving with the Ala Augusta, based in Britain in the late first century AD. This is a reconstruction of Insus based on his *tombstone found at Lancaster.*

19 Fresco from Dura Europos, Syria, *c.*AD 239 showing Julius Terentius at the head of Cohors XX Palmyrenorum. © Yale University Art Gallery. (*See (71) in the colour catalogue.*)

20 Wall painting from the Synagogue at Dura Europos, known as the Ezekiel fresco. © Yale University Art Gallery. (*See (76) in the colour catalogue.*)

21 Reconstruction of Tribune Julius Terentius, commander of Cohors XX Palmyrenorum. All of the clothing and equipment is based as near as possible on finds from Dura Europos itself.

22 Hat found at Mons Claudianus in Egypt dating to the Hadrianic period. *Photograph courtesy Lise Bender Jørgensen*

23 Reconstruction of a hat found at Mons Claudianus which had been partially made up from a re-cycled garment.

24 Reconstruction of two legionaries from Legio II Parthica based on finds from Syria, including Apamea and Dura Europos. The figure on the left is mainly based on the tombstone of Aurelius Mucianus, a trainee *lanciarius* at Apamea. Although the helmet is a copy of a type from Germany, pieces of a similar helmet were found at Dura Europos. The figure on the right is based on another Apamea tombstone, that of Petronius Proclus. Both men wear red tunics decorated with purple trim and have integrally laced boots.

25 Roman period hat found in Egypt. ©
Bolton Museum and Art Gallery

26 Detail of a fresco from Pompeii perhaps showing what may be a hat worn as helmet padding.

27 Broad brimmed hat depicted in the Imperial palace mosaics at Constantinople, now Istanbul.

28 A late Roman hat found in Egypt.

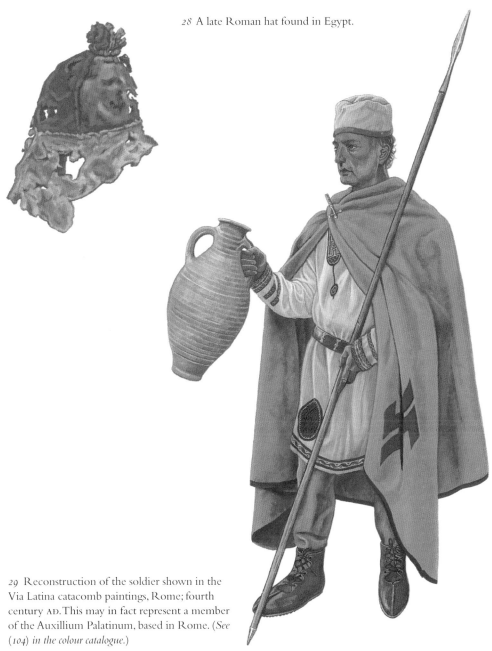

29 Reconstruction of the soldier shown in the Via Latina catacomb paintings, Rome; fourth century AD. This may in fact represent a member of the Auxillium Palatinum, based in Rome. (*See* (*104*) *in the colour catalogue.*)

30 Restored section of the fresco which once covered the central shrine of the standards built into the Temple at Luxor. *Photograph courtesy of Robert B. Partridge, Editor of* Ancient Egypt *magazine*

31 Tombstone of an unknown soldier from the third century AD now in Alexandria, Egypt. It does show one important detail and that is the remains of the yellow brown colour on the cloak. © *Jenny Cline*

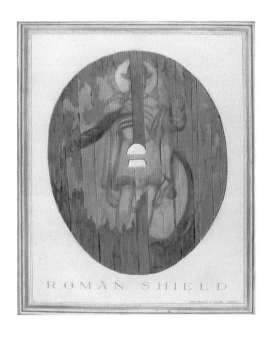

ROMAN SHIELD

32 Modern watercolour painting of a shield discovered at Dura Europos which featured at its centre a warrior god wearing a blue long-sleeved tunic and a beige cloak. © *Yale University Art Gallery*

33 Reconstruction of the soldier depicted in the Via Maria, catacomb painting, Syracuse, Sicily; fourth century AD (*see (108) in the colour catalogue*). Maximianus was a member of an unknown *numerus*. His helmet is an Intercisa type clearly illustrated in the original painting. His red tunic is decorated with purple trim and *orbiculi*. The painting shows blue leg wrappings that are tied with red straps fastened with small buckles.

34 Reconstruction of the soldier from the Via Latina catacomb paintings, Rome, fourth century, depicting a soldier representing the Egyptian army of Pharaoh. The original painting may have been based on the appearance of a *centenarius* of *palatini* serving in Rome. Early Christian art often depicted Roman soldiers as the villains.

35 Late Roman period tunic found in Egypt.
© *Bolton Museum and Art Gallery*

36 Tunic decoration showing hunting scenes found in Egypt. *Courtesy of Raffaele D'Amato*

37 Reconstruction of a military officer serving in Egypt *c.*AD 550–600. He holds one of the splendid Persian-style riding coats while wearing a white linen hooded *dalmatica* over a linen under-tunic, both of which are decorated with purple wool bands. On his legs over his trousers are a pair of wool and silk leggings decorated with Persian motifs

the fleece but could also be left in its variety of natural colours from the sheep of different regions. Checked effects such as those popular with the Celts could therefore be produced by mixing the wool of different sheep breeds.

The selected dye was added to water in vats of either stone or metal placed over a furnace. After treating with a mordant the wool fibres were dipped in the vats, boiled and stirred with a long pole. Getting the right shade was a matter of careful timing and sight on the part of the dyer, but achieving uniform shades would have been practically impossible. As each dye required a slightly different time we find that dyers specialised in certain colours. Plautus lists these specialists; reds were produced by *flammarii*, yellow by *cerinarii*, blues by *violarii* and safrons by *crocotarii*.

(Plautus *Aul.* 510). Other dye specialists include *spadicarii* who produced browns and *purpurarii* who produced the highly prized purple.

The development of Roman 'living history' groups since 1972 has increased general interest in the colours of Roman clothing and textiles. Unfortunately, due to the scarcity of accessible published material, and a former trend amongst historians to relegate or even ignore the study of textile finds, there has been a tendency to follow preconceptions rather than specific archaeological data.

Undoubtedly one of the most controversial aspects today of Roman military history is the answer to the question 'what colour was the military tunic?' The long standing view was that legionaries wore red, and this was the colour adopted by the first Roman re-enactors. Contrary to this, Fuentes later suggested that legionaries and senior officers wore white tunics, and only centurions dressed in red to make them instantly recognisable. To judge from recent publications, both popular and academic, this view seems to have been widely accepted. However, many re-enactors do not concur with this viewpoint, and as a result the public is now presented with a confusing array of groups in tunics coloured red, white, blue, green or yellow.

While there is no doubt that the Romans had the capability of producing all these colours, the issue is whether any or all were adopted by the army. It should be remembered that it is virtually impossible to specifically identify textile fragments as belonging to military tunics, including those from supposedly military sites. There is a tendency to forget that there were many civilians present living both in and around forts; and that the Romans had as many uses for textiles as we do today. The main colours connected with the military will now be discussed and their merits for and against assessed.

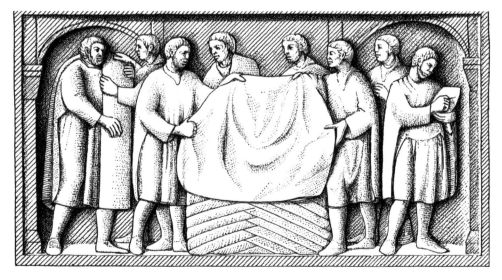

91 The Igel monument set up near Trier in Germany shows details of the local wool industry, including the buying and selling of cloth. The military was the largest purchaser of wool goods and would have dealt with merchants like those depicted on the monument. © *Rheinisches Landesmuseum Trier.*

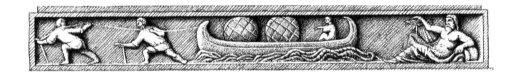

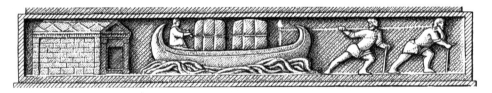

92 The Igel monument also shows wool being prepared for transportation into large bales and then being transported by both land and by water. © *Rheinisches Landesmuseum Trier.*

White

To the casual observer white may seem an odd colour for military uniforms. However there is plenty of evidence for its use as such even in fairly recent times. The Bourbon and Habsburg armies of France and Austria in the eighteenth and nineteenth centuries equipped large numbers of troops in white wool uniforms. A relatively clean appearance could be maintained by using chalk as well as regular washing. Remarkably there is evidence from French sources that when the Republican blue uniforms replaced the Royalist white, the soldiers found the blue uniforms harder to keep clean! As the Romans had well established methods of whitening garments perhaps they did not find it too much of a problem either.

Of course an even simpler solution is to provide regular changes of clothing and the surviving pay accounts seem to indicate that a great deal of the soldiers' pay was deducted at source to provide new clothing. Common sense would also dictate that soldiers had more than one tunic or cloak at any one time and the lists in the *Scriptores Historiae Augustae* certainly indicate that officers owned large amounts of clothing.

Un-dyed wool would provide a variety of colours ranging from a yellowish off-white to a brownish shade. A number of frescoes and mosaic scenes appear to show soldiers wearing these colours both for tunics and cloaks, sometimes together. Other literary sources refer to shining white garments, which are obviously garments that had been specially bleached. These seem to have been worn on special parades and references to this practice can be found from the earliest times into the late Imperial period. The soldiers in the Egyptian portraits all have pure white tunics and brightly coloured cloaks, posing perhaps in their best uniforms as soldiers did with the advent of photography. One of the Vindolanda tablets and the *Scriptores Historiae Augustae* also refer to special dining tunics, the Roman equivalent of a modern officer's mess dress. Vegetius gives a list of legionary officers, *principales*, and includes the ranks *candidati duplares* and *candidate simplares*. *Principales* were excused some of the more laborious army fatigues perhaps so that these particular soldiers could keep their tunics clean and white.

Red

Madder (*rubia tinctorum*) was the commonest red dyestuff known to the Romans. The Romans would have imported it in dried root form to places like Britain where it was unknown at that time. On the other hand local alternatives, including bedstraw – a herbaceous plant – in particular 'lady's bedstraw' (*galium verum*), could be used instead. After the mordanting process, madder could also be used to make other colours in a range from peach-yellow to brown-purple. It is easy to see why red was a popular colour with ancient Italian armies including the Romans and not just because of its associations with the war god Mars. Pliny informs us that Italian madder was the most highly prized dye and the best of all was grown around Rome itself (Pliny. *Nat Hist*. XIX, 47–48).

The colour red has therefore been perceived as the traditional colour of Roman soldiers, something which has persisted into modern times, although ironically not as a result of Hollywood, as many classic epic movies, including *Ben-Hur* (1959) show soldiers in white tunics and red cloaks, which is not too far off the mark as we shall see. In the seventh century AD Isidore of Seville wrote a history of the world up to his own times. Referring to a period when Rome was 'under the Consuls' – presumably the Republican era – he wrote that there was a dye, *russata*, which was called '*Phoenicea*' by the Greeks and was known as *coccina* in his own day. He claimed it was invented by the Spartans to conceal their blood when they were wounded in battle, so as not to give any encouragement to their enemies (*Origines*, XIX, xxii, 10).

We must therefore conclude that the dye Isidore is describing was red in colour and he later adds that Roman soldiers also used it and because of this they were called '*russati*'. This can be taken literally to mean that the soldiers themselves were nicknamed '*russati*'; but can also be translated as 'whence the *russati* took their name', which could point instead to the red circus faction. Isidore goes on to say that Roman soldiers only wore this colour on the eve and actual day of battle, and that before a battle the same colour was somehow displayed in front of the headquarters tent. This reminds us of the actions of Caesar (*Gallic War*, II, 4, & *Civil Wars*, III, 89, and Plutarch, *Pompey*, 68), who hoisted a battle flag, Shakespeare's 'bloody sign of battle' (*Julius Caesar* Act V scene 16). This occurred both when the Nervii attacked his camp and before the battle of Pharsalus. Therefore it is extremely interesting to note that in Plutarch's account of Pharsalus he says that it was a tunic itself that was displayed as the battle sign.

Taken at face value, Isidore suggests that Roman soldiers wore red only into battle, and presumably therefore did not wear clothing of this colour for normal everyday wear. Although it is believed that Isidore based his narrative on ancient Roman sources which are now lost, and authors such as Tacitus and Suetonius, he is not always considered to be very reliable. Therefore we have no idea of the accuracy of his observations or his grasp of military matters. Nonetheless there are indeed plenty of written and pictorial references to support the theory that the Romans regarded red as their traditional military colour and Isidore's reference to the red battle sign may have been copied directly from Plutarch.

Cicero made a derogatory comment that wool taken from sheep reared in Canusium – which was brown with a reddish hue – acted as the poor man's purple (*Pro Sestio* 8.19). This is a reminder that not all red colours observed in Roman art need be the results of dyeing, as many reddish-brown shades could be achieved from natural shades of wool. Un-dyed wool would also retain the natural lanolins which would make them even more suitable for military garments. Indeed many of the textile fragments from the isolated site of Mons Claudianus – an Imperial quarry site supervised by a military garrison – were brownish in colour.

Purple

Pliny the Elder writes extensively about the use of purple in Roman times. True purple could only be produced by specialist dye workers working around the Mediterranean coast, particularly in the area around Tyre, home of the shellfish *murex brandaris* and *murex trunculus* – two types of whelk which secreted the precious dye fluid. Their rarity, together with the dye's fastness to light and washing, was the reason why purple was so prized as an exclusive status symbol. According to Pliny one Cornelius Nepos, who died during the reign of Augustus, was supposed to have said that in his youth violet-coloured shellfish dye was fashionable in Rome and cost about 100 denarii a pound; however, this was later followed by the double-dyed Tyrian variety which could not be bought for less than 1,000 denarii a pound (*Nat. Hist.*, 137).

Such garments were clearly well beyond the reach of the average legionary, who in the late first century AD earned about 300 denarii a year. However, senior officers came from senatorial families, whose wealth during the early years of the empire might be extraordinary, and even the topmost levels of the centurionate sometimes accumlated considerable wealth. From the third century onwards military garments were wrought with purple decoration in the form of *clavi, orbiculi* and *tabulae*. Purple cloaks remained popular with senior commanders and Egyptian portraits even show some cloaks of lower ranks in purple shades of red.

Nevertheless, the insatiable demand for purple clothing inevitably led to the creation of a number of cheaper alternatives, and a counterfeit industry like that which exploits the modern hunger for designer labels. The poet Ovid remarked that it was madness to wear expensive purples when there were so many cheaper alternatives, but as we have already noted there were those like Cicero who were quick to mock those who could not afford the best types of purple-coloured clothes. A purple of sorts could be achieved by simply over-dyeing red from madder with blue from indigo or woad, and archil – a purple dye obtained by fermenting lichen in stale urine – was also widely used. Evidence of some of this faked purple clothing was brought to light by the excavations in the Bar Kochba caves in Israel.

The *Scriptores Historiae Augustae* makes frequent references to the association of the colour purple with the Imperial throne. This includes the usual portents of future greatness, and occasions when pretenders to the throne – who would usually be proclaimed emperor by placing a purple cloak on them – had none to hand, so had to make do with purple handkerchief instead. Hardly an auspicious start!

Green

Given the Romans' obsession with colours in the red to purple range, it is perhaps not surprising that other colours are under represented in both the archaeological and pictorial record. In addition traces of green dye are very difficult to detect even with modern tests on textile finds. All the same, considering its application for camouflage by the military in recent times, one might have expected to see more use of green by Roman soldiers. There might be two explanations for the apparent lack of evidence for green garments. Firstly green may have been an unfashionable colour for clothing; the examples in the Fayum portraits of green clothing worn by women are negligible compared to the reds and purples. Secondly green colours were most likely achieved by over-dying cloth dyed yellow with woad. Double dying would therefore make green coloured clothes more expensive.

For all that, some evidence for the use of green clothing by Roman soldiers does exist. If green was a more expensive colour to produce then that might have made it appealing to officers or guards. Indeed one of the most famous images from the Roman world, the mosaic from Ravenna showing the Emperor Justinian surrounded by his court and guards, shows one guard in a green tunic, and at least one of the late Roman period Persian-style riding coats perhaps belonging to an officer was also green.

The well known properties of concealment attached to green coloured clothing might have been utilised during off-duty hours when out hunting rather than as camouflage on the field of battle. There are a few representations of soldiers engaged in hunting wearing green tunics, including soldiers on the Gamzigrad mosaic and in one of the mosaics from Olmeda, while a fresco from Aquincum shows a man with a bow wearing green. The tunics in these sources are very similar in style and decoration to a green tunic found in Egypt, although that has been recently carbon-dated to the seventh century AD. Other instances of green being used in a military context are two saddlecloths in green, one from Luxor, the other on the tombstone of the first-century cavalryman Silius, whose attendant is also dressed in a green garment of some sort, which will be discussed in the colour catalogue.

Yellow

Some Romans may have deemed yellow inappropriate as a martial colour because of its associations with the veil traditionally worn by brides on their wedding day. This prejudice is highlighted by Virgil (*Aeneid*, XI, 777) when Chloreus, a former priest of Cybele and therefore a eunuch, assumes the role of a soldier. Because Chloreus wears a cloak of yellow and other bright garments he is described somewhat disparagingly as a fop rather than a true warrior. Pliny too describes yellow in a similar light, saying that in earlier times yellow was the most popular colour but since it was used as the bridal veil it was no longer regarded as one of the principal colours, at least for men (*HN*, XXI, 46).

Nevertheless in spite of this apparent prejudice, yellow-brown cloaks appear to have been extremely popular amongst military personnel, although this was probably a natural wool colour retaining its lanolins rather than a dyed colour. If dye was used, a yellow colour could be achieved by using weld (*Reseda Luteola*) and dyer's green weed (*Genista tinctora*). Weld itself appears to have been introduced into Britain specifically for its use as a yellow dye. One of the tunics found in the Nahal Hever cave had been dyed yellow by using saffron.

Blue

Cloth could be dyed blue by either woad or indigo. However there is even less proof for soldiers wearing blue tunics than there is for green, though there are some notable pieces of evidence. These include an early frieze from Praeneste which shows a cavalryman and some soldiers in blue garments. One Imperial tombstone of Druccus a cavalryman, whose portrait only shows a head and shoulders, nevertheless still reveals traces of blue paint on a garment around his neck. It is frustrating that so little of his body is visible since it is not possible to tell whether this garment is a tunic, a scarf or a cloak. In view of some of the other evidence presented below, a cloak might seem the most plausible suggestion.

Some of the frescoes from Dura Europos are a further source for blue tunics. The Ebenezer fresco shows two cavalrymen fighting each other, dressed very similarly in blue tunics with red leggings or trousers. The Ezekiel fresco shows an armoured figure, possibly an officer, in a blue tunic and pinkish red cloak.

Otherwise a blue colour is limited to a number of cloaks, most of them from the Egyptian Fayum portraits. Some of these portraits can be identified as belonging to men of centurion rank. Perhaps not surprisingly the remaining evidence points to a naval connection. There are a couple of literary references to either blue flags or cloaks being awarded for naval victories. The nautical association is continued by Vegetius, whose famous reference to sailors of the British fleet wearing *Venetian*, therefore dark blue, clothing might be a distant echo of the description of naval uniform from Plautus.

Conclusion

To summarise, the evidence suggests that generally soldiers wore an off-white tunic which was suitable for everyday wear and fatigue duties. It is possible this white tunic was replaced for military action by a red tunic which might have come in a range of shades, perhaps depending on the wealth or rank of the individual. This could mean anything from a salmon pink to a dark purple-red. Equally possible is that un-dyed tunics of reddish brown wool were worn alongside the off-white ones for everyday wear or even as battledress.

On dress occasions such as parades or religious festivals a white tunic – in all probability specially whitened – was worn, and this could apply to all ranks although needless to say those belonging to officers would have been made from finer material. It is tempting to suggest that some naval personnel wore blue or blue-grey clothing but the evidence is scarce and is contradicted by a tombstone of a sailor dressed entirely in red. Some soldiers appear to have worn green tunics alongside the other well known colours when hunting, and special hunting dress is referenced in a description of the portraits of the Emperor Tacitus. Guard uniforms seem to have consisted of red, green, blue and white tunics, often elaborately decorated. Not surprisingly these are probably directly linked to the four main circus factions, which assumed an even greater political significance in the early Byzantine era. Guard uniforms would naturally be made from and dyed with, the more expensive materials.

There is no clear pattern as to whom or why some soldiers wore certain cloak colours. A yellow-brown colour is by far the most common for both *paenula* and *sagum* style cloaks for officers and ordinary ranks but off-white, white, red and blue are also fairly well represented too. The most common 'uniform' in the pictorial sources appears to be a white tunic with either a red or yellow-brown cloak. This is generally what could be termed an 'undress' uniform, as the soldiers wearing this combination are depicted without any armour.

As stated above a number of possible centurions in the Egyptian portraits wear blue cloaks but also apparently some ordinary soldiers do as well. However one would imagine the centurions' cloaks would be produced from more expensive fabrics and dyes. A tribune and perhaps the senior cohort centurion wear white cloaks in the Terentius fresco from Dura Europos while the rest of their men wear yellow-brown ones. Perhaps the deciding factor was something that is not always visible in the pictorial sources – the quality of the material not just the colour. This is just about indicated in the Dura fresco. The soldiers' cloaks in the rear rank of the Dura fresco wearing yellow-brown cloaks were given a hashed texture by the artist to indicate that they were made from a rougher material than those worn in the front row, presumably by the officers.

The range of evidence for tunic colours is vast and increasing all the time. As much as possible of this corpus of material is presented next. Readers not happy with the summary outlined above are therefore invited to read through it themselves and by and large, are ultimately left to draw their own conclusions as to how this evidence is to be best interpreted. Needless to say the countless ancient references to the emperors wearing purple garments of any kind have been omitted, as the association of that colour with the Imperial rank is well known and beyond any doubt.

5

EVIDENCE FOR THE COLOUR OF MILITARY CLOTHING

(Colour Catalogue (Col. Cat.))

THE REPUBLIC

Cum tot prodierint pretio leviore colores, quis furor est census corpore ferre suos!

When so many cheaper colours walk abroad, what madness to carry whole incomes on ones body! (Ovid. Ars. Amat.III. 170)

(1) Painted terracotta, Esquiline, Rome; c.500 BC. (La Rocca, E. 1990: fig 112)

The terracotta body of a warrior remains from the pediment of a temple once on the Esquiline in Rome. Underneath the linen armour the warrior wears a blue tunic edged with white and red bands.

(2) Fresco, Lucanian tomb, Paestum, Italy; c.321 BC. (Rouveret, A. 1997: pp.104–107)

A fresco which it has been suggested commemorates the victory of the Samnites over the Romans at the battle of the Caudine Forks shows a naked warrior carrying spoils from the battle. These include a white tunic carried on a spear.

(3) Historical fresco, tomb on the Esquiline, Rome; Republican period. (Bandinelli, R.B. 1970: p.117)

This fragment of a tomb fresco is probably amongst the oldest surviving examples of Roman painting, and provides us with the earliest clues for the colour of Roman military tunics. It appears to illustrate an event around 326 BC during the Samnite wars showing the surrender of the Samnite general Marcus Fannius to Quintus Fabius the Roman consul. Around the main central group of figures can be seen a number of warriors, both Roman and Samnite, in short white tunics and kilts.

Becatti dated this fresco to the first century BC, but concluded that it appears to be a copy of a far earlier work.

(4) Livy (IX, 40, 2–3 & IX, 40, 9)

Livy says that one division of the Samnite army wore bleached white linen tunics. This was because they had consecrated themselves and white was the colour of the priesthood. Unfortunately Livy neglected to leave any description of contemporary Roman army tunics.

(5) Etruscan fresco; fourth century BC. (Torelli, M. 2000: pp.8–9)
The so-called 'François' tomb shows a legendary battle possibly between the Etruscans and the Romans, or perhaps their Latin allies. A soldier wearing a bronze muscle cuirass and a red tunic is shown being killed by a naked opponent. As the defeated warrior is unlikely to be an Etruscan this could reasonably be seen as evidence for the colour of Roman tunics at this period.

(6) Etruscan urns; Republican period.
A number of these urns found in Etruria survive, many with most of their original colour paint surviving. They appear to follow a standard formula showing a central battle scene between two warriors, both of whom generally wear red tunics.

(7) Historical fresco, tomb of the Statilii, Rome; Republican period. (Bandinelli, R.B. 1970: p.121)
This fresco may also show Roman soldiers from the early Republic. The details of the costumes, such as the short white kilts, are similar to the earlier Esquiline fresco, so it is likely that this too may be a copy of a much earlier work. It is conceivable that this painting also represents another legendary battle between the Romans and Samnites, but there is no general agreement amongst historians as to which historical event is being depicted.

(8) Plautus, *Miles Gloriosus* 1179; Republican period.
Plautus describes a sailor's uniform as consisting of a broad brimmed hat and a cloak which are both described as *ferugineum* which Plautus says is the maritime shade. This was interpreted in the past as being rust coloured but iron coloured would be a better translation, perhaps meaning a blue grey colour.

(9) Silius Italicus, *Punica* IX, 420; Republican period.
The poet Silius Italicus records that the cloaks worn by the *Lictores* were red as opposed to those worn by senior commanders which were either purple or white.

(10) Fresco, Tomb of the Scipios; late Republic. (La Rocca, E. 1990: figs 156–163)
Belonging to the most famous family connected with the Punic War, their tomb was lavishly decorated with scenes from both that conflict and the Hispanic Wars. Parts of the fresco still show half a soldier in a red tunic tied with a yellow belt. Elsewhere other soldiers are dressed in white tunics with black boots, but the paintings are generally too poorly preserved to offer any interpretations.

(11) Frieze, Praenestae, Italy; second century BC. (Pensabene, P. 1992: pp.117–120)
An important pottery frieze which depicts the procession of a *Praetor*, shows *Lictores* and soldiers including cavalry evidently dressed in ceremonial attire. The *Lictores* are in short red sleeveless tunics which are open at the breast, that hang in V shaped folds and are tied with a white girdle (*cinctus*). They also wear a *sagum* tightly wrapped around the waist, knotted at the front and falling down in two folds. The other men have blue and red tunics.

(12) Fresco from the Areti Tomb, Rome, Italy; second century BC. (La Rocca, E. 1990: figs 165–169)
The tomb of the magistrates on the Esquiline hill known locally as the Sepolcro Areti dates from around 133 BC. It depicts scenes of warfare and the triumphal procession of a Roman general. The *Lictores* wear short red tunics again but this time with a yellow belt and the addition of a single wide white vertical band (*clavus*).

(13) *The African War* LVII, 54–6; late Republic.
Q. Caecilius Scipio, commander of the Pompeian forces in Africa, always wore a purple cloak. This angered his African ally, the Numidian King Juba I, because this naturally was his own normal royal attire. Therefore Scipio was in future obliged to dress in white.

(14) Fresco from Stabiae, Italy; late Republic.

A detail of a boar hunt shows a group of figures armed with spears and shields. The shields are oval with a barley-corn type boss that can be corroborated with known examples and archaeological finds. The central figure wears a pinkish-red tunic with a yellow-brown cloak, while two of his companions appear to have off-white/yellowish tunics. In the background is another hunter wearing a purple-red tunic, a yellow-brown cloak and a cream coloured pointed hat with a brim.

(15) Quintilianus (*c.*AD 35–95?), *Declamationes*, III Declamatio, 'Pro Milite Contra Tribunum'.

The rhetorician Quintilianus, in the passage 'For a soldier against a tribune', set during the period of the army of C. Marius, presents us with a detailed picture of the dress of a Roman soldier of the late Republic, perhaps even of the first century AD. Quintilianus relates how the soldier's body was protected by a sword, hard iron armour and a helmet which covered the face. He adds that the helmet crest was designed to 'strike terror' into the enemy, and that the name of the Consul Marius was inscribed upon their shields. Finally he declares that the soldiers also wore 'the terrible dress of the god of war'.

   Mars is shown in Roman art wearing a red tunic as for example in the mosaic preserved in the Villa Borghese, Italy, where priests offer a sacrifice before a painted statue of the god. Another is the painting of Mars in Region IX in Pompeii, which shows the god amongst the other gods wearing both a red tunic and cloak. The red tunics of the notorious circus faction were also dedicated to Mars, so the obvious understanding of this passage is that soldiers wore red tunics into battle.

(16) Plutarch (*c.*AD 50–120), *Lives, Crassus*, 23.

Crassus wore a black cloak on the eve of the fateful battle of Carrhae in 53 BC. With the benefit of hindsight Plutarch naturally interpreted this as a bad omen, and says that Crassus realised his mistake and reverted to wearing a purple cloak. Why he should have chosen to wear a black cloak in the first place instead of a general's purple colour is not explained.

(17) Valerius Maximus I.6.11.

Maximus describes the same incident of Crassus wearing a black cloak before the battle of Carrhae '*pullum ei traditum est paludamentum, cum in proelium exeuntibus album aut purpureum dari soleat.*' His version is slightly different from the account of Plutarch and he explains how Crassus was offered a black cloak rather than the white or purple cloak that was normally worn into battle.

(18) Appian, *The Civil War*, V. 100.

After naval victories over Octavian, Sextus Pompeius called himself the son of Neptune and according to Appian 'became so conceited that as a result of these events he changed the colour of his military cloak from the normal purple of a commander-in-chief to dark blue, thus signifying that he was Neptune's adoptive son.' Chronicling the same events and perhaps using Appian as his source, the later writer Cassius Dio also mentions the incident with the blue cloak (XLVIII).

THE EARLY EMPIRE

(19) Mosaic from Palestrina, Italy; date uncertain. (Goldsworthy, A. 2000: p.16)

The Palestrina mosaic shows an exotic Egyptian landscape with the Nile clearly in flood. At the lower centre a group of soldiers are gathered in front of a temple. Various dates have been but forward for the date of this mosaic, ranging from anywhere between the first century BC and the third century AD. The mosaic has also undergone some extensive restoration work in the last few hundred years and some figures may have been slightly altered from their original state. Fuentes believed that the mosaic documented a visit to Egypt by Octavian (later the Emperor

Augustus) after the battle of Actium in 31 BC. Octavian's visit coincided with an abundant flooding of the Nile and this remains the most popular date for the mosaic.

Nevertheless, other scholars – including Meyboom who made an extensive study of the monument – are of the opinion that the mosaic is in fact a copy of a much earlier work by an Alexandrian school, which now no longer survives. There are some slight discrepancies in the details of uniform colours between the observations of Fuentes and Meyboom, in particular regarding the figures Fuentes believed to be the admiral Agrippa and his centurion bodyguard. For example, Fuentes described one man (Agrippa) wearing a very pale blue tunic and moulded cuirass, accompanied by another figure dressed in a red, sleeveless, knotted tunic (a centurion). However, when Meyboom describes the same two figures, he refers to one soldier wearing a white leather or linen muscle cuirass over a white *chiton* (a Greek-style tunic) and the other dressed in a brownish-yellow *chiton*. Fuentes believed that the figure wearing what he thought was a blue tunic could well have been the admiral Agrippa because he associated the blue colour with the navy.

One of the central figures in the Palestrina mosaic that has been restored is the character Fuentes identified as Octavian. He appears to wear a green moulded linen or leather cuirass, possibly with *pteryges* attached, over a white *chiton*. While moulded linen or leather cuirasses are not always thought of as being Roman, these details do correspond to Macedonian tomb paintings from Egypt. Taking this into consideration with the other evidence, including details of the soldiers' dress (Greek-style boots, *embades*, rather than Roman *caligae*), Meyboom came to the conclusion that the figures on the mosaic represented not Roman soldiers at all but members of the elite troops of the Ptolemaic army, the Macedones.

The popular alternative suggestion however is that the scene does indeed represent Octavian/ Augustus perhaps with Agrippa, surrounded by praetorian guards who are known to have worn the scorpion device as depicted in the mosaic and which they adopted around this time.

93 The 'Judgement of Solomon' fresco from Pompeii. *(Col. Cat. 20)*.

(20) 'The Judgement of Solomon' fresco, Pompeii, Italy; late Republican/early Imperial. (Feder, T. 1978: p.127)

Fuentes argued that this court scene recreating the Old Testament story of the Judgement of Solomon as performed by pygmies actually shows them dressed in contemporary clothing. However it has been suggested elsewhere that this fresco is a copy of a much earlier Alexandrian work which no longer survives and that therefore the contemporary dress is Ptolemaic rather than Roman.

Fuentes pointed out that two of the soldiers wear white tunics, although at first glance the tunic of the soldier about to cleave the baby in half may be light blue and Sekunda in fact states that this tunic is indeed blue. However, the fresco is badly damaged in parts, including the areas around this figure. So what appears now as blue may in fact be an attempt to render shading on a white garment, a technique that is evident elsewhere on this and other frescoes. The second soldier has a salmon pink cloak while a third soldier wears both a dark red tunic and cloak, which Fuentes believed marked him out as an officer, in his opinion a centurion. Nevertheless all three soldiers have similar red helmet crests, which would seem to weaken this theory, as according to Vegetius centurions wore transverse silvered crests to distinguish them. Vegetius also does not mention centurions wearing any different tunic colour. The helmet crest of the third soldier is clearly not transverse or silvered, nor does he show any of the usual attributes associated with centurions at this date, such as a vine stick or silvered greaves. However, this soldier's armour and helmet are different in colour from those of his companions, so perhaps Fuentes is correct in identifying this man as an officer.

(21) Tavern sign, Pompeii, Italy; late Republican/early Imperial. (Gusman, P. 1900: pl.III. See also Baldassare, I. & Pugliesse Carratelli, G. 1993: p.1011 Vol IV Regio VI)

A wall painting shows a soldier being offered wine by a landlord. The soldier is apparently off duty because he wears only a tunic and cloak but appears to carry a spear which looks like a weighted *pilum*. If this identification is correct, this soldier could be a legionary or a praetorian rather than a local policeman. He is in fact dressed very similar to other contemporary soldiers, also probably praetorians, on the Cancelleria relief in Rome. The soldier's cloak is clearly of the *paenula* style and is yellow-brown in colour decorated with thin dark red *clavi*. The cloak is apparently worn over a grey-green scarf.

(21a) Fresco, Pompeii, Italy; Late Republic/early Imperial. (Maiuri, A. 1953: p.144)

A tavern scene from a Pompeian fresco which shows a group of men playing dice has sometimes been put forward as evidence of military tunic colours. One man in particular wears a dark red belted tunic and a grey paenula. However there is no obvious indication of side arms or a military belt to confirm whether this individual, or any of his companions, is a soldier or not.

(21b) Fresco, Pompeii, Italy; Late Republic/early Imperial. (Baldassare, I. & Pugliesse Carratelli, G. 1993: p.304 Vol VI)

A better example of evidence for clothing colour perhaps is provided by the painted frieze of peristillium 19 in Regio VII. It represents gladiatorial equipment but also includes what looks more like military armour, including a mail shirt with shoulder doubling, a red tunic and orange-red cloak.

(22) Wall painting, House of Valerius Rufus (or of the Trojan Shrine), Region I, Ins. GA., Pompeii, Italy; late Republican/early Imperial. (Dersin, D. 1997: p.102)

In the upper registers of the painting can be seen two figures, a male and a female. The man is armoured and wears a Montefortino-style helmet with a red crest, a white (linen?) cuirass and has bronze greaves on his legs. He carries a large oval shield and a spear in his left hand, and casually adjusts his cloak with the other. His tunic is a pinkish-red and the cloak is white. Although the figure is probably meant to represent a deity or a hero he appears to be armoured in a contemporary panoply. The similarity between his equipment and that of an officer or tribune supposedly represented on the famous Altar of Domitius Ahenobarbus is indeed quite striking. The inclusion of a Montefortino helmet – well known from other sculpture and archaeological evidence – rather than the stylised 'attic' type helmet, adds an extra touch of realism.

(23) Fresco, Pompeii, Italy; Late Republic/early Imperial. (Werner. P. 1977, p.102)

The man is wearing a short white belted tunic under a yellow-brown cloak and he rests on a spear or staff. The similarity between his apparel and that of off-duty soldiers is obvious, although this figure is generally described in modern texts as simply a traveller. It may in fact simply illustrate that there was little difference in basic outdoor clothing recommended for travelling and military dress. Similar parallels can be drawn with modern military clothing and hiking clothes worn today.

(24) Fresco, Domus Aurea, Rome, Italy; early Imperial. (Ministero per I Beni e le Attività culturali, *Domus Aurea Calendar*, Rome, 2001: plate for the month of June)

An armoured figure is depicted in a fresco from Nero's Golden House which possibly represents the Trojan hero Hector. Although the overall impression of the warrior's panoply is Hellenistic, his helmet is of a pseudo-Corinthian design. He carries a long spear and his shield is oval, but the body armour appears to be a Roman '*lorica segmentata*'. *Lorica segmentata* is considered a purely Roman invention but Mike Bishop's work on this armour has uncovered possible evidence for Hellenistic origins.

   The warrior wears a green tunic and helmet crest and is wearing a red cloak draped like a *paludamentum*. If the colour green was normally considered rather expensive for soldiers' uniforms, this need not of course apply to a profligate ruler like Nero, and by extension to his Praetorian Guard. Given the clear association of the Golden House with Nero, it is very tempting to speculate that the figure represents a member of the Guard, and that during the reign of Nero the praetorians were dressed not only in Hellenistic style reflecting Nero's passion for all things Greek, but also in the colour of the circus faction that he fanatically supported, the Greens. The *paludamentum* cloak would suggest that the man is an officer of some sort, although if he was a centurion then we would have expected to see the usual attributes that went with that rank, such as a transverse silvered crest.

(25) Tacitus (*c.*AD 56–?), *Histories*, II, 89.

Describing the triumphal entry into Rome by the Emperor Vitellius in AD 69, Tacitus relates how all the legionary camp prefects, tribunes and senior centurions were dressed in shining white *candida vesta*. Fuentes consequently argued that if the centurions and other senior officers were specially dressed in shining white at this parade, then they must therefore have worn another colour on other occasions. Using his previous interpretations of the evidence from the Palestrina mosaic and the 'Judgement of Solomon' fresco, Fuentes seems to have ignored the possibility that the other colour could have been off-white or unbleached cloth, and concluded that the alternative colour for centurions' tunics was red.

   What is in fact more obvious is that soldiers clearly had additional tunics, one of which could be specially whitened for events like the triumphal parade of Vitellius. One other occasion when soldiers would be expected to wear their best uniforms was at the Saturnalia festival. In a list of household goods and clothing uncovered on one of the Vindolanda writing tablets there is a mention of a tunic for dining, possibly belonging to the Cohort commander and conceivably for the Saturnalia dinner or some other special banquet.

(26) Vindolanda writing tablet, Britain; late first century AD.

An alternative colour for the *paenula* is supplied by one of the Vindolanda writing tablets, which refers to a white *paenula* (Tab.196). In view of some of the later evidence from Dura Europos discussed below, this conceivably belonged to the commanding officer of the cohort.

(27) Textiles, Vindolanda, Britain; late first century AD.

A sample of nearly 50 textile fragments recovered from Vindolanda were analysed for dye but evidence was found on only nine of these. Many of the textiles were of un-pigmented wool, and although suitable for dyeing they had been too heavily stained from burial to show any traces of dye. Of the nine textiles which had positive results, eight had been dyed red; the remaining piece actually appeared to have been a purple stripe. The red dye used was almost certainly madder, *rubia tinctorum*, which as mentioned previously would have been imported into Britain. The report on the Vindolanda textiles by George Taylor concluded that the image of Roman soldiers in red tunics may well be correct. Nevertheless we should remember that the textile fragments are extremely small and may not even be from tunics at all. Evidence of this came to light in another recently translated document from Vindolanda that refers to red and purple curtains!

(28) New Testament Gospels, Matthew, 28, 28; first century AD.

It is interesting that the cloak the auxiliary soldiers of the Jerusalem garrison used to mock Christ with as recorded by Matthew, was a red one. All the other Gospels say it was a purple cloak or robe but under the circumstances a red cloak is far more likely to have been left lying around. The other Gospel writers however clearly felt a purple garment was far more significant.

(29) Martial, *Epigrams*, XIV, 129; first century AD.

When the poet Martial described red Canusian cloaks he said that 'Rome wears more brown, Gauls red, and boys and soldiers like this colour.' – '*Roma magis fuscis vestitur, Gallia rufis, et placet hic pueris militibusque color.*'

(30) Pliny the Elder (AD **23/4–79), *Natural History*, XX, 3; first century** AD.

Pliny records that scarlet dye from the kermes was used for dyeing the *paludamentum*. He mentions that the most commonly used red dye was madder, which was grown near Rome. He adds that the most prestigious red dye was obtained from the kermes (*kermococcus vennilio*), a parasitic insect which infected the kermes oak throughout southern Europe. However he wrongly believed that the dye itself came from the berries of the tree when it is in fact obtained from the female insects' egg sacks!

(31) Tombstone (Cn. xiii 6277), Mainz, Germany; first century AD. **(Junkelmann, M. 1992: abb.46)**

A rare example of a tombstone that when excavated still had surviving traces of it original colouring and may possibly indicate that the practice of wearing red cloaks was more widespread among ordinary soldiers. Sadly although the paint did not survive for long it was recorded and a watercolour copy was made. The tombstone shows Silius, a cavalry trooper in the *Ala Picentiana* and either he or more likely his attendant (*calo*), had a red cloak. Silius himself is shown reclining on a couch at his funeral banquet and is dressed in a toga.

The remainder of what the *calo* is wearing is also interesting. He has a plain garment coloured green with a red fringe at the bottom. This garment is similar to others shown on Auxiliary tombstones elsewhere. Without the paint what he is wearing may well have been labelled as a mail shirt. An alternative explanation was discussed in the section on the *subarmalis*.

(32) Tombstone, Germany; first century AD.

There were remains of original paint on another tombstone belonging to Gnaeus Musius, an *aquilifer* standard-bearer, with Legio XIIII Gemina Martia Victrix. This led the German archaeologists who were creating a reconstruction of the monument to make the tunic white.

(33) Pay receipt and textiles, Masada, Israel; first century AD.

A recently excavated receipt sheds light on military tunics and clothing. For instance it seems to confirm that even ordinary soldiers owned more than one tunic and had special garments

94 Detail of the tombstone of Silius a cavalry trooper with the Ala Picentiana now in Mainz *(Col. Cat. 31).*

for specific occasions. The receipt below belonged to C. Messius, son of Gaius of the Fabian tribe, recruited from Beirut. In spite of his local origin it is believed that he served in Legio XI Fretensis as a legionary cavalryman, rather than in an auxiliary cavalry or unit.

The fourth consulate of Imperator Vespasianus Augustus
Accounts(?). salary
C. Messius, son of Gaius, of the tribe Fabia, from Beirut.
I received of my salary   50 denarii
Out of which I have paid:
Barley money   16 denarii
m.   )rnius
Food expenses   20 denarii
Boots   5 denarii
Strapping (*lorum fasciari(um)*)   2 denarii
Linen tunic (*tunica linia*)   7 denarii
I received of my salary   60(?) denarii
Out of which I have paid:
Barley money   16 denarii
Food expenses   20 denarii
C. Antonius
Overall cloak (*pallium opertoriu(m)*)   ? denarii
Publius Valerius
White tunic (*tun(i)ca alba*)   ? denarii

(Trans Cotton & Geiger 1989)

Among the list of compulsory deductions from his pay it can be seen that 7 denarii was taken for a linen tunic, and an unknown amount for a white tunic. Cotton and Geiger noted that as linen would have been an expensive item to purchase, this garment would have been used for special occasions. However, we might also expect that in eastern climates soldiers may have even preferred linen garments to wool. For instance, during the Persian wars of the fourth century, Ammianus Marcellinus (XIX, 8.8) describes how he and a companion tore up their linen clothes to make a line in order to obtain water from a well.

Both linen and wool fragments were uncovered during the excavations at Masada. Many of these textiles may have come from clothing belonging to the Jewish defenders and civilians present at the famous siege. It can also be argued that some of these fragments were clearly not from clothing at all. It is no surprise to discover that nearly all of the linen textiles were left un-dyed, but it was not clear how white they would have been. It is therefore fairly safe to assume that the linen tunic mentioned in the Masada pay receipt was originally white. A true white had probably only been achieved by one textile fragment found at Masada which had been made from lambs wool.

In contrast, over half of the 105 wool textiles analysed had been dyed. Of these 14 were red, ranging in shade from a salmon pink to dark maroon. Six other textile fragments had been dyed plain blue or blue-green. Contrasting colour bands in dark blue, purple or mauve which may have been *clavi* were observed on several fragments.

It was noted that most of the coloured textiles would originally have been worn by women as this is supported by Jewish literature and the Egyptian funerary portraits where men's tunics are almost without exception white. However, one textile fragment, consisting of two thick selvedges that had been sewn together and dyed red, was believed to come from a man's tunic, possibly a military one. However at least one Egyptian funeral portrait shows a woman wearing a scarlet tunic, so once more this evidence is inconclusive. In addition, while Jewish law forbade men from wearing coloured tunics, there is evidence that Jewish people – like the Romans with their sizes of *clavi* – did not always follow the rules. The Babylonian Talmud actually mentions a Jewish man who wore a new Roman red tunic while in a period of mourning.

(34) Josephus, *Jewish War*, first century AD.

We owe much of our knowledge on the Roman army to the Jewish historian Josephus, who at first fought against the Romans, was captured, and then collaborated with them. When he documented the fall of Jerusalem he states how one of the main Jewish leaders, Simon Bar Gioras, tunnelled his way out of the city but was unable to get past the Roman lines. He then appears to have tried to bluff his way past the Roman guards by disguising himself as a Roman soldier or an officer, for he wore a number of white tunics and a reddish purple cloak (*BJ*, 7.26–36).

(35) Tombstone, Vienna, Austria; first century AD.

One example of the 'Cimmerian' tunics might be illustrated on the tombstone of T. Flavius Draccus, who served with the Ala I Flavia Domitiana Britannica MCR (see 38 below for a description of *Cimmerian*). His tombstone retained evidence of its original colouring, but unfortunately only the head and shoulders of the deceased are shown. Draccus appears to wear something blue around his neck and shoulders. It could be a tunic or a scarf, but might equally be a blue cloak. The latter would certainly be in keeping with many of the painted wax portraits from Egypt.

(36) Papyri, *BGU VII* 1564, Egypt; early second century AD.

Among the vast collection of ancient documents discovered in Egypt are at least two papyri which refer to the delivery of clothing to provincial armies. BGU VII 1564 and the following P.RYL 189 confirm that local communities supplied the army. Nonetheless it is interesting to discover that villages in Egypt were supplying clothing to troops based as far away as Judaea in one case and Cappadocia (now part of modern Turkey) in the other.

> Copy of order for payment. Ammonius, son of Polydeuces, Syrion, son of Heras, Heraclides, son of Heraclides, all three collectors of clothing (in requisitions), and Hermes, ex-agoranomos, to Heraclides, banker, greetings. Pay to Heraclides, son of Horgias, Heron, freedman of Publius Maevius, and Dioscorus, freedman of the mighty god Serapis, weavers of the village of Philadelphia,

95 Part of the tombstone of Titus
Flavius Druccus from Vienna,
Austria. *(Col. Cat. 35).*

for them and the other weavers in the same village on their mutual responsibility, (these sums) as an
advance payment of the cost of the clothing which is part of that which his Excellency the prefect
Avidius Heliodorus ordered to be prepared for the requirements of the soldiers in Cappadocia: one
white tunic with belt, 1.55m (3½ cubits) long, 1.40m (3 cubits, 4 dactuloi) wide, weight 1.6kg (3¾
minae) – 24 drachmae on account; four white Syrian cloaks, each 2.66m (6 cubits) a long, 1.77m
(4 cubits) wide, weight 1.6kg (3¾ minae) – 24 drachmae on account for each; total 96 drachmae;
combined total 120 drachmae; for the requirements of the hospital in the Imperial camp, one plain
white blanket, 2.66m (6 cubits) long, 1.77m (4 cubits) wide, weight 3 pounds 9 ounces (4 minae) –
28 drachmae on account; total of payment order – 148 silver drachmae; but from the advance of 28
drachmae in respect of the blankets, 6 drachmae were deducted for the Imperial treasury. It is agreed
that they are to make the clothing of good soft pure white wool without any kind of stain and that
it is to be well-woven, firm, with finished hems, satisfactory, without damage, and not in value below
the price paid to them in advance for the clothing. If, when it is handed over, any of the clothing
is missing or is held to be of inferior value, they shall on their mutual responsibility repay the value
of the missing clothing, together with dues and expenses, and the deficit in respect of clothing of
inferior value. And they shall deliver them promptly with the established specifications and weights,
separate from other public clothing requirements which they owe. The second year of Emperor
Caesar Titus Aelius Hadrian Antoninus Augustus Pius, Thoth 12.

There is, however, more evidence that the sending or collecting of military supplies over great
distance was not a unique occurrence. A strength report (*pridianum*) of *c*.AD 105 relating to
Cohors I Veterana Hispanorum Equitata, although found in Egypt probably relates to a period
when the unit was based in Macedonia. It records that soldiers had been sent all the way to
Gaul to collect clothing! (Fink 1971, No 63).

(37) Papyri *P. RYL.*189, Egypt; early second century AD.

We, Dionysius son of Socrates and the associate collectors of public clothing for the guards, have received from the weavers of the village of Socnopaei Nesus nineteen … tunics, total 19, and for the needs of the soldiers serving in Judaea five white cloaks, total five. The 13th year of the emperor Caesar Trajanus Hadrianus Augustus, Choiak 22. (signed) received by me, Diogenes. Received also by me, Onesas. Received also by me, Philoxenus.

(Trans Campbell 1994)

Fuentes found it surprising that this document referred to five white cloaks because in his opinion the pictorial evidence largely suggested that military cloaks should be yellow-brown. However, the papyrus document *BGU VII* 1564 also refers to four white cloaks, providing in addition the term 'Syrian' to describe them. To this reference can be added the white *paenula* cloak from the Vindolanda document and two white cloaks illustrated on the fresco from Dura Europos (see below). Finally another papyrus from a slightly later date in fact mentions the 'controllers of tunics and white cloaks'.

As Roman military documents are quite minute in their detail, even to the point of documenting individual nails for boots, there is another point that is raised by these papyri. There are two references to supplying the soldiers in Judaea and one to the armies in Cappadocia but there is no mention as to whether these garments are for citizen legionaries or non-Roman auxiliaries. It is known that at the date of the papyri in question both provincial garrisons were comprised of legionary and auxiliary troops.

It is a matter of debate, therefore, whether any attempt was made to differentiate between citizen and non-citizen soldiers by them wearing differently coloured tunics. In one famous incident Tacitus informs us as to how two soldiers in the civil war of AD 69 passed through enemy lines by the stratagem of using captured shields and he also states on several occasions distinctive weapons and equipment used by auxiliaries (*Hist.*, I, 38; III, 47). So it seems that it was the type of equipment and weapons that were used which distinguished the two troop types not their clothing. Certainly in the overall style of clothing depicted on their tombstones it is often difficult to tell them apart and without any surviving inscriptions sometimes impossible. In contrast Tacitus also alludes to a policy of Romanising the allied armies by giving them Roman armour and standards.

If both types of soldier received all their clothes from the same supply source it was likely that both legionaries and auxiliaries wore the same colour of tunic. On the other hand, Fuentes suggested that locally recruited auxiliaries might have worn their own traditional clothing. As an example he noted that in the early first century the Greek historian Strabo had described the men in a number of Spanish tribes dressing in black (*Geog.*, 3. 3.7). He therefore suggested that this may have been reflected in the colour of the tunics of the tribesmen recruited into the Asturian infantry and cavalry units raised in Spain, but there is no firm evidence for this. If there was any designated colour difference between citizen and non-citizen soldiers it is not known how this applied to the citizens who chose to serve in the Auxilia or if the cohorts of citizens were distinguished in any way.

The best evidence for the colour of auxiliary tunics are the frescoes from Dura Europos, ironically dating after the *Constitutio Antoniniana* when the Emperor Caracalla (AD 211–217) granted Roman citizenship to all free-born inhabitants of the empire. Officially at least this wiped out at a stroke the traditional differences between citizen legionaries and non-citizen auxiliaries.

(37b) Papyrus. Egypt, *c.*second century AD, Bibliotheque Nationale Paris. cod. suppl. gr. 1294 (various, le tre vite del Papiro di Artemedoro, voci e sguardi dall 'Egitto Greco-Romano, Milan, 2006. cat 109 p.280)

The Romance papyrus, also known as The Alexander Papyrus, is an extremely rare fragment of a once illustrated manuscript. One of the surviving illustrations shows the judicial case between a soldier, Demetrios and an old woman over a considerable amount of money. The soldier wears a blue *paenula* decorated with purple *clavi*.

(38) Arrian (*c.*AD 129–130), *Ars Tactica*, 34.6.
When he described the spectacular training displays carried out by the Roman cavalry, Arrian said that

> instead of corselets they wear Cimmerian tunics, similar in size to corselets, some scarlet, others
> blue and others in a variety of colours. On their legs they wear trousers, not loose ones like the
> Parthians and Armenians but tight round the legs.

Arrian was a provincial governor so one would expect he knew what he was talking about.

The Romans frequently named things after what they believed was its place of origin and the Cimmerians were an ancient tribe of steppe nomads mentioned by the Greek historian Herodotus. It is possible therefore that the '*Cimmerian*' tunic looked like something worn by the steppe peoples of Arrian's day and may have been a thick type of riding coat.

(39) Antonine Wall distance slab, Bridgeness, Scotland; *c.*AD 142 (Clarke, D. *et al.* 1980: 15).
The scene on the distance slab represents a military sacrifice or *suovetaurilia*, with the legionary legate dressed in a toga and four other figures including a *vexiliarius* holding the flag-type standard standing behind. One of these soldiers has a *paenula* and scarf while the other wears a *sagum*. The *sagum* retained traces of red paint, and Fuentes believed that this man was therefore a centurion.

Wild points out that when painted colour survives on tombstones of civilians in the north-west provinces their tunics, capes, cloaks and scarves are generally yellow or yellow-orange which has then been outlined in red. So it is not clear if the traces of red paint on the cloak of a soldier on the Bridgeness distance slab came from a similar outline or from the cloak itself. The cloak might originally have been yellow or yellow-brown although in the light of some of the evidence cited elsewhere a red cloak can not be ruled out either. Yellow-brown or red cloaks seem to have been quite common so it would be difficult to say what rank this soldier would have been.

(40) Tertullian (born *c.*AD 160/170), *De Corona Militis*, 1.3.
Tertullian describes how a soldier was accused of being a Christian because he refused to wear a military crown. Before his trial commenced the accused was stripped of his military insignia which included his cloak, sword and sandals. Finally he was left clad 'only in red' which could be taken to mean either a tunic or a cloak. Of additional interest is Tertullian's description of the soldier's boots which he calls *caliga speculatoria*. This suggests that the unfortunate soldier was a member of the emperor's own elite cavalry bodyguard, the *Speculatores Augustii* or 'Augustan Scouts'.

(41) *Scriptores Historiae Augustae*, *Clodius Albinus* II. 5.VI. 4.
The SHA states that the Emperor Commodus when designating Clodius Albinus his successor gave him the privilege of wearing a scarlet cloak (*coccinum pallium*) which he could even wear at court.

(42) Encaustic portrait, Antinoopolis, Egypt; second/third century AD (Doxiadis, E. 1995: pl. 2).
Hundreds of painted portraits have been discovered in the Fayum district of Egypt. They are painted on linen or in wax on wood panels, a technique known today as encaustic. They were probably executed during the lifetime of the sitter because some show evidence of alterations, perhaps because the client was displeased with the likeness. The portraits were presumably displayed like modern photographs are today around the house, but when the person died the portrait would be placed over the face of the deceased and incorporated into the funeral wrappings around the body.

96 Detail from the Antonine Wall in
Scotland *(Col. Cat. 39).*

In a letter from Apion, a young recruit into the imperial fleet to his father, he says that he
has 'sent you by Euctemnon a portrait of myself' (BGU 423). This clearly illustrates that these
works of art were within reach of even the humblest soldier and it comes as no surprise that
several portraits have been identified as being members of the military.

Principally this identification rests on the studded red leather baldrics and swords that are
sometimes visible. Also in sharp contrast to the plain white tunic and cloak that most males in
these portraits wear, the 'soldiers' have brightly coloured cloaks generally draped over the left
shoulder. A comparison with early imperial tombstones would suggest that those males with
sword baldrics crossing from their right shoulder to their left side are centurions while those
crossing in the opposite direction are possibly legionaires.

They were also undoubtedly many portraits of the Emperors depicted in military garb.
The Augustan History informs us that one of these portraits depicted the Emperor Tacitus in
various types of dress which included a *toga*, a military cloak, full armour, a Greek cloak and
hunting dress (SHA. *Tacitus*, XVI. I). Sadly all but one are lost and that, an image of Septimus
Severus and his family, adds a little to this study.

One of the most well known of these encaustic portraits is called 'The Tondo of the Two
brothers' and is on display at the Cairo Museum. The younger looking of the two men wears
a white tunic edged around the neck with a thin reddish purple line and dots. Extending from
the neck down the shoulder is a small notched band also in reddish purple and below that a small
swastika motif. The man wears a reddish purple cloak fastened over the right shoulder with an
elaborate brooch fitted with a gemstone. This ensemble is clearly similar to other illustrations and

descriptions of contemporary military dress so it is possible the man was an officer in the local garrison.

(43) Encaustic portrait Hawara, Egypt; *c*.AD 160–180 (Doxiadis. E. 1995: pl. 3).
A painted portrait now in the Manchester Museum shows a man with a very fashionable Antonine curly hairstyle and beard. He wears a plain white tunic with a red cloak and baldric crossing over his left shoulder down to a sword worn on his right side. The sword pommel is just visible. The baldric is decorated with alternate bronze and silvered discs.

(44) Encaustic portrait, Egypt, now in Moscow; possibly Trajanic (Doxiadis, E. 1995: pl.4).
Judging by his hairstyle this man is from the Trajanic period. He wears a white tunic with a blue cloak draped over the right shoulder like a *paludamentum*.

(45) Encaustic portrait, Philadelphia, Egypt; Trajanic, *c*.AD 100 (Doxiadis, E. 1995: pl.15).
A portrait now in Berlin showing what appears to be a centurion wearing a white tunic and a dark cloak almost black, pinned on his left shoulder in the style of a *paludamentum*. He has a sword baldric also in black with white (silver?) discs crossing from his right shoulder to the sword worn on his left, which at this date should identify a man of centurion rank. He wears a gold wreath in his hair.

(46) Encaustic portrait, Philadelphia, Egypt; Trajanic-Hadrianic *c*.AD 110–130 (Doxiadis, E. 1995: pl.16).
Another portrait now in Berlin but the man is slightly more gaudily dressed than the previous example. Again he has a white tunic but a single black clavus is visible on his right shoulder. Over his left shoulder is a blue cloak with what appears to be a silver *fibula*. His baldric crossing from his right shoulder to his left side again indicating centurion status is red with gold or bronze coloured discs.

(47) Encaustic portrait, Philadelphia, Egypt; Antonine *c*.AD 138–192 (Doxiadis, E. 1995: pl.17).
This is one of the most spectacular portraits and is a classic work of ancient art. The man with his Antonine hairstyle and beard has an almost cavalier attitude far removed from the stereotypical image of a Roman soldier. He wears a white tunic with a black *clavus* visible on his right side. Over his left shoulder he has a blue cloak fastened with a bronze brooch. He wears a black baldric crossing from under the cloak on his left shoulder to behind the sword pommel worn on his right which would indicate that this is an ordinary *miles*.

(48) Encaustic portrait, Philadelphia, Egypt; *c*.AD 117–138 (Doxiadis, E. 1995: pl. 18).
Now in the British Museum collection this portrait appears to be an ordinary soldier because of the position of the sword on his right. He is wearing a white tunic with blue cloak and red baldric decorated with alternate yellow and grey discs presumably representing bronze and silver.

(49) Encaustic portrait, Philadelphia, Egypt; *c*.AD 125–150 (Doxiadis, E. 1995: pl.19).
Portrait of a soldier wearing a white tunic and a dark almost black, olive coloured cloak. Part of the red leather baldric crossing from the man's left shoulder, decorated with yellow discs is just visible. The painting is now in Berlin.

(50) Encaustic portrait, Philadelphia, Egypt; *c*.AD 138–192 (Doxiadis, E. 1995: p.34).
Also in Berlin, this portrait is of a man in white tunic and dark almost black tunic. This man wears a baldric crossing from his right shoulder, indicating another possible centurion.

97 Funeral portraits from Roman Egypt
that appear to illustrate soldiers.

Col. Cat. (46).

Col. Cat. (47).   *Col. Cat. (53).*

 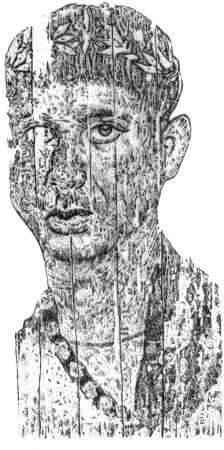

Col. Cat. (61).   *Col. Cat. (62).*

(51) Encaustic portrait, Egypt (Doxiadis, E. 1995: p.36 fig 6).
A double portrait of a man and a woman generally identified as Mars and Venus but apparently wearing contemporary dress. The military garb of Mars is therefore of special interest. He is wearing a red garment and some form of head gear.

(52) Encaustic portrait, Egypt, now in Moscow; c.AD 161–180 (Doxiadis, E. 1995: pl. 122).
A man with a golden wreath, white tunic and red purple cloak fastened on his right side with an elaborate silver *fibula*.

(53) Encaustic portrait, Er-Rubayat, Egypt (Now in Wurzburg); c.AD 300 (Parlasca, K. 1969–1980: n.497).
This is a remarkable portrait as it appears to show a Jewish man in military costume. He wears a white tunic with a yellow-brown cloak fastened over his right shoulder with a disc *fibula*.

(54) Encaustic portrait, Er-Rubayat, Egypt (Now in Melbourne National Gallery); late third century AD (Parlasca, K. 1969–1980: n.546).
This man wears a white tunic with a black cloak edged with white fastened over his right shoulder with a red brooch. Just below the brooch a small notched band can be seen extending down the shoulder. A black cloak is unusual but a black tunic is also known from Egypt on the Temple Fresco in Luxor (see (81) below).

(55) Encaustic portrait, Egypt (now in Boston); *c.* first half of the third century AD **(Parlasca, K. 1969–1980: n.389).**
Portrait of a man with a white tunic and a violet red cloak fastened over his right shoulder with an elaborate circular *fibula* with a gemstone. The tunic neck has a coloured border with small regular spaced lines extending down.

(56) Encaustic portrait, Er-Rubayat, Egypt (now in Vienna); *c.* second quarter of the third century AD **(Parlasca, K. 1969–1980: n.409).**
A slight variation on the common colour combination is displayed by this man. He wears a white tunic with a purple decoration around the neck and a notched band extending down the shoulder from the neck, but instead of a red-purple cloak he has a yellow-brown one fastened over the right shoulder with a round fibula.

(57) Encaustic portrait, Hawara, Egypt (now in Chicago); *c.*AD 170–180 (Parlasca, K. 1969–1980: n.345).
This is a fascinating portrait and is quite unlike any other example. As is normal in these portraits only the upper body of the individual is shown. Therefore in this particular case it is difficult to understand what the man is actually wearing. An educated guess would suggest that he is dressed in a red *paenula* which has been folded up onto his shoulders, as is commonly seen in many monuments. Another alternative preferred by D'Amato is that he is wearing a *subarmalis* decorated with studs. Around his neck is a large scarf possibly decorated with white pearls, which has been knotted below the neck and covers the neck opening of a *paenula*, if that is indeed what is worn.

(58) Encaustic portrait, Er-Rubayat, Egypt (now in New Haven); *c.*AD 160–180 (Parlasca, K. 1969–1980: n.354).
Sadly only fragments survive of this portrait but enough to indicate that this man wears an almost identical costume to (55). His red cloak is fastened with a disk fibula on his right shoulder.

(59) Encaustic portrait, Er-Rubayat, Egypt (Now in Milwaukee); *c.*AD 170–180 (Parlasca, K. 1969–1980: n.364).
Portrait of a man wearing a white cloak with the upper edge decorated with triangles and fastened with a circular fibula.

(60) Encaustic portrait, Er-Rubayat, Egypt (now in Stockholm); (Parlasca, K. 1969–1980: n.180).
Portrait of a man wearing a white tunic and a dark cloak.

(61) Encaustic portrait, Egypt, (now in Cambridge, Mass); *c.*AD 120–130 (Parlasca, K. 1969–1980: n.177).
A portrait of a man, very similar to (45); presumably another centurion.

(62) Encaustic portrait, El-Fayyum, Egypt (now in Cairo); *c.*AD 120–130 (Parlasca, K. 1969–1980: n.169).
One more apparent centurion as this man too wears a white tunic, an ornamented red baldric over the right shoulder and has a light medium blue cloak.

(63) Encaustic portrait, Antinoopolis, Egypt (now in the Louvre, Paris); *c.* second quarter of the third century AD **(Parlasca, K. 1969–1980: n.421).**
Like (57) above this portrait might show a man wearing a *paenula*. It is decorated with two small rosettes on either side above the breasts just below the v-shaped neck opening.

98 A funeral portrait
found at Deir El
Medineh, Egypt _(Col.
Cat. 65)._

(64) Encaustic portrait, Tanis/Manashin, Egypt; _c._AD 218–235 (Parlasca, K. 1969–1980: n.469).
Now in the Ashmolean museum in Oxford, this painting shows a man with a yellow-brown cloak wrapped around him with a red band – possibly the tunic – visible around his neck underneath the cloak.

(65) Portrait, Deir-El-Medinah, Egypt; mid-third century AD (Luxor, J. 194: Q 1512).
Although the Fayum portraits generally depict only the subject's head and shoulders this portrait – found near Luxor dating to the mid-third century AD – shows the soldier down to his waist. Like the men in the other portraits he too wears a white tunic, although it can be seen that the sleeves are long with fringed cuffs. He wears a red cloak. His sword can be clearly seen worn on his left side, but by this later date this feature is no longer unique to centurions and he has a belt decorated with silver-coloured plates.

(66) Painting of the god Heron, Egypt; third century (Kiss, Z. 1996: fig.3).
The warrior god is depicted wearing a stiff white cuirass, possibly linen or leather, decorated with _clavi_ each one outlined with two thinner lines. This is worn over a white tunic decorated in the same manner. The upper part of the cuirass appears to be scale armour, perhaps an additional chest defence over the stiff garment underneath and this is partially covered by the god's white, purple-bordered cloak, which is fastened in the centre by a circular fibula.

(67) Painting of the god Heron, found in situ painted on wall of house B50, Karanis, Egypt; third century (Thomas, T.K. 2001: fig.57).
A very similar depiction of the god to that discussed above, but there are some interesting differences in the detail. The armour looks more like it is quilted and is coloured grey. The tunic just visible below the white _pteryges_ is pinkish with dark purple _clavi_ each outlined with a thin purple line. The only visible tunic sleeve has a thick and a very thin purple band with

99 Painting of a warrior god from
Egypt *(Col. Cat. 66)*.

perhaps another single purple band at elbow height. He is wearing a pink-purple cloak with no
obvious sign of a brooch.

(68) Painting of the god Heron, Egypt; third century (Breccia, E. 1926: pl LVIII).
In this example the warrior god is shown wearing a sleeveless red tunic over a longer sleeved
blue tunic. The over tunic has purple *clavi*.

(69) *Scriptores Historiae Augustae, Sev Alex*. **XLII. 2.**
The Emperor Severus Alexander wore a scarlet cloak (*lacerna coccea*).

(70) Tombstone, Haghia Triada, Crete; late second/early third century AD **(Liberati,
A.M. 1997: 45–93: p.72).**
A tombstone shows a marine named Sabinianus who was detached from the fleet based at
Misenum. He wears a *paenula* over a tunic and there were traces of red paint on both. Recent
research has also revealed traces of orange/red wool on the body of the possible marine
discovered at the Herculaneum dating to AD 79.

(71) *Scriptores Historiae Augustae. The Two Gallieni*. **VIII.1.**
The Emperor Gallienus celebrated a decennial festival, 'he repaired to the capitol with the
Senators and the Equestrian order dressed in their togas and with the soldiers dressed all in
white' – '*iam primum inter togatos patres et equestrem ordinem albato milite*'. Gallienus himself liked
to dress in a purple cloak with a long-sleeved tunic also in purple decorated with gold. He had
a jewelled sword belt and even had jewels on his boot laces! As a further affectation Gallienus
also liked to sprinkle gold dust in his hair.

(72) Fresco, Dura Europos, Syria; *c.*AD **239.**
Unlike most of the other pictorial evidence that portrays anonymous soldiers, this fresco depicts
a known historical unit, the auxiliary Cohors XX Palmyrenorum and names and illustrates the

tribune of the cohort, Julius Terentius. Terentius and the other soldiers are all depicted wearing white long-sleeved tunics with purple decoration. The tunic of Terentius has a purple band around the neck and hem and two cuff bands which probably did not go entirely around the sleeve. Instead of *clavi* this tunic had short notched bands coming down from the shoulder, only one of which was originally visible as the other was obscured by the cloak. The other soldiers appear to have worn similar decorated tunics but one individual – perhaps a senior centurion – had two swastika devices on the skirts of his tunic.

The cloak worn by Terentius is white and has a purple fringe along the bottom edge. Only one other soldier wears a white cloak, the same soldier who has the swastikas on his tunic, the rest have yellow-brown coloured cloaks and those of the other soldiers in the background are covered with hatched lines to indicate a coarser material.

All the soldiers appear to wear very tight fitting dark blue-grey or grey-brown trousers. The contemporary and distinctive ring belt buckles and wide red or brown leather belts and baldrics with metal fittings, all appear to be portrayed reasonably accurately. James has suggested that at least two of the soldiers may have a fabric waist sash which in one case might be white.

100 Fragment of a fresco from Dura Europos (*Col. Cat. 73*).

(73) Fresco, Dura Europos, Syria; mid-third century AD.
A figure attending a sacrifice on a fresco on a wall close to the Terentius fresco and possibly contemporary, wears a white tunic and a red cloak. Because of the red cloak Fuentes considered this man was a centurion.

(74) Fresco, Dura Europos, Syria; third century AD.
A badly damaged fresco that may originally have depicted an entire battle scene includes a cavalryman, perhaps a horse archer, in combat with an infantryman. The infantryman's tunic is white edged in red-purple. A third figure dressed in a red-brown tunic looks to be carrying off a young captive.

(75) Tunic, Dura Europos, Syria; third century AD.
A number of textile fragments were recovered during excavations at the site including a near complete wool tunic. It was un-dyed with narrow purple stripes on the cuffs of the sleeves with three small 'z's near each cuff. The neck opening and cuffs had been hemmed and finished off with an embroidered cord. Apart from the long *clavi* the tunic looks like those rendered in the Terentius fresco but this does not positively identify it as a military garment.

Nevertheless the dimensions of the tunic are interesting; it was 92cm long and 65cm wide. The sleeves were 33cm wide and 17cm long. It had two purple *clavi* 8cm wide and two purple bands on the sleeves each of them approximately 1.1cm wide and 21cm long. The tunic is virtually the same width as the one from Thorsberg but it is much smaller than those from Nahal Hever in Israel so it is possible that this tunic either did not belong to a mature adult or was very tight fitting.

(76) Synagogue frescoes, Dura Europos, Syria; third century AD (Bellinger, A. 1956).
The figures in the Synagogue frescos are depicted in contemporary dress, which not surprisingly for a frontier city reflects Roman, Palmyrene and Persian influences rather than the days of the supposed Old Testament setting of the scenes illustrated. Some of the armour and equipment illustrated has attracted attention, especially the mail or scale coifs.

    a) One scene illustrating the Israelites crossing the Red Sea depicts them as two phalanxes of infantry. Although the soldiers all carry large oval shields that obscure most of their bodies it is just possible to see that they all wear white or light pink-red tunics.

    b) The 'Ebenezer' fresco shows two un-armoured light cavalrymen armed with two-handed spears facing one another as if in a duel. Both men however have blue tunics with white bands possibly an under tunic visible beneath the short sleeves. They both wear red trousers.

    c) In the 'Ezekiel' fresco there is also a mixture of eastern and western style dress. There is a large figure wearing a muscled cuirass while a group of smaller figures wear scale armour, *lorica squamata*. All have the classic leather or white linen *pteryges* worn from the waist. The larger figure seems to have a bronze helmet, while his companions have what looks to be iron ones; he also has a long-sleeved blue tunic and pinkish-red cloak, while they wear pinkish-red tunics. Only one cloak is visible in the group of soldiers and that is a yellow-brown colour. On the legs of the large figure are greaves which are clearly tied with laces. The other figures in this scene are all wearing eastern style dress with long-sleeved tunics tied tightly at the waist with trousers tucked into boots.

(77) Fresco, Dura Europos, Syria; third century AD (James, S. 2004: pl.3).
A portrait of Heliodorus who was a clerk, *actuarius,* shows him wearing a white tunic with purple trim around the neck and a yellow-brown cloak.

(78) Praetextatus catacomb painting, Rome; third century AD (Bisconti, F-Mazzei, B. 2002: fig 10).
Believed to be one of the earliest representations of the Passion, this painting shows two men presumably Roman soldiers crowning Christ with the crown of thorns. Both have off-white tunics and sagum cloaks.

(79) Fresco, Castellum Dimidi, Algeria; mid-third century AD (Picard, G.C. 1947: pp.159–72).
A poorly preserved painting survived at this isolated desert outpost. It might originally have come from a similar scene to that represented in the Terentius fresco. It was only possible to reconstruct a couple of figures; one is wearing a white tunic with a blue-grey cloak. While another man has a white tunic and a red cloak that is outlined in black. Originally these paintings may have been on a similar scale to those at Luxor, but sadly little remained.

101 Praetextus catacomb detail *(Col. Cat. 78)*.

102 Wall paintings from Castellum Dimidi
depicting soldiers *(Col. Cat. 79)*.

(80) Mosaic, Dougga, Tunisia; mid-third century AD (Fradier & Martin. 1989: p.164).
A scene depicting Odysseus and the sirens with Odysseus tied to the mast of a ship surrounded by his crew. The sailors on the ship are dressed in white possibly linen tunics with red *clavi* and cloaks in blue green (*venutus*) which would tie in well with the later description of Vegetius. Odysseus is wearing a white tunic worn off one shoulder and a white *pileus* cap. Other figures possibly soldiers have a *chlamys* knotted on the left side, white tunics with red *clavi* and they carry what appear to be polished bronze shields, an item of equipment still used by the Byzantine navy in medieval times.

(81) Fresco, Luxor Temple, Egypt; mid/late third century AD.
A series of wall paintings were uncovered in 1859 dating from the time when the famous temple had actually been converted into a Roman fort! The wall painting in the central chapel was originally thought to depict Christian saints, but archaeologists now agree that it formed part of the fort's shrine of the military standards dating to the time of Diocletian (r.AD 284–305). Unfortunately the Victorian excavators were more interested in the Pharaonic relief's underneath, so the majority of the paintings only survive today in the form of watercolour copies made at the time. What survived into modern times was until recently faded and obscure and one recent guidebook showed the same casual indifference, stating that 'fortunately what little is left is wearing off'. Thankfully what remains of the paintings have now undergone restoration and transformed them back to their former glory.

   The paintings on one wall originally appear to have represented cavalrymen, one of whom wears a red tunic, the other a white tunic. Other figures were too badly preserved to indicate what colour tunics they were wearing. It is clear from the remaining characters on the main central wall – which have now been restored – that the Roman military tunics displayed the contemporary civilian fashion for decorative patches. They include patterned borders at the neck, sleeves and hem, and large medallions on the lower part of the tunics and cloaks. All the visible tunics on this wall are white and the cloaks are yellow-brown with dark green, almost black, patches decorated with faint white designs. Fuentes suggested the figure on the previous wall scene was a centurion because of his red tunic. However, if he was an officer his tunic is the least decorated of all those in the entire series of paintings.

(82) Mithraic temple frescos, Italy; third century AD (Vermaseren, M.J. 1971: & Daniels, C. 1989).
Mithras was a deity of Persian origin and many of his worshippers were from the military. The followers of the cult were divided into seven grades and each grade was represented by a specific character. One of these was the soldier, *miles*, and on special occasions the worshippers dressed in costumes to portray this character. We should expect that the military costume was something that would be easily recognisable to contemporaries.

   Some paintings from Mithraic temples have survived. They either show the events taking place or pictures of the individual characters themselves. In the temple at Capua Vetere in Italy there are two paintings that show initiates into the grade of *miles* undergoing ordeal by fire. In both paintings the initiate is held by a man wearing a white tunic with red stripes on the sleeves while another figure wearing a dark red tunic, red cloak and red crested helmet comes towards the initiate holding burning torches.

   Daniels identified the figures wearing the white tunics as the *milites*; however Vermaseren said that they were the figures in red. Further support for the latter assertion is provided by another fresco in the Mithraeum at Santa Prisca in Rome. This shows a procession of the seven grades and the costume of the *miles* also appears to be reddish-brown, with two rows of purple bands on the tunic cuffs. Nevertheless, to confuse matters in one more procession scene at the same Mithraeum it is possible the *miles* wears an olive-green tunic with brown bands on the tunic sleeves. Vermaseren was however not so sure of this identification.

(83) Dio's Roman History, *Epitome* of Book LXXIX, 2–3; third century AD.
Caracalla is recorded as wearing at least three other conventional types of coloured cloak as well

as the *caracalla* with which he is normally associated. Dio – who was a contemporary – says that
Caracalla wore a purple cloak, a purple cloak with a broad white stripe down the centre and
another cloak which was presumably white because the stripe itself was purple.

(84) *Scriptores Historiae Augustae*; written c.AD 390? *The Two Gallieni*, VB, 4 – VIII, 1.
The Emperor Gallienus (r.AD 253–268) celebrated a Decennial festival and the soldiers who
attended the parade all dressed in white. This event was therefore similar to the triumphal
parade of Vitellius described earlier by Tacitus.

(85) *Scriptores Historiae Augustae, The Deified Claudius*, 2–10.
In two quoted letters supposedly sent by the Emperors Valerian (r.AD 253–260) and Gallienus
(r.AD 305–311) the equipment owned by Claudius when he was a tribune serving in Syria in
c.AD 255 is itemised. In the first letter the following clothing items are recorded.

> two red military tunics each year; two military cloaks each year; one white part-silk garment
> ornamented with purple from Girba (modern day Djerba, Tunisia); one under-tunic with Moorish
> purple; two white undergarments; a pair of men's leg bands; and one toga to be returned.

(85b) *Scriptores Historiae Augustae, The Deified Claudius*, XVII. 6–7.

The second letter lists

> two cloaks with purple borders; 16 garments of various kinds; a white one of silk; one tunic with
> bands of embroidery, three ounces in weight; three pairs of Parthian shoes; ten Dalmatian striped
> tunics; one Dardanian greatcoat; one Illyrian cloak; one hooded cloak; two shaggy hoods; and four
> handkerchiefs from Sarepta, near Sidon in Phoenicia.

(86) *Scriptores Historiae Augustae, The Deified Aurelian*, XIII, 24, and XLVI, 1–6.
According to the Augustan History, as a reward for his victory against the Goths c.AD 255, the
Emperor Valerian presented Aurelian with various military decorations and 'four red general's
tunics; two proconsul's cloaks; a bordered toga; a tunic decorated with palms; a toga decorated
with gold; and a long under tunic.'

(87) *Scriptores Historiae Augustae, Probus* IV, 3–6.
Probus (r.AD 276–283), like Claudius II before him, also served as a military tribune before
becoming emperor. A similar clothing list to that of Claudius is also documented allegedly in
another private letter sent by the Emperor Valerian. Valerian, aware that Probus is not a wealthy
man, orders the Prefect of the Guard to supply him with all the necessary clothing suitable for
someone of his rank. Probus is therefore supplied with 'two red tunics; two 'Gallic cloaks', and
two under tunics with decorated bands.'

(88) Synesius of Cyrene, *De Regno* 12 OP., m.66, 1804.
Synesius writing about AD 400 glorifies the simple lifestyle of ancient emperors and describes how
Carinus (r.AD 283–285) dressed only in 'red commonplace wool' before a gaudily clothed and hence
degenerate Persian embassy. Historians can not agree whether Synesius actually means Carinus at all
and other contenders have included Probus who concluded a peace treaty with the Persians, or Carus
(r.AD 282–283). Synesius further describes how the Roman emperor attempted to hide his baldness
with a hat and of the three men only Carus is shown in his coin portraits as being bald.

(89) Fresco, Aquincum, Hungary; late third century AD (Szilagy. J. 1956: pl.iv).
Excavations at the legionary fortress discovered fragments of a wall painting which showed the
top half of a man, possibly hunting because although he was un-armoured he was equipped

103 Fragement of a
fresco in Aquiuncum,
Hungary *(Col. Cat. 89)*.

with a bow. He wore a green long-sleeved tunic possibly with dark green *clavi*. It is possible the
man was a soldier or officer from the local garrison.

(90) Mosaics, Olmeda, Spain; late third century AD **(Fuentes, A. 1997: p.318 fig.7).**
Some spectacular late third century mosaics exist at a villa which had earlier origins. Two main
panels exist, one depicts a hunting scene, the other a story from the Iliad showing Odysseus
discovering Achilles who is hiding to avoid the Trojan War. Various figures are shown in military
garb, including one figure, presumably Odysseus, wearing an old fashioned off the shoulder
white tunic with red *clavi* down to the hem. He also has a red cloak and a white pointed hat.
There are two armoured figures in the background. Both have an iron cuirass with white
yellow-edged *pteryges*, but one man wears a short-sleeved red tunic and cloak and is playing a
tuba-like instrument. The other man – perhaps dressed as a senior officer – has a long-sleeved
red tunic with two yellow gold bands on the cuffs. In art at least, old fashioned clothing can be
seen quite happily worn alongside contemporary styles and which might even reflect reality.
    The hunting scene shows a number of men both mounted and on foot. There are two
mounted figures. One man appears to wear a long-sleeved light blue tunic with yellow gold
decoration on the hem with what seems to be a brown over-tunic. He has yellow-brown, fairly
loose fitting trousers. The second rider has an off-white long-sleeved tunic with two greyish
bands on the cuffs over grey trousers. The four men on foot also have long-sleeved tunics. One
tunic is green with red *orbiculi* at the shoulder, short red *clavi* and two red bands on the cuffs
and the wearer also has orange-red trousers. Two other tunics are white both with red *orbiculi*
at the shoulder, one on the skirts of the tunic as well, short red *clavi* and two red bands around
the cuffs. One of the men wearing white tunics has orange-red-brown leg wrappings instead of
trousers. The last tunic is red and is worn with green trousers.

(91) Mosaic, Palmyra, Syria; late third century AD **(Gawlikowski, M. 2005: pp.26–32).**
The Bellerophon mosaic has two central panels with mounted figures. In the first Bellerophon
mounted on Pegasus spears the Chimera. Bellerophon wears a red riding coat of the Persian
type over a green tunic. The coat has a single white band both around the cuff and the upper
sleeve. Further decoration is indicated on the front of the coat almost like the regimental facings
of eighteenth century military coats. The outfit is completed with blue Persian style trousers.
    The second panel shows a rider shooting an arrow at a rearing tiger. This rider too wears a
red riding coat which billows behind. The decoration of the coat is similar to Bellerophon's
although the band around the cuffs is green. He also wears blue trousers although these have

a yellow band down the front. These costumes can be seen as typical of the aristocratic officer class of the Palmyrene army.

THE LATER EMPIRE

(92) Mosaic, Gamzigrad, Yugoslavia; late third/early fourth century AD (Mano-Zisi, D. 1955).

Part of a mosaic showing two soldiers protected by a large oval shaped shield hunting a lioness. Both of the men wear long-sleeved green tunics which are decorated with red *clavi,* sleeve cuffs, and *orbiculi* with yellow motifs. The *clavi* themselves are in turn also decorated with a yellow vine branch pattern. If soldiers they might have belonged to a *vexillatio* (detachment) from Legio III Gallica and their elaborate costume emphasises the importance the military held at this period. The tunics themselves may be compared with examples on other mosaics including those from Piazza Armerina, and with the surviving textiles from Antinoe and other sites in Egypt.

(93) Mosaic, Piazza Armerina, Sicily; fourth century AD (Carandini, A. 1982).

One of the most important sources of evidence for late Roman costumes are the mosaics at the magnificent villa of Piazza Armerina. Numerous theories have been put forward as to who the villa owner was and what the relationship was between the mosaics and their owner. The most popular candidate is the Emperor Maximian due to the likeness between three figures wearing pillbox hats in the 'Great Hunt' mosaic and the co-Emperors Diocletian and Maximian in the famous Tetrarchs statue now in Venice. Other historians point out that Piazza Armerina is by no means a unique villa in Sicily or even the largest villa complex on the island. The praetorian standard painted above the main entrance however lends some support to those who argue in favour of the villa's Imperial ownership.

What is not in doubt is that the owner had considerable wealth and an interest or connection with the wild beast trade from North Africa. The great hunt mosaic alone includes over seventy figures who are engaged in various activities associated with the hunting and transportation of animals destined for the circus. It is generally assumed that most of these figures are soldiers because as part of their training, as a way of supplementing their diet and as a leisure activity, soldiers took part in hunting. The military were probably involved in expeditions to maintain the supply of wild animals needed for the arena. A further example of this involvement was that the navy provided sailors to rig the awnings at the Colosseum. More relevant perhaps, an altar found at Montana (Mihailovgrad) in Bulgaria relates how Cohors I Cilicum and detachments from Legio I Italica, Legio XI Claudia, and even the Danube fleet, Classis Flavia Moesica, from Lower Moesia in Bulgaria supplied troops to catch wild animals for the Emperor Antoninus Pius in AD 147!

The clothing colours worn by a number of the men are the common combination of white tunic and yellow-brown cloak. Of particular interest is the fact that many of the figures serving on board the ships wear blue or light blue tunics, although other individual sailors wear red tunics. These men Fuentes identified as the ships' centurions. However, at least one ship is entirely manned by three figures dressed in white tunics which are highly decorated with *orbiculi*, decorated hems and closed with red military belts. There are other figures shown in the mosaic who may not be soldiers and they include men leading ox wagons, who wear yellow-ochre tunics. Although Fuentes thought those wearing yellow tunics were civilian porters there is one man who stands out in a golden-yellow tunic with a red belt decorated with 'propeller' shaped fastenings, a well authenticated piece of military equipment. He also has yellow-gold hair which overall together with the tunic of the same colour might even suggest he was an Imperial German guard.

There is one strange incident depicted in the mosaic. One man in a white tunic and yellow-brown cloak beats another man with a staff. The unfortunate individual wears a red tunic but other than this there is nothing which could be said to be military. Unlike many of the other so-called soldiers who have broad belts, this figure has none visible as his tunic is bloused up and over whatever belt he is wearing. Perhaps this figure is a soldier undergoing punishment.

(94) Mosaic, Piazza Armerina, Sicily; fourth century AD **(Carandini, A. 1982).**
A smaller mosaic at the villa shows the legendary tasks of Hercules. Some armoured figures are equipped in a similar fashion to soldiers presumed to be praetorians on the Arch of Constantine. The crested iron helmets are attested by archaeological and other pictorial specimens and if the villa has Imperial connections the soldiers could mirror contemporary praetorian uniforms. The only tunic visible is red with a white border around the lower hem.

104 Part of the Triconchos mosaic at Piazza Armerina in Sicily *(Col. Cat. 94).*

(95) Mosaics, Tellaro villa, Sicily; fourth century AD **(Moscati, S. 1982; pl 121).**
There are other elaborate mosaics at the villa at Tellaro. One mosaic in particular has figures which could be identified as soldiers as they wear almost identical clothing to the figures on the Great Hunt mosaic at Piazza Armerina. Another mosaic scene – perhaps from the Iliad depicting the recovery of the body of Hector – shows a variety of clothing styles. One man has the traditional old fashioned tunic worn off the shoulder with a white pointed cap. The central figures appear as two senior officers; one dressed in the style of an emperor has a peacock crested helmet and a short-sleeved white tunic beneath his armour decorated with a red band above the hem. The other 'officer' has a white tunic with a red cloak but his sleeves or arms are not visible due to a mixture of damage to the mosaic and the composition of the other figures. The fourth figure has a long-sleeved white tunic decorated with three red bands around the cuffs and possibly a yellow-brown cloak with a brooch on the right shoulder.

(96) Mosaic, Bone Algeria; fourth century AD **(Hadas, M. 1966: pp.467).**
Another hunting scene on a mosaic probably contemporary with the mosaics from Piazza Armerina, shows at least five figures on foot. All of them wear white tunics with black decorated patches, while at least two men have dark yellow-brown cloaks. One mounted figure wears a cloak of the same shade, but the cloak of another rider is a reddish hue. Fuentes correctly noted that the only readily available published picture of the mosaic appears to be in reverse.

(97) Mosaic, Tipasa, Algeria; fourth century AD **(Blas de Roblès, J.M. & Sintes, C. 2003: p.78).**
A mosaic, depicting scenes from the legend of Achilles shows some figures contemporary dress. One man in particular also appears to wear the same type of clothing visible in the Piazza Armerina hunting scene, and archaeologists have in fact dated the mosaic to the fourth century because of this. Not surprisingly, historians have suggested there were links between these African mosaics and those from Sicily and that perhaps they were even products of the same mosaic school.

(98) Mosaic, Centcelles, Spain; fourth century AD **(Bou, F.T.).**
The domed ceiling at the Imperial Mausoleum near Tarragona in Spain is very well preserved but sadly the mosaic in the cupola is little more than scattered fragments. On one of the restored panels from the central section one can see enthroned figures surrounded by courtiers and perhaps guards. What details remain of their tunics indicate they were decorated with *clavi* and *orbiculi*. Other details of late Roman clothing is visible elsewhere, including short hooded capes with fringes along the lower edge.

(99) Mosaic, Cologne, Germany, fourth century AD **(Borger, H. 1974: p.157).**
A male figure wears the familiar colour combination of white tunic, yellow-brown cloak and dark coloured trousers. This clearly indicates that this type of dress was not just confined to the Mediterranean and North African provinces.

(100) Mosaic, Leptis Magna, Libya; fourth century AD **(Polidori, R. 1999: p.43).**
Two huntsmen appear in this mosaic which archaeologists have again dated to the fourth century AD because of the similarity in costume to those seen in other mosaics. One peculiarity at this later date is the short-sleeved white belted tunic one man wears beneath his cloak. Otherwise his companion sports the more fashionable long-sleeved white tunic complete with decorative patches. The cloaks of both men are a reddish colour. A shield carried by the man in the short-sleeved tunic is strikingly reminiscent of those depicted on Trajan's Column.

(101) Mosaic, Ayios Iakovos, Chios, Greece; fourth century AD **(Xeroutsikou, L. 1997: p.26).**
A mosaic, comprising eight panels filled with gladiatorial and hunting scenes. In one of the panels there is a man dressed in a white long-sleeved tunic decorated with purple *orbiculi* and *clavi* who is shown killing a lion with a spear. His costume has many similarities with those on the Piazza Armerina mosaics.

(102) Fresco, Vibia Ipogeum, Appia Antica, Rome; fourth century AD **(Pavia, C. 1999: p.223).**
A warrior, possibly a mythological hero, appears in the lower register of a fresco found in the temple of Sabbatius. His tunic is red but unusually for this date it has short sleeves, rather than the more common long sleeves.

(103) Fresco, Massimo Vinyard catacomb, Rome; fourth century AD **(Bisconti, F. 2000: pl.IIB,III,IVA).**
Two deceased soldiers are depicted. One has an off-white tunic, yellowish trousers and a red brown cloak. Only the red brown cloak of the other soldier is now visible.

(104) Via Latina catacomb paintings, Rome; fourth century AD **(Ferrua, A. 1990).**
Although the scenes in this fresco illustrate stories from both Old and New Testament stories, the characters are all wearing contemporary dress. Therefore of special interest are the following military figures. Two soldiers are illustrated casting lots for the clothes of Christ as described in the account of the crucifixion in the Gospels. Part of the painting of one soldier is very badly damaged but his companion wears a pill box hat, white tunic and yellow brown cloak decorated with a small swastika device.

In a dramatic scene in another painting a column of cavalry meant to represent Pharaoh's Egyptians, chase after Moses and the Israelites as they cross the Red Sea. The helmets worn by the cavalry bear a remarkable likeness to those on the Arch of Galerius, and are coloured light blue to represent iron. Their cloaks are yellow-brown and their tunics are an ivory white colour.

The same Old Testament story is also repeated in one more painting in the catacomb. The cavalry may have been painted by the same artist as they are identical with the exception that they have yellow helmets presumably meant to depict bronze. Finally, a single figure in a separate decorated panel stands in for the Egyptian army. He is wearing a reddish-brown cloak with either a crested helmet or a Phrygian cap. It appears that the artist has attempted to show him wearing a mail shirt and a narrow white band just visible below this shirt and around the neck may be the tunic worn underneath.

(105) Domitilla catacomb paintings, Rome, Italy; fourth century AD? **(Bisconti, F. 2000: pl XIIA)**
A graffito shows an armoured cavalryman, possibly a cataphract, who wears an orange-red tunic, cloak and a red crested helmet.

(105a) (Bisconti, F. 2002: fig 18.)
A second fresco represents Moses touching the rock with his staff so water flows out. A soldier clad in a red cloak and tunic with a white or very light blue Pannonian cap drinks from the water.

(106) Fresco. Barcelona, Spain; late fourth century AD **(de Heredia Bercero. 1997: fig.12).**
Only the upper portion of a mural now survives of a once elaborate design which is now displayed at the Placa del Rei Museum. A rider, possibly a hunter, is depicted wearing a white tunic decorated with black *orbiculi* on the shoulders, short *clavi* and a single band around the tunic cuffs. The ancient artist has attempted to show that these decorations were themselves further decorated. Part of a horse head also survives and this reveals elaborate horse furniture. Clearly this man was a wealthy individual.

(107) Mosaic, Meroth, Synagogue, Israel (c. fourth/fifth century AD **(Ilan, Z. & Damati, I. 1984: 265–68, pl.34C).**
Perhaps the most remarkable aspect of this mosaic is the helmet which is not being worn by the soldier but is positioned alongside him with his shield and sword. It is as close a likeness to an actual helmet as one could possibly expect in a mosaic medium. It can be identified with a series of helmets that Robinson classified as Cavalry type 'H', the best example of which came from Heddernheim; it is as if the ancient artist traced over a photograph from Robinson's book!

The soldier, possibly a representation of Goliath himself wears an off-white belted tunic which is decorated with black circular star-like *orbiculi* on the upper arm and on the lower skirt of the tunic. He is wearing a red-brown cloak which is fastened over his right shoulder with a circular brooch. Unfortunately as most of his legs are now completely missing, it is not possible to ascertain for certain whether he was wearing any trousers or not. If he was then they were a very light brown colour close to the colour tone of his face.

(108) Via Maria, catacomb painting, Syracuse, Sicily; fourth century AD **(Bishop, M. C. & Coulston. J.C.N. 2006: pl.6c).**

This painting is often seen as the best and sometimes the only evidence for Roman soldiers in red tunics. The soldier's red tunic is further decorated with dark red or purple decorated patches. The painting has for many years only been familiar as a photograph of the soldier's upper body.

However thanks to Raffaele D'Amato who was able to photograph the entire figure it is now possible to say that the soldier is in fact equipped with blue leg wrappings so his 'uniform' is pretty similar to that of another soldier in the Mosaics of Sta Maria Maggiore described below (131). One soldier seen there is also wearing a red tunic and blue leg wrappings. Another remarkable detail of this painting is the crested 'ridge' helmet, which like the helmet in the Beth Alpha synagogue can be matched with an excavated helmet, this time from Intercisa, and to yet another which is worn by a soldier on a tombstone from Aquileia. This is further proof that Roman art can sometimes be very accurate in its depiction of military equipment and should not be dismissed as easily as it often is.

(109) St Callistus catacomb paintings, Rome; fourth century AD **(Schug-Wille, C. 1970: p.15).**

A man in short belted tunic, off-white in colour, with decorative *orbiculi* and a red cloak collects water in his hands after Moses has struck a rock with his staff. A sword scabbard is just visible which lends support to the theory that he is a soldier.

(110) Papyrus document, Egypt; *c.*AD **320.**

Circumstantial evidence for red clothing or tunics in particular can be found in a will drafted by Valerius Apion. Apion was a centurion who served with a *vexillatio,* or detachment, from the Equites Promoti of Legio II Traiana that was based in Egypt. His will lists the possessions he left behind to his heirs, including his military equipment. Among the latter items can be found something Apion calls an *alabandicum,* which is not heard of anywhere else. Given the Roman habit of naming things after their place of origin it is possible the *alabandicum* had something to do with the city of Alabanda, now in Turkey.

In Roman times Alabanda was famous for producing reddish-purple gemstones, as recorded by Pliny. Some fine examples of late Roman helmets have been recovered which are lavishly decorated with gemstones. To date none of them have been decorated with a single type that warrants any being given a nickname which relates to a particular gemstone. David Woods has therefore offered an alternative explanation. He suggests the term actually refers to the military tunic because of the red colour. As additional support for this theory he cites a reference to St Jerome who referred to the tunic of a state official as '*Punic*', a term that derived from the old Roman name for Carthage. Furthermore it is intriguing to learn that Pliny the Elder also mentions another red gemstone that was called 'Carthaginian' (*Nat. Hist.*, 37.25, 92–96).

If this is indeed the correct interpretation the nickname *alabandicum* may only have had regional connotations, because Woods also supplies yet another term for tunics that appeared in late antiquity which is the Greek word *blattea*. This also appears to be connected with red or purple-red clothing, for it is used in connection with the tunics worn by King Clovis when he was made consul in AD 507 (*Gregory of Tours*, III': 2.38). It can also be linked with the military martyr St Theagenes of Parium (BHG, 2416). The latter reference is very intriguing because by a curious coincidence, St Theagenes was a recruit into Legio II Traiana, the very same legion as Valerius Apion.

(111) Decorated shields, Egypt; fourth century AD? **(Junkelmann, M. 1996: pp.115–124)**

    a) This shield was originally comprised of four rectangular panels with figures, two of which now survive. The shield theme appears to be hunting and one of the figures is mounted on a horse. He is wearing a green tunic and has a pink-red cloak fastened by a disc fibula. He appears to be bare legged with red boots that have black laces. The second figure is posed resting on a shield and holding a spear that looks very similar to the famous image of Stilicho. His costume is less elaborate however, comprising a dark red cloak with a black *tablion* held in place with a large crossbow brooch, which is worn over a pink-red tunic and white trousers.

b) Another restored shield shows a battle scene. This is between three figures, one of them mounted, and dressed in pink-red tunics and white trousers, two of whom wear black leggings and three native African warriors two of whom are dressed in exotically coloured kilts and two in green tunics. The mounted warrior has a blue cloak. Above the place where the shield umbo would have been stands an officer type dressed in a pink-red tunic and a blue cloak decorated with a black *tablion*. Just about visible are dark brown trousers.

(112) Mosaic, Low Ham Villa, Somerset, England; mid-fourth century AD (Toynbee, J.M.C. 1962: pl.235).

This late Romano-British mosaic illustrates the story of the romance between the Trojan hero Aeneas and Queen Dido of Carthage. The mosaic artist may have drawn inspiration for the male military costumes from the nearby presence of Legio II Augusta. In particular the character of Ascanius – the young son of Aeneas – in one scene is wearing a red Phrygian cap and a cloak over a long-sleeved white tunic with three bands around the cuffs. The same costume is worn in another panel when he is mounted on a horse. The hero Aeneas is portrayed wearing a cuirass over a red tunic.

(113) Fresco, Santi Giovanni e Paolo, Rome; late fourth century AD (Graber, A. 1967: figs 240–241).

Part of a wall painting showing the death of saints but all that remains of one of the Roman soldiers carrying out the execution is part of his red cloak.

(114) Mosaic, Croughton, England; late fourth century AD (Neal, D. & Cosh, S.R. 2002: 86.1).

This mosaic shows Bellerophon slaying the Chimera. Bellerophon is dressed in a white tunic decorated with black *orbiculi* and a band around the shoulders and cuffs. He has a red cloak.

(115) Vegetius, *Epitoma Rei Militaris*, II.7; c.AD 390.

Vegetius gives a list of titles and grades of officers that served in a late Roman legion. Immediately ranking above the ordinary soldiers called by Vegetius *munifices* (because they did fatigues, *munera*), are the *candidati duplares* and the *candidati simplares*. Fuentes believed that due to their rank both these grades of soldier were spared the unpleasant duties carried out by ordinary soldiers. As a result of this they possibly always went about in relatively clean tunics. It was probably natural that the other ranks gave them a slightly derogatory nickname and the term '*candidati*' may be a colourful example of military slang.

(116) Vegetius, *Epitoma Rei Militaris*; IV, 37.

In one of the most famous references to clothing colour Vegetius records that the sails and rigging of small patrol vessels were dyed 'Venetian' blue. This was a colour that according to Vegetius 'resembles the ocean waves'. Some modern commentators have taken this to mean anything from sea-green to blue-grey, but *Venutus* is in fact the same dark blue shade that was used by the blue circus faction. The ships' crews also wore 'Venetian' blue uniforms as camouflage. Although the exact translation is not especially concise, Vegetius adds that the Britons called the small scouting vessels *picati* possibly a misspelling of *pictae* – 'painted' – presumably because the wax that was used to paint the ships' sides was a blue colour.

(117) Mosaic, Rielves, Spain; fourth century AD (Blazquez, J.M. 1982: lam.50).

Occupying the central panel of this mosaic is a scene showing warriors dressed in an archaic style; all the men all wear short-sleeved tunics rather than the contemporary long-sleeved type. It has been suggested that the figures are in fact gladiators rather than soldiers, although their armour looks more military. In spite of the fact that it is coloured yellow their armour does not look like scale or even metal and has more of a draped fabric effect.

(118) Mosaic, Halicarnassus, Turkey; fourth century AD.
A mosaic shows the hero Meleager spearing a panther. Meleager wears a white tunic with black *clavi* reaching the hem. There are black *orbiculi* and two bands on each cuff. He has a grey cloak and socks with black sandals.

(119) Claudianus, *Opera Omnia, Contra Rufinum* II,108–109; c.AD 404.
During the reign of the Emperor Honorius the Roman poet Claudianus wrote a poem in praise of the *Magister Militum* which includes some brief descriptions of Roman uniforms. A unit of Armenians, possibly the Comites Sagitarii Armeni, are described as having grass coloured cloaks.

Claudianus in *De Quarto Consulatu Augusti* also refers to the 'white cohorts', probably a unit of the Auxilia Palatina and in another work *De Sexto Consulatu Honorii Augusti* he describes cavalrymen wearing purple-red sashes or ribbons on their shoulders.

(120) Mosaics. Antioch; fourth–fifth century (Doro. L. 1971).
   a) Dumbarton Oaks Mosaic.
      Various hunters are shown; one wears a greyish tunic, red cloak and green bracae. Another wears a grey tunic with a yellow cloak, purple bracae and red-purple boots. A third man wears a greenish tunic with decorated trim in yellow outlined in red. His colourful costume is completed by a dark red cloak and violet bracae.
   b) The Worcester Hunt Mosaic.
      1. A horseman is dressed in a red cloak over a dark grey tunic.
      2. One spearman on foot has a violet tunic, grey *bracae*, red boots and white socks.
      3. A man armed with a sword sports a violet red tunic with white vertical bands coming from the shoulders that end in roundels. He has white breeches and red boots.
      4. Another horseman is dressed in a white tunic, green cloak, yellow bracae and red boots.
      5. One other man on foot has a grey tunic, violet bracae and red boots.
      6. Yet another horseman wears a white tunic with round trimmings on the lower edge, green bracae and a red cloak.
      7. A final horseman wears both a grey tunic and bracae with black boots.
   c) Mosaic of Megalopsychia and the Hunting Heroes.
      A number of figures and heroes are wearing various types of colourful clothing.
      1. Narcissus has a pink tunic decorated with *segmenta* with one of a pair of vertical bands ending in a roundel just visible beneath a yellow cloak. He wears red boots.
      2. A hunter with a green tunic and yellow cloak with white boots.
      3. Acteon the hunter has a pink tunic with round *orbiculi* and yellow-brown cuffs, a white cloak and green socks.
      4. Hippolytos is dressed in a white tunic with the typical decorations of this period on the cuffs, shoulder and breast. He has a violet cloak fastened with a brooch.
      5. Adonis wears a red tunic and boots with grey socks and sports a narrow scarf.
      6. Meleager has a white tunic and red cloak with white boots.
   d) House of the Amazonomachy.
      A mounted Amazon is portrayed in battle with an axe wielding warrior on horseback who is wearing armour over a long-sleeved green tunic. He has a red cloak. A fallen figure lies below them, who like the warrior is also wearing a green tunic. A third figure is wearing a red cloak but as a result of damage to the mosaic nothing else is visible.
   e) Hunting Mosaic, Constantinian Villa.
      1. A bearded hunter sitting on a rock wears a light yellow tunic with green *clavi*. A companion is dressed only in a dark violet cloak wrapped around the upper body that is held in place around the waist by a white waist band. The only other item of clothing he has is a scarf or small cloak hanging from his left arm.

2. Two other hunters, one of them has a red tunic and a green cloak the other a yellow tunic and a red cloak. An attendant has a green-violet tunic worn off the right shoulder.

3. A horseman in a red tunic and cloak with a yellow lining. He has grey-green leg bindings.

4. Another rider wears a white tunic with violet decoration including *orbiculi*. He has tight fitting trousers, *anaxyrides* and a red cloak.

5. A horseman in a green tunic.

6. Another horseman, this time in a yellow tunic, blue cloak, and tight-fitting white trousers.

7. One more rider in a light yellow tunic but this time with black and dark purple *orbiculi*. He also has tight-fitting white trousers.

f) The Jugglers mosaic, Constantinian Villa.

Three figures that have been interpreted as jugglers and yet their costumes are almost identical to those worn by three figures in the Piazza Armerina mosaic that were identified by Speidel as members of the Imperial guard! Their tunics are white with a black belt that has a thin strap hanging from it, black tunic trimmings and *orbiculi* that are in turn decorated with white wavy lines or spots.

(121) Great Hunt Mosaic, Apamea, Syria; fourth/fifth century AD **(King, A. 1982: p.123).**
Two hunters wear a red tunic with either short or rolled up sleeves, brown bracae and leg bindings. Of more interest are the white waistband and white knotted scarf.

(122) Mosaic, Faenza, Italy; fifth century AD **(Brogiolo, G.P. & Chavarria Arnau, A. 2007: pp. 140–141).**
A crudely executed mosaic probably made to celebrate the victory of Stilicho at Pollentia. The figure on the left is believed to be Stilicho himself, standing before the Emperor Honorius who sits on a throne flanked by armed guards. Stilicho wears a white tunic which is decorated with a single broad black stripe down the middle, edged with red. The sleeve cuffs have two black bands which are again edged with red. The red bands may represent an actual colour but could alternatively be an outline. Stilicho wears a brown-purple cloak that has a striped effect, but rather than reflect actual colours this may in fact be a crude attempt to show folds. The Stilicho figure also wears long purple-brown trousers decorated by a thin row of alternate black and white squares. This somewhat gaudy costume is completed by a garish orange-brown cap of Phrygian style. The Emperor Honorius is naked except for his cloak and boots but still demonstrates one costume detail worthy of mention as he clearly wears white socks, which are visible through the gaps in his leather boots.

In contrast to the slightly exotic garb of Stilicho are the two fully armoured guards wearing the classic muscled cuirass who have old-fashioned short-sleeved white tunics, one of which appears to have the fashionable circular type of applied decoration. It is immediately obvious that neither of the guards wears trousers. This is perhaps in keeping with a law banning them, that Honorius himself had introduced. It is conceivable that the artist was aware of the wave of anti-Germanic feeling that was was sweeping the court and which would ultimately topple Stilicho and lead to his execution. Stilicho – if indeed it is he who is represented – is hardly presented as a heroic warrior in this mosaic; in fact he has a slightly comic air.

Another fragment of the mosaic shows two other armed guards. One man is naked but has a red–brown cloak; the other also has a red brown cloak and a white short-sleeved tunic beneath a muscled cuirass.

(123) Fresco, Sta Maria in Stelle, Verona, Italy; fifth century AD **(Dorigo, W. 1971: pl.213–4).**
A little known but important site that was originally an underground Mithraeum and was later converted into a church. The fresco shows the biblical 'massacre of the innocents', with two of Herod's soldiers dressed as contemporary Romans. They have short off-white *Dalmatica* or *linea* decorated with *clavi* and *orbiculi* at the shoulder and over the thighs. One man has an orange cloak,

the other a brown. While the man in the orange cloak has two bands on his cuffs the man in the brown cloak has four bands. Both men wear tight fitting off-white *anaxyrides* and black *campagi*. Herod himself is shown in another scene with a single guard who has a yellow-brown cloak.

(124) Dome Mosaics, the Rotunda, Thessaloniki, Greece; *c.*AD 400.

The soldiers wear belted tunics with tight fitting sleeves under cloaks with broad purple *tablia* that are fastened by gold crossbow brooches. One tunic is off-white with *tablia* and *orbiculii* in purple and gold. Two cloaks are brown the other white with blue, gold, green and violet *tablia*. Black *campagi* are worn with white socks or *anaxyrides*.

(125) Mosaics, Argos Museum, Greece; *c.*AD 400 (Iacovidis, S.E. 1988: pp 88–89 figs 55–56).

A soldier, possibly a *Flammoularios*, is shown wearing a red long-sleeved tunic underneath iron armour and a helmet. Another figure, perhaps a pioneer, is shown un-armoured in a short, long-sleeved orange-red tunic with dark leg wrappings or bindings. He carries a *dolabra* or axe over his left shoulder. Other figures in the mosaics such as hunters wear various types of late Roman garments including white tunics and red or reddish trousers and short hooded capes *aliculae* in off-white or brown, decorated with red and blue *clavi*. These capes also have loose hanging sleeves with decorated cuffs – much like the riding coats from Egypt – and are worn over white tunics and red trousers. One hunter in particular deserves note as he holds a bird of prey in his left hand which is covered with a brown glove. Footwear includes high black boots and pointed brown boots remarkably similar to excavated examples from Panopolis. Trousers are either tucked into the boots or worn over them. Other examples of footwear include *campagi aeticulati* or brown laced *cothurni*.

(126) Mosaic, Thebes, Greece; *c.*AD 400.

A figure in a hunting scene wears a white tunic outlined in red with either a green hat or a helmet covered with green cloth. The tunic has a panel which is green that extends down each shoulder from the neck and down the front of the tunic forming a 'T' shape. Part of a light coloured cloak is also visible.

(127) Mosaic, Grue, Tunisia; fourth/fifth century AD (Ville, G. 1965–6: pp.139–181 fig.9. p.163).

Two officers from Carthage are shown on a hunting expedition. They wear white, possibly natural linen tunics and are further distinguished from their servants by their grey white trousers. One rider wears light purple *femoralia*, while their cloaks are light purple or red-orange.

(128) Mosaic, Grue, Tunisia; fourth/fifth century AD (Bèjaoui, F. *et al.* 1994: pp.144–145).

Six cavalrymen are shown in either orange, red, yellow or grey-brown tunics all decorated with dark purple *clavi* and *orbiculi*. They all have grey-brown military neck scarves (*maphorion*) and thigh or calf length brown boots.

(129) Mosaic, Djemila. Algeria; fourth/fifth century AD (Blas de Roblès, J.M. & Sintes, C. 2003: p.124).

Amongst a number of *bestiarii* equipped with decorated red leather *pectoram* a splendidly dressed rider stands out. He wears a green tunic with red *clavi* and *orbiculi*, a red brown *sagum*, high leggings, perhaps in leather, and brown *calcei* worn over green socks.

(130) Mosaic, Qsar Lybia, Lybia; fourth/fifth century AD. (Bussoni, M. 2004: pp.52–119, p.63).

Amongst a number of mosaics dating to the re-conquest of North Africa under Justinian, one in particular seems to illustrate a cavalryman from the *Libyi Justiniani*. He is dressed in a red tunic with a yellow cloak, white *anaxyrides* and black *cothurni*.

(131) Mosaics, Church of Sta Maria Maggiore, Rome; AD 432–440 (Hack, B. 1967).
There are hundreds of military figures in these spectacular mosaics representing Biblical scenes so an individual figure description would be extremely lengthy and repetitive.

Suffice to say the officer types wear white tunics with gold embroidered elements or bright scarlet tunics also decorated with gold. The tunic decorated with *segmenta* of Joshua also has red and black chequers on its lower hem. Large gold *tablia* are visible on purple cloaks and red and purple trousers are common. Footwear is highly elaborate with boots encrusted with red gems or even silver boots tied with gold laces.

The infantry wear red or white tunics, perhaps a distinction between the *Palatini* and *Comitatenses* units of the fifth century Western army. Some of these tunics have either two yellow or purple bands around the cuffs but only the white tunics have dark purple *orbiculi* and *tabulae*. The military belts are red. Cloaks are chiefly red or red-brown but there are others in yellow-brown, green, green-blue, blue and dark blue. *Anaxyrides* are mainly green brown or sky blue some with red vertical bands down the front. One soldier has wide white trousers, *sarabara* of Persian type also with a red vertical band while another has tight fitting white *anaxyrides* inside black *campagi*. Some soldiers have *femoralia* which are either white or green, while leg wrappings are dark blue.

The footwear is quite varied with blue or brown *calcei* on display. Others have black or red-brown *campagi* or even the old fashioned brown *caligae*. One cavalryman appears to wear very high white boots, perhaps made of felt. White or natural coloured wool socks are often depicted worn inside the boots or visible through the open footwear.

(132) Mosaics, Great Palace of Constantinople; late fifth/early sixth century AD **(Jobst, W. & Behçet, E. 1997).**
Imperial *doriphoroi* or *hypaspistai* engaged in hunting wear garments in colours associated with the Circus factions, a practice amongst guards that probably stretched back for centuries. Here the predominant colour is green, which may be associated with the Emperor Anastasius who was a supporter of the green faction. However it might just be because the soldiers are out hunting and green colours appear in hunting scenes more than anywhere else.

Other images include:
a) A rider with a red tunic decorated with purple and white cuff stripes, worn under a white-fringed green cloak. He has rough green trousers tucked into brown boots.
b) An officer wears metal armour over a white under armour garment, *peristithidion,* with *pteryges*, a dark green tunic, and black leggings tied up with yellow strapping.
c) Two *doriphoroi* wear short knee-length *bracae* in yellow and white which are tied at the thigh by broad green and red garters. They both have loose sleeveless leather *pectoraris* that are decorated with *tablia* and *orbiculi* also in green and red. They have short-sleeved under tunics of ochre and white and small cloaks or wide sashes in white and green that are wrapped around the waist.

(133) Procopius of Caesarea, *De Bello Vandalico*; **sixth century** AD.
Procopius describes the dress given to military leaders of Libyan tribal *Symmachari* as comprising '…a silvered cap (*pilos*) that did not cover the whole head, but was held in place like a crown by bands of silver; a white cloak known as a *tribon* that was gathered at the right shoulder by a golden fibula, like a Thessalian cape; a white embroidered chiton, and gilded boots (*arbuti*) …' (BV, III, XXV, 5–8). The term *pilos* refers to a cylindrical cap that was tightened by laces. *Arbuti* were high, tough boots suitable for travelling or hunting made of un-tanned leather and fastened at the front.

(134) Mosaic, Church of St Vitale, Ravenna; AD **532–547 (Graber, A. 1966: pp.159–160, fig.171).**
Perhaps one of the most famous images from the Roman world shows the Emperor Justinian surrounded by his court, including guardsmen. The clothing worn by two of the guards is visible.

a) One guard wears a red *paragauda* with purple panels around the neck and shoulders, two bands around the cuffs and around the lower edge of the tunic. The bands are embellished with gold decoration that takes the form of arrowheads. He has very white *anaxyrides* as one would expect, and black *campagi*.

b) The other guard wears a similar costume except his tunic is green with gold ornamental bands. Both men wear the jewelled gold collar of their *ordo* (probably Protectore Primoscutarii). Just behind the guard in the red tunic is just visible the clothing of another guard. He appears to also have a green tunic, but the band around the neck appears to be red rather than gold.

c) In the same mosaic are two officers of patrician rank in similar style clothing but with slightly different ornaments. One of them is possibly Justinian's great general Belisarius who wears a white *chlamys* pinned by a gold 'crossbow' brooch that has a squared purple *tablia* at the breast. His white *paragauda* has a squared dark purple and white panel on the shoulder. He has white trousers worn inside black *campagi*. The shoulder decorations are probably an indication of military rank and if this man is indeed Belisarius, then the large squared appliqué would illustrate the rank of a *Magister Militum*.

(135) Stobi frescoes, Vardar valley, Macedonia; sixth century AD **(Hoddinott, R.F. 1963: pls.43–44).**
Fragmentary remains show figures in white tunics and cloaks fastened on the upper chest with a round brooch. Some men are bareheaded while others have red Phrygian caps and one even wears a low pink turban! This is perhaps the first representation of the *phakeolion* mentioned by some sources. Tunic sleeves have the usual *segmenta* on the cuffs which as mentioned previously may be a sign of rank. The men in the fresco may have been soldiers of the *Magister Militum per Illyricum*.

(136) Mosaics, Church of the Deacon Thomas, Ayoun Mousa, Mt Nebo Jordan; *c.*AD **500–550 (Piccirillo, M. 1993: figs 252).**
This mosaic may show men from the local garrison hunting. An archer wears a short off-white tunic, tied up for shooting and crossed diagonally on the front by a yellow border and with the left front overlapping the right. He wears tight yellow orange *anaxyrides* with black and white chequered decoration worn with light brown *calcei*. A spearman wears a linen *armilausion* that is decorated with red *clavi* and *orbiculi* and which also reveals an archaic feature because the back of the tunic is knotted, recreating the old fashioned 'bunching'.

(137) Mosaic, the old Diakonikon, Mt Nebo; Jordan AD **530 (Piccirillo, M. 1993: figs 165, 167, 168, 169, 174).**
A number of military figures are illustrated hunting with spears. One sports a Phrygian cap that is orange with a red stripe. He has a red Gothic tunic with dark green decoration at the neck and cuffs, wide light red-brown trousers that are edged at the bottom in black or dark green decorated further with small white circles. The trousers are worn over short red boots.

One of the two cavalrymen represented is evidently of Germanic origin due to a likeness with the Vandal mosaics at Carthage. This Germanic aspect is further enhanced by the white Gothic tunic he wears. This has wide gold embroidery on the lower hem and light brown *segmenta* on the sleeves. He has a green *sagion*, wide orange trousers embroidered at the bottom in black and white, and red boots.

In the same church a mosaic in the Basilica of Moses shows a mounted hunter perhaps yet another Germanic *foederatus,* because of his blond hair, wears a light red-brown tunic, red cloak and white trousers with a yellow trim at the bottom.

(138) Mosaic, Martyr Theodore chapel, Madaba, Jordan; *c.*AD **562 (Piccirillo, M. 1993: fig 101).**
A soldier is clad in a white tunic tied up with knots to allow freedom of movement. Underneath his tunic can be seen a light *kamision* which is tied up in the same way.

(139) Mosaic, Chapel of Suwayfiyah, Jordan; *c*.AD 550–600 (Piccirillo, M. 1993: fig 452).
An archer has a white tunic that is edged at the neck and cuffs with a red and white lozenge decoration. This is an important detail which can be matched to actual tunics found in Egypt.

(140) Mosaic, Hippolytus Room, Church of the Holy Virgin, Madaba, Jordan; mid sixth century AD (Piccirillo, M. 1993: fig 5).
An officer is depicted wearing an ochre brown tunic with white and purple *clavi*, *orbiculi* and segmentata at the cuffs. He has a light blue chlamys fastened with a red and gold brooch. The officer wears red boots with a white lining or socks visible.

(141) Mosaic, Church of Al-Khadir, Madaba, Jordon; *c*.AD 530 (Piccirillo, M. 1993: fig 143).
A soldier carrying a shield is dressed in an off-white tunic worn over wide ochre coloured trousers. He also sports a red Phrygian cap.

(142) Encaustic painting, Egypt; sixth century AD (Rutschowscaya, M.H. 1992: cat.41).
A painting on a wood panel of a cavalryman leading his horse. He has a Persian style tunic decorated with a 'T' shape panel made up of brown-purple stripes and white dots that might even be pearls.

(143) Wall paintings and frescoes from Bawit, Egypt; sixth–seventh century AD.
  a) A hunter or soldier illustrated in Chapel 18 has a long-sleeved knee-length white tunic with red 'T' shaped trim, white trousers, a composite belt set, and enclosed shoes.
  b) Two angels, Chapel 3, represented as Imperial guardsmen with long white *paragauda* wrought with gold *clavi* and *orbiculi* on the lower leg and with *segmenta* on the cuffs. They wear gold *taenia* headbands and have off-white *anaxyrides* that are neatly tucked into their silver boots (Cledat, J. 1904: pls.LXV XCVIII).
  c) David fully armoured before Saul. Under the lamellar armour he wears a pinkish-red tunic, and has high yellow coloured boots that are possibly covered with gold leaf (Cledat, J. 1904: pl. XVII).
  d) Goliath is portrayed fully armoured wearing a pink-red *peristithidion* with attached *pteryges* visible underneath a muscled cuirass. A pink-red cloak, linen *anaxyrides* and green boots completes his costume (Cledat, J. 1904: pls. XVIII–XIX).
  e) Four cavalrymen depicted in Chapel 26, all of whom have 'T' shaped tunic trim.
    1. One has a green tunic with red purple trim while the lower edge is black purple with pink roundels. He has white trousers and a white cloak with red *tablion*.
    2. A second cavalryman has a white tunic with grey purple ornaments, white trousers, black leggings, brown boots and finally a cloak with red *tablion* and black spots.
    3. Sadly only fragments survive of the next painted figure but enough to indicate that he had red boots, *toubia* decorated in white, and a white tunic.
    4. The fourth cavalryman wears a white garment embroidered in red and white, a light brown cloak, light green trousers but more likely leggings which are outlined in red and worn over a second white pair, and black boots that are identical to specimens found at Panopolis (Cledat, J. 1904: pls. LXXXVIII–LXXXIX).
  f) Saints represented as two cavalrymen wearing tunics that are off-white or ochre with T-shaped blue-green decoration showing roundels. One cloak is ochre and the other brown. Both men wear off-white trousers with black boots. The 'Byzantine horseman' found by Gayet was also dressed in this way (Cledat, J. 1904: pls. XXXIX, LIII,LIV & LVI).
  g) Abu-Hennis sanctuary, Egypt. sixth–seventh century AD (Zibawi, M. 2003: pp.58–61, figs. 54–59). Herod's soldiers are shown wearing long-sleeved white or red–brown tunics with red-purple T-shaped trim and they have yellow-ochre trousers. The guards wear

105 Figure from a fresco in Chapel 37 at Bawit in Egypt. *Charles W. Evans-Gunther.*

helmets, while the executioners are depicted bare-headed, perhaps distinguishing Roman guardsmen from Gothic or Asiatic mercenaries.
h) Military saints, paintings, Kellia, modern Qocur el-Izeila (Rassart-Debergh, M. 1993: p.389. figs 2,3).
Three soldiers in one painting have yellowish or brown tunics and each has a purple cloak fastened with a large brooch and are further equipped with a muscled cuirass and a *thoracomachus* with two or three rows of *pteryges*. Another painting shows a figure wearing a natural linen coloured cloak apparently covered with floral decoration. This is worn over a red-pink tunic with yellow *clavi*, *orbiculi* and cuffs.

(144) Clothing finds from Egypt; fifth–seventh centuries AD.
Perhaps for Roman military studies it is a misfortune of history that these garments were found at the wrong time and in the wrong place because Roman period artefacts discovered in Egypt have rarely received the attention that they deserve, as they are overshadowed by the remains of the much earlier culture. Sadly these garments were also discovered before the advances in modern archaeology, and were not treated with the respect one hopes they would get if found today. Thanks to the work of Fluck and Eastwood they may now be better appreciated.

At least 32 late Roman Persian-style riding coats were found by Gayet and Schmidt and fragments of a further fifty! The majority were either in red-purple, blue-green or green. They were decorated with silk brocade embellished with a rich variety of patterns and ornament including lions and birds on different coloured backgrounds.

A number of late Roman cavalry tunics in the Gothic or Persian style were also found. These had either a wool tablet woven trim or like the riding coats, in silk brocade. A whole depository of other clothing uncovered at this time included the familiar 'Coptic' linen tunics with *orbiculi, clavi* and *tablia*; cloaks in purple dyed linen, leggings of green grey felt edged with silk; wool socks dyed black; officers belts in yellow dyed leather; officers' and soldiers' boots of various styles in brown leather; and numerous belt fittings, buckles in gold and silver alloy and many bronze and iron brooches.

(145) Encaustic portraits, icons of military saints, Egypt; fifth–seventh centuries AD (Banck, A. 1966: pls. 113–114).

Hundreds of these military icons survive. Originally they were displayed in army camps. The most striking example left today is from the Sinai Monastery, representing the saints Sergius and Bacchus who are portrayed as sixth or seventh century Roman officers. They both wear a white *chlamys* with dark brown *tablion* and have a red *chiton* with gold shoulder bands. Their neck *torques* which are set with three gems classify them as either Imperial officers or guardsmen.

(146) Codex miniatures, fifth–seventh centuries AD.

a) Quedlinburg Itala codex, Italy; AD 425.

This manuscript is contemporary with the Sta Maria Maggiore mosaics and very similar in artistic style. Roman generals wear red *chlamys*, red *anaxyrida* and have cloth-lined boots. The white under-cuirass garments are decorated with purple *segmenta* on the *pteryges*.

b) Codex Vergilius Romanus, Britain, Gaul or Italy; fifth century AD (Grilli, A. 1990: figs 386, 389, 390, 392 & 395).

It has recently been proposed that this manuscript has a British origin which would therefore suggest that this is a unique representation of sub-Roman or even Arthurian warriors! Rich white *paragaudia* decorated with gold are worn by officers with yellow, orange and brown Phrygian caps which can be compared to the use of Phrygian caps by Romano-British soldiers from the fourth century mosaic at Low Ham Villa in Somerset. Brown tunics are decorated with red trim; *sagula* are orange, red-purple, red brown, red and green. All the *anaxyrides* visible are either brown or mauve, decorated with small *orbiculi* and lines on the front; this unusual feature is only found elsewhere on the Ravenna mosaics.

c) Codex Rossanus Purpureus, Constantinople; sixth century AD (Graber, A. 1966: p.207, fig 232).

A rich variety of military uniforms are on display highlighting the fact that the tunic colours of Imperial *semeiophoroi* followed those of the Circus factions. Furthermore, the white tunics are associated with the blue and the red with the green. In early medieval Byzantium the white and blue factions opposed the red and green, and from the end of the seventh century their militia gave rise to two different regiments, the *Teichista* and the *Noumera*.

d) Genesis of Vienna, Syria or Constantinople; sixth century AD (Wickoff, F. 1895: folio 7).

The Melchisedec image wears high red-purple boots that have pearls on the edges. These *tzangia* are a unique illustration of the Imperial boots that are described by Theophanes and which were worn in battle by the Emperor Heraclius himself.

e) Ashburnham Pentateuch, sixth-seventh centuries AD.

Although disputed by some scholars, this document is perhaps a rare source from the North African province re-conquered by Justinian; nevertheless identification of figures with units listed in the Notitia Dignitatum is open to interpretation. Many types of troops and commanders are illustrated; some wear armour and have multi-coloured tunics. A few men have cylindrical caps and leg wear which can be associated with other sources. Some tunics have trim at the lower edge, and/or two segments at the wrists. In addition some soldiers have trousers in the Gothic style, with decoration at the ankles. Perhaps the most striking aspect is that very few tunics and cloaks have any of the decoration we would expect to see at this period.

f) Rabula Gospel, Syria, preserved in the Biblioteca Laurenziana, Florence; seventh century AD (Schug–Wille, C. 1970; p.144).

Imperial Guardsmen wear pinkish *paragauda* decorated with gold while an executioner is illustrated wearing a red tunic, green trousers and off-white *fasceola* as described by Paulus Diaconus. These are tucked into brown *calcei*. Elsewhere a *centenarius* wears a red tunic, white *sarabara*, light purple leggings and black *cothurni*. Other soldiers display what can best be described as typical Persian costume, used by Anatolian Roman soldiers, while a senior officer has a red tunic, gold lamellar armour, violet *chamlys*, white *fasceolae* and brown *corthurni*.

g) Codex of the Syrian Orthodox church of Mar Jacques de Sarug (Leroy, J. 1964: pl.44). A general wears a red tunic, violet *chalmys*, white *fasceolae* and brown boots.

(147) Mosaic. Church of St Demetrios, Thessaloniki. Greece; seventh century AD (Τηεολογου, M. 1995: p75).

A saint is portrayed in the military dress of a senior officer. He wears a white *chlamys* decorated with gold rhomboids and a red *tablion* decorated with white rhomboids. The inside of the cloak is light blue with the same rhomboid pattern on a red background like the *tablion* which forms a border along the bottom edge. The saint's tunic is light brown with dark blue-purple panels at the shoulders and on the lower part of the tunic. Patterns on these panels are picked out in white.

Contributory Evidence for Clothing Colour

A group of late Roman and early medieval manuscript copies of earlier Roman originals could additionally be included as evidence of Roman tunic and cloak colours. Perhaps the most famous of these manuscript copies is the anonymous De Rebus Bellicis, now in the Bodleian Library in Oxford. An illustration purporting to represent a garment known as a *thoracomachus* worn under armour also shows an un-armoured soldier standing close by. The accessories illustrated – including his pillbox hat – are quite accurately observed and provide a touch of authenticity to the drawing. The soldier's tunic is a red-orange; he wears white *bracae*, and black leg wrappings tied with red thongs.

   The results of early discoveries and excavations are now virtually forgotten or generally ignored by the majority of modern scholars, and this is especially true in the study of Roman army equipment. A totally dismissive approach is hard to justify, when this includes discoveries that no longer survive or which were in a better state of preservation when they were first recorded. For instance, many early antiquarians must have seen surviving traces of the paint that once decorated all Roman sculptures and monuments.

   A good example is perhaps provided by the reconstructions of a Republican triarius from the altar of Domitius Ahenobarbus by the nineteenth century scholars Racinet (in Le Costume Historique, Paris, 1883), and Hottenroth (in Costume, Le armi, gli Utensili dei Popoli Antichi e Moderni, Rome, 1887–92). In both publications this figure wears a blue tunic. This source material was obviously used for the same soldier in a reconstruction that appeared in Forestier's *The Roman Soldier* (London, 1928). Nevertheless both Racinet and Hottenroth depicted a first century legionary in marching order wearing a red tunic. Many of these drawings and illustrations were clearly used by the costume makers on early Hollywood movies. For example a Roman legionary soldier in dark blue tunic, crimson red cloak and high laced boots stuffed with wool painted by Forestier was almost certainly the model for the soldiers featured in the *The Robe* starring Richard Burton.

   Old Welsh genealogies list a native chieftain of North Britain named 'Pattern Pesrut' or 'Paternus of the red tunic', who possibly lived in the fourth century. The Welsh word 'Peis' could possibly have derived from the Latin *Tunica Pexa* (soft furnished tunic) while the colour red (old welsh rut) could be one of the many shades of red purple. Sir Ian Richmond believed this was 'strangely suggestive of Roman investiture' (see also SHA *Probus* 4, 5; *Aurelianus* 13,3. 46,6).

More intriguing, perhaps, is the discovery made by Abbot Rudolph at the monastery of St Trudon in Cologne, Germany, in 1121. When a large sarcophagus believed to belong to St Gereon was opened, the saint's remains and clothing were found to be in an excellent state of preservation. It was recorded that the saint was wearing an under tunic which had apparently been of fine white cloth but had been stained a reddish colour by the red over tunic: '*subitus ad carnem … vestis serica albi maxime coloris sed tamen sub rubea.*' This discovery is of interest because Gereon was a soldier, who had served in either Legio III Diocletiana Thebaeorum or Legio Maximiana Thebaeorum. He was martyred in *c.*AD 304 on the orders of the Emperor Maximian for refusing to sacrifice to pagan gods. We are left with the intriguing possibility that he may even have been buried in his military clothing.

PART THREE

OTHER GARMENTS AND CLOTHING

6

OTHER GARMENTS

HEADGEAR, HATS AND HELMET LININGS

Roman soldiers are rarely depicted in any form of hat until the late third century. Indeed it is rare to see any type of hat worn by Romans at all. However Etruscan urns show a Greek style hat called a *kausia*, the use of which seems to have persisted into late Republican times. A painting from Pompeii shows a scene from *Miles Gloriosus* – the famous play by Plautus – and the leading character himself is shown wearing one of these hats with his cloak and tunic.

A slightly mysterious type of head gear has been discovered at Vindolanda on Hadrian's Wall. Known today simply as the 'hair moss cap', it is made from stems of hair moss and is woven into a cap shape from which strands extend like a fringe. A similar parallel exists from the fort at Newstead and they may be examples of a native style worn on the frontier. No one seems quite sure whether it is a basket or hat. It might be the Roman equivalent of the Australian bush hat with corks hanging from string to keep away flies. Anyone who has visited Vindolanda will be well aware of how useful this hat, if that is what it was, might have been!

According to Synesius of Cyrene, the Emperor Carinus (r. AD 283–285) wore a hat to hide his baldness when he met some Persian ambassadors (*De Regno*, 12 OP., m66, 1804).

Nevertheless, it is surprising that Vegetius – writing around the end of the fourth century – states that in earlier times soldiers always wore hats. He explains that this was so that they would become accustomed to wearing something on their heads to prepare them for when they wore helmets in battle. According to Vegetius these hats were known as 'Pannonian' (*pileus pannonicus*) and were made from leather (Epit., 1.20). Modern historians believe that when Vegetius refers to 'earlier times' he sometimes simply means before his own lifetime, rather than the Republican and early Imperial periods. The hats described by Vegetius are probably those now known as 'Tetrarchic caps' because of their appearance on the statue of the Tetrarchs now in Venice. They frequently appear in late Roman art and complete the military style uniform worn by soldiers and civil officials.

They are generally of a round 'pillbox' shape, and artistic representations give them either a smooth or rough textured finish. The smooth versions seem to have been made from either leather or felt while those of a rougher appearance from wool or fleece. In fact the edict of Diocletian describes how sheepskin with the wool left on was used to make these hats. When depicted in Roman art they sit high on the head so that the wearer's hair is visible below the lower edge. As well as different materials they also seem to come in a variety of heights. It is conceivable that the design of these caps developed from the Persian *tiara*. The Lex Suidas: Poll.,

106 Hats in ancient art.
Left: Greek *petasus* or *kausia* from an Etruscan urn representing the death of Enomaos; second century BC
from Casaglia, Italy.
Right: Phrygian hat, Column of Marcus Aurelius, Rome.

107 Green felt hat *pileus pannonicus* from
Mons Claudianus in Egypt. *Photograph courtesy
Lise Bender Jørgensen.*

108 The Didymoi hat, Egypt. ©
Dominique Cardon.

7,58 says that *tiara* was indeed another name for the *pilos*, which could support this idea. The Christian Eusebius of Samosata fled the persecutions of the Emperor Valens and is described as disguising himself as a soldier and wearing a *tiara* (HE,IV,13,4). Another Christian – this time a young woman – escaped her punishment of being raped in a brothel by wearing military clothing, including one of these hats. Because of its height she was able to conceal her hair inside it, and by wearing it low on the brow was able to hide her face (Euseb.Hem., *De Matre et duabus filiabus martyribus*, c.19).

The hats shown on the tetrachic monument have slots in them, perhaps for the addition of jewels or metallic crowns. This would certainly be in accord with the modern perception of a *tiara* but is also what we have now come to expect from late Imperial costume. A Pannonian hat has recently been found at Mons Claudianus in Egypt. It is made from green felt at least two millimetres thick. While exceptional in itself the real surprise is that it is dated much earlier than expected, to the second century AD. This may have been a freedman's hat, as there were undoubtedly slaves and civilians working there, but as there was a military presence at the site the possibility exists that it belonged to a soldier.

Many soldiers may only have worn hats previously as part of the padding under their helmets. This practice could account for their rarity in the surviving pictorial sources. The type of headgear we might expect to see is shown on a fresco from Pompeii. It is a white cap possibly in linen or felt resembling an arming cap of the Middle Ages. Such a garment would be necessary beneath a helmet to prevent the effects of blunt trauma caused by a blow to the helmet. Traces of what seemed to be a padded lining made from wool was discovered attached to the inside of an iron helmet found at Newstead in Scotland. The remains had been glued inside with a resin-like substance because incredibly when hot water was applied to it, it became sticky! A similar lining was also found at Vindonissa – a military fortress in Switzerland.

109 Senior officers or officials, taken from the Great Hunt Mosaic at the Piazza Armerina villa in Sicily. All of them wear the *pileus pannonicus* type of hat. The figure leaning on a staff is often identified as the emperor Maximian and it is sometimes suggested that he was the owner of the original villa

Remains of leather hats of the type known as *petasi* have also come from Vindonissa, and what appears to be a *petasus* hat is shown worn by a shepherd on a relief from Trier. Its flat cone shape neatly resembles a felt hat found in Egypt, now in Bolton Museum in England. However it is also a reminder that these items need not be exclusively military and were also worn by civilians.

Archaeologists working in Egypt have identified several well preserved helmet-shaped hats made of wool, as likely candidates for soldier's hats. There are at least two types. The first are divided into triangular sections which are coloured alternately in two different shades finished off with a small pom-pom on the apex. The second type is tri-coloured red, green and yellow. A spectacular and rather garish example of the latter also has ear and neck flaps. This hat is made from damask twill and one of the front red triangle segments appears to have originally been the *clavus* from a tunic. The Roman writer Statius says that hats made from cloaks were suitable as a cheap gift but this would still seem to be a rather expensive item to give away. Another less well preserved example was found at the same site so it was not a unique item and this also had a segment decorated with part of a *clavus*. These hats look too colourful to hide away beneath a helmet in spite of their helmet-like shape, but perhaps that sort of extravagance might be expected of a soldier!

Another segmented hat, but this time only in four triangular pieces in red and yellow, has also been discovered in Egypt. It is conical in shape but does not appear to have been as tall as the pointed hats awarded to freed slaves. One other surviving example is from Dydimoi, another desert site from Egypt. This hat has side cheek pieces and is made from felt and wool dyed red with thin yellow stripes. The design itself is very like an attic helmet. Perhaps the most famous hat is the one discovered at Dura Europos. This fragile relic was immediately photographed worn on the head of a local! It was well padded with extra pile added to the ear flaps and would appear ideal for wearing under a helmet. In fact as its pointed top was bent over and folded, James suggested that was 'consistent with being worn inside a helmet'.

In the Odysseus and the Sirens mosaic at Dougga, Tunisia, Odysseus wears a white, slightly pointed hat. A cap of the marines in Britannia was similar to the ancient Greek *kausia*. It is visible on the coin of Carausius but also on the reverse of the famous Arras medallion showing the relief of Londinium by the fleet of Constantius Chlorus in AD 296. Both the victorious Constantius Chlorus himself and his sailors are wearing them.

Other military personnel of the army based in Britannia perhaps influenced the artists working on the fourth century Low Ham mosaic, illustrating scenes from the Aeneid. In this instance the men wear dark red Phrygian caps. More Phrygian type hats are worn by irregular auxiliaries on the earlier Column of Marcus Aurelius and other Antonine monuments appear to show Phrygian hats with metal fittings worn as helmets. Red Phrygian caps also appear in Mithraic scenes, worn by his attendants and by the young god himself, and are still worn in late Roman Vatican manuscripts.

The 'horsemen's graves' from Antinoopolis yielded a felt helmet-like hat with plumes. In spite of the plume Gayet believed this hat might be worn as helmet padding. However plumed hats were shown on the now lost Column of Theodosius, possibly worn by militia units. Caps were sometimes replaced by or wrapped with a *phakeolion* making a kind of turban. This was usually linen wound around the cap and head with complex folds with an end falling over the shoulders, like the modern day Havelock, to protect the neck from the sun. This arrangement would also allow a helmet to be worn over the top.

THE WAISTBAND (*FASCIA VENTRALIS*)

A study of grave stelae of the early Empire – in particular those of P. Flavoleius Cordus from Legio XIIII Gemina and Daverzus from Cohors IIII Delmatarum – appear to indicate that a waist sash was worn underneath the military belt. Waist sashes like cummerbunds certainly existed in Roman times and Pliny the Elder for instance records waist sashes (*ventralia*) made from rough wool (*Nat. Hist.*, VIII, lxxiii, 193). In a further passage he specifies a *ventrale* was sometimes used for medical purposes, because wormwood (Nat. Hist., XXVII, 52) was inserted inside it as a prevention against groin cancer! The sashes on the tombstones look like those also worn by the *lares* or household gods such as illustrated on the well known fresco in the House of the Vettii in Pompeii. This shows two *lares* with purple coloured sashes worn around the waist over a white tunic. Other supportive bands around the waist can be seen being worn by manual workers including two dock workers on a monument from the Moselle region of Germany.

Nevertheless until recently there was no mention in ancient literary sources of these waistbands with reference to military men. However a newly discovered document from Vindolanda (*Tab. Vin*, 607) records that a soldier called Taurinus bought *acia* thread to repair and re-stitch his *ventralis*. The purpose of these waistbands would be twofold. Firstly they would act as a back support and secondly they would protect the tunic from any sharp edges on the back of the belt. The fact that Taurinus needed to repair his waistband could be seen as evidence for this. Furthermore the band, like the scarf mentioned below, might have been used to identify individual units by different colours or was simply another way of enhancing the military belt or showing off the soldiers rank and status.

110 Soldier wearing a fabric waistband or *fascia ventralis*. From an Etruscan cinerary urn, Volterra, Italy.

111 A Gallic noble from the Roman period known as 'the Vecheres warrior', Musée Calvet, Avignon, France. A fabric waistband is just visible below the figure's right arm.

112 Figures from the Augustan arch of Susa, Italy. The figure on the left appears to be wearing the famous strip armour or *lorica segmentata*, while the man on the right has a fabric waistband.

113 Statue from Cassaco, Italy, possibly first century AD, showing a waistband beneath the belt.

114 Figures from the Great Hunt Mosaic in Apamea Syria. Both men have white fabric waistbands. (*See (121) in the colour catalogue.*)

The best sculptural example of one of these waistbands appears to be the broken *stele* of a soldier found at Cassaco in northern Italy, although similar belts can be seen worn by civilian labourers (*fasciae interulae*) wrapped around the belly. This was also the function of the *semicinctium*, a short waistcoat (Mart., *Apoph.*, 153). The origins of these waistbands might go back as far as Etruscan times – a warrior is wearing one on a cinerary urn from Volterra. Something similar also appears to be worn beneath the belt of the Celtic warrior in the Avignon museum. In both cases these sashes are worn with mail shirts. Perhaps they added a dash of colour to a fairly bland piece of military equipment.

Some practical experiments were carried out by the Dutch re-enactor Peter de Haas with a length of material 350cm long and 30cm wide. When worn with replica armour he observed that the waistband supported the back which helped the wearer to endure the weight of the armour over a long period of time. The waistband also prevented any rough edges from the back of the belt – such as the rivets which held the belt plates in place – from damaging the tunic. This could be why the waist belt at Vindolanda needed repair which would certainly be more economical than repairing or replacing a tunic. A waistband would also hide the tucks that are found on many surviving tunics which had come about if they were shortened. Finally if the last turn of the waistband was doubled, Haas found that it made an ideal pocket about 15cm deep. The tombstones that appear to show these waistbands also depict a rectangular object tucked into them. Often assumed to be the auxiliary military diploma, perhaps a better explanation might indeed be a purse or a writing tablet, because legionaries (who did not get diplomas) are shown with these rectangular objects too.

A late Roman mosaic from Apamea shows hunters in red tunics with what appears to be a white scarf and a white waistband. This is a rare illustrated example from later times. One other possible example is on the Terentius fresco from Dura Europos discussed above. It is possible that the practice of wearing a fabric waistband survived into Anglo-Saxon times. A Saxon grave from Market Lavington (Wi5 G32) displayed signs of a linen tabby repp lying over much courser twill around the waist.

Sashes

From earliest times senior officers and emperors are often represented wearing a knotted sash over the muscle cuirass, sometimes with each hanging end being finished with a fringe. They were probably introduced to the Romans by Hellenistic armies – Alexander the Great can be seen wearing a green version in the famous Alexander mosaic in Pompeii. In later Byzantine times the historian John Lydius described a *zona militaris*, made of red leather, *puniceus,* decorated with gold (*De Magistratibus*, II; 9, 13). The expression 'cut the belt' (John of Ephesus, V 1,2) meant to degrade a senior commander and in AD 573 the officialis Acacius cut the *zona* from the breast of the *Magister Militum per Orientem Marcianus*, signifying his removal from command of the troops besieging Nisibis.

A sash of rank was also called a *loros*; this was a long embroidered cloth, sometimes ornamented with precious stones. In special ceremonies some guardsmen and senior officers wore the *loros* fan-folded and wrapped around the body (Lydus, *De Mag.*, 11,2) like a shawl, in the shape of the *trabea*, the last survival of the ancient toga. Wide sashes were also worn in the same way as protection against the cold.

SUBARMALIS, THORACOMACHUS AND ARMOUR COVERINGS

Pteryges

While he was opposed to the idea of leather armour used by the Romans, Russell Robinson nonetheless suggested that leather garments could be worn either under or over the armour. Evidence for a garment or 'arming doublet' worn under the armour he argued could be seen on numerous Roman monuments showing the so called muscled cuirass. This type of armour is further distinguished by the thin strips worn in a skirt sometimes of two rows seen around the waist or hanging from the shoulders. These strips or *pteryges*, familiar from countless Hollywood epics, were either made of layers of linen or leather and sometimes appear to be reinforced by metal plates or other decorative elements.

The *pteryges* would have provided protection to the upper thighs and arms and were almost certainly attached to whatever was worn under the armour. Evidence of this is provided by a statue in the Museo della Terme in Rome which shows one of these garments with *pteryges* attached hanging over a tree stump. The garment is clearly flexible to bend almost in half and appears to be rendered to look like soft leather. A further example can be seen in the Bergama Museum in Turkey dating to the Antonine period. This shows another flexible garment with *pteryges* attached, although Travis Lee Clark argues that this is not an under-cuirass garment but the actual cuirass itself.

Although mail armour might prevent a cutting blow, the force delivered could still cause an injury resulting in broken or smashed bones and internal bleeding. Mail also provides little defence against stabs from pointed weapons such as swords and spears and is especially vulnerable to arrows. Scale armour, although slightly more effective, can also be pierced by stabs or hits coming from slightly below, and the soldier wearing plate armour would not be immune to blunt trauma either. Therefore a padded undergarment of some sort which would help to dissipate the force of a blow as well as providing an extra protective layer would be a vital piece of equipment.

Subarmalis and Thoracomachus

In medieval times padded garments were known as either 'aketons', 'brigandines', 'gambesons'; 'pourpoints' or 'jacks', and there was another variation called the 'joupon' or coat armour. It is possible that the Romans equally described their own under armour garments with a variety of names and at least two possibilities exist, the *thoracomachus* and the *subarmalis*. The best known example is the *thoracomachus*, which is described in great detail by the anonymous author of *De Rebus Bellicis* although Wild believes the author invented the term (XV 1–2). The work is a fourth century collection of often-fantastic inventions designed to restore the superiority of the Romans over their barbarian adversaries. The author admits that the *thoracomachus*, unlike many of his other ideas, already existed and was indeed known to the ancients who in their foresight

> devised for use in war … the thoracomachus to counteract the weight and friction of armour. It is amazingly useful for protecting the body. This type of garment is made of thick cloth to the measure and for the protection of the upper part of the human frame; fearful apprehension, guided by cleverness, devised it, so that, after it has been put on first, the *lorica*, or *cliuanus*, or something similar, cannot injure the frail body by its roughness and weight; and again, the limbs of the wearer, helped by this means of relief, will be able to do their work, amidst the difficulties of warfare and cold weather.

The anonymous author adds that to prevent it getting wet a second garment made of Libyan hide was also required. As confirmed by a modern reconstruction made of linen stuffed with wool, if the *thoracomachus* was made this way and it did get wet it would make the wearer thoroughly uncomfortable, as it takes an awful long time to dry out. The hide covering, therefore, was probably treated with tallow to make it waterproof. These hide coverings may have been termed 'Libyan' because they originated in the leather clothing worn by Libyan mercenaries during the Punic Wars. The Latin poet Silius Italicus refers to the red-dyed leather worn by Libyans, as does the Greek historian Herodotus, who also adds that they were made from goatskin with the hair removed (*Histories*, 4 & 7). It is of further interest that Pliny the Elder comments that madder could also be used to dye leather as well as textiles, while Apuleius in *The Golden Ass* refers to a red Moroccan saddle.

Illustrations from early medieval copies of *De Rebus Bellicis* depict both the *thoracomachus* and the hide covering as T-shaped tunics, while those from later editions – perhaps influenced by contemporary *aketons* – show them as quilted. These descriptions are nevertheless remarkably similar to garments mentioned in an account by Caesar, who records that during the battle of

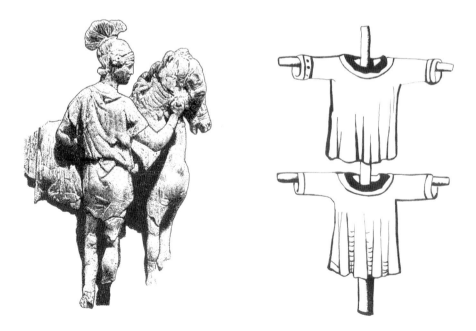

115 The *subarmalis* or armour cover. Left: Ivory carving of Trajanic date, Ephesus, Turkey.; right: Depictions of a *thoracomachus* and hide covering in an early medieval edition of *De Rebus Bellicis*. *After M. Daniels.*

Dyrrachium his soldiers made tunics and other protection from arrows out of felt, quilt, and hide (*Civil War.*, III, 44).

magnusque incesserat timor sagittarum, atque omnes fere milites aut ex coactis aut ex centonibus aut ex coriis tunicas aut tegimenta fecerant, quibus tela vitarent.

The Spanish conquistadors also considered armour made from quilted and rolled cotton suitable protection against the darts and arrows of the Aztecs. On the other hand the fact that Caesar draws attention to these garments could be interpreted as evidence that it was not normal practice or at least somewhat unusual to wear them. Archaeologically there is very little conclusive evidence but the mail armour called the 'Persian shirt' found beneath tower 19 at Dura Europos was mixed up with a light brown fibrous material that James suggests could conceivably have come from under armour padding.

There are a few surviving examples of medieval *aketons* which are usually vertically quilted linen stuffed with tow or wool rags. 'Aketons' could also be long-sleeved and an Etruscan period sculpture now in Volterra Museum in Italy seems to show the same thing. Furthermore it is known that the 'aketon' could be worn without any armour above and could be used as a protective garment in its own right, especially by the lower ranks. The fact that they were used by common soldiers does not mean that all these garments should be considered as cheap alternatives to armour. One such surviving medieval coat covered with red damask silk was considered fit for a king!

There are tantalising pieces of evidence from Roman sculpture to suggest that the practice of wearing padded garments instead of armour was familiar to them too. It would certainly help explain away some of the more bizarre attempts to render mail attributed to Roman sculptors by modern historians. One such example is on a panel from the Arch of Marcus Aurelius, later incorporated into the Arch of Constantine where it still remains. In this particular scene the emperor addresses his soldiers with three figures prominent in the foreground. Each are equipped differently in scale, plate and apparently mail armour which Robinson suggested indicated that they represented a *praetorian*, a *legionary* and an auxiliary. Apart from the fact that they could all represent *praetorians*, what interests us most here is the representation of the so called mail armour. The effect is created by a garment divided up into small squares in the centre of which is a small circle.

Roman sculptors were more than capable of achieving very detailed mail effects. Even on extremely large projects like Trajan's Column, mail was indicated by a herringbone method; indeed many illustrators use the same technique today. Therefore the method used in the Arch of Aurelius would be an extremely lazy way of achieving a mail effect and not what one would expect to see on a major Imperial sculpture. Perhaps it is not a mail shirt that is being shown. In fact it looks remarkably similar to medieval padded garments illustrated by the late fifteenth century Flemish artist Memling. These garments are quilted in small squares and are also fitted in at least one case with small circular metal rivets.

A third century tombstone now in Istanbul depicts the 'armour' worn by Severius Acceptus, a soldier serving with The VIII Augustan Legion. The armour is in fact not any of the usual types one would expect. While the upper arms and lower waist would have been protected by the common *pteryges*, the torso is covered by a series of vertical lines divided by a horizontal band below the arms. There are eight panels around the lower torso and five wider panels covering the upper torso and shoulders. This could quite easily be a quilted garment rather than armour. An almost identical garment is worn by a figure of Mars depicted on a building inscription from High Rochester on Hadrian's Wall also dating from the third century AD.

Another figure of Mars found on a votive tablet from Bisley near Gloucester, also wears a striped upper garment rather than the expected traditional muscled cuirass. The lower half of this particular garment extending over the abdomen is semi-circular and plain. The *pteryges* are either attached to the bottom of this or are worn underneath. The Bisley tablet is the work of Iuventinus, a Celtic sculptor, and J.F. Rhodes commented that his style was so crude it was obvious he had had no classical training. It is possible therefore that Iuventinus perhaps like many other frontier sculptors, was working from something he had seen rather than making any attempt to follow a classical convention he was not familiar with. D'amato has also pointed out another possible example of a *subarmalis* which is shown on a frieze illustrating the equipment of a Roman warrior, perhaps a Centurion, from Sora in Italy. It shows a cuirass composed entirely of narrow vertical lines again indicative of a padded garment.

Robinson suggested that some sculptures showed covers over the armour. In particular he identified the first century AD tombstones of Firmus an auxiliary infantryman and an unknown soldier, both from Andernach in Germany. They appear to wear a plain garment over the torso with what looks like another garment underneath, which has a zigzag pattern on its lower edge and is in turn worn over a curved draped tunic underneath. Robinson's interpretation was that the smooth garment was the cover while the zigzag pattern was the mail. However, when only the plain garment was visible on other tombstones this was seen as the mail shirt the texture of which had originally been painted. The tombstone of the cavalryman Silius mentioned previously which had surviving paint on it might seem to contradict this idea because the plain garment was coloured green and the fringe was red. This does not suggest mail but perhaps the individual portrayed was not Silius himself but his servant. Nevertheless for all intents and purposes he is wearing a garment that could easily be mistaken for what is being worn by soldiers on other monuments. Both versions described by Robinson therefore could possibly just be variations of padded protective garments worn without any armour at all.

Indirect evidence for the wearing of padded undergarments has been provided by modern reconstructions of the plate armour known today as '*lorica segmentata*'. Observers of Russell Robinson's reconstruction of this armour and those made by the re-enactors who followed, discovered that the two chest pieces crossed together at an angle meaning the strap and buckle fittings on them did not fit squarely. Even more alarming was the fact that openings were left both below the neck and above the upper girth strips! At first it was thought that Robinson had perhaps missed out a piece of as yet undiscovered armour, but there was a more obvious solution to the problem. The modern reconstructions had simply been worn over a tunic so the armour naturally followed the downward sloping line of the shoulders. Therefore if another garment was worn under the armour one which was especially padded at the shoulders, it would in turn raise the armour up so the two central plates sat vertically together.

It is quite possible that in the earlier Imperial period what Anonymous calls the *thoracomachus* was known by another name. The Emperor Septimius Severus once had the Praetorian Guard parade in what is described as a *subarmalis* to humiliate them (SHA, *Severus*, 6.11). This name clearly suggests something that is worn under armour. A *subarmalis* is also mentioned in a list of clothes on one of the wooden writing tablets from Vindolanda (*Tab. Vind.* II, 184, iii, 38).

One other problem remains. This is whether the garment made of Libyan hide was worn directly over the *thoracomachus*, or over armour in turn worn over the *thoracomachus*. The latter arrangement would be familiar to students of thirteenth century arms and armour, as it parallels the medieval surcoat and could be put on and taken off as required without too much effort. D'Amato believes that the meaning of *thoracomachus* derives from 'fitted to the thorax', thus explaining both the muscular shape of many Roman armours represented in art and the description in De Rebus Bellicis of the hide garment as being 'the same shape as the thoracomachus' and 'well worked'. D'Amato therefore believes that the hide garment was worn directly over the *thoracomachus*, both with and at times instead of metal armour on top.

An anonymous author of Justinian's time (*De Re Militari*, XVI, 20 if.) describes among other items of Roman equipment the garment worn under the cuirass by infantrymen. He refers to felt and leather armour worn by soldiers instead of metal, or used underneath metal armour. The author writes that armour 'should not be worn directly over ordinary clothing, as some do, to keep down the weight, but over a himation at least a finger thick.' These garments were not worn under metal armour alone, but also under leather lamellar defences, when their protective function took on more importance.

A passage of Procopius (BV, III, 23) mentions Roman bodyguards preparing to fight by first putting on their *himatia* and then taking up their weapons. Padded undergarments of this kind (*himatia* or *peristithidia*) are often represented in pictorial sources with hanging fringes of *pteryges* attached at the shoulders and abdomen. Such garments are still visible on many monuments, for example under the muscled leather cuirass worn by Palatini infantry in the surviving fragments of the Theodosius Column. The mosaics of Sta Maria Maggiore also show them finished off with double layers of *pteryges* so thick that the under-tunic itself is not visible.

The material of such strap work fringes might have been silk and coarse cotton stitched in layers, as in later periods. A good example of a *peristithidion* worn by an infantryman is visible on a terracotta plaque from Vinicko Kale; and decorated fragments of similar garments have been found in the Ballana graves, entirely in red leather, including fragments of *pteryges*.

Much as any important person today might wear a bulletproof vest, some of the emperors, especially the more paranoid ones, are know to have worn protective garments under their everyday clothes. Caracalla – after the murder of his brother Geta – attended a meeting in the Senate '*tunc sub veste senatoria loricam habens cum armatis militibus Curiam ingressus est*' – 'wearing a cuirass under his senator's robe and accompanied by an armed guard.'

Caracalla, in constant fear of assassination, took to wearing a long-sleeved tunic fashioned to look like armour. This was probably a fabric padded garment or linen cuirass, familiar from Greek sources and certainly in keeping with Caracalla's passion for Alexander the Great. Inspired by his hero and his conquest of Persia, Caracalla went ahead and equipped 16,000 of his own troops as Macedonian pikemen for his proposed Persian expedition (Dio, Epit., LXXVIII).

In what can best be described as an early attempt at historical re-enactment, the emperor dressed his soldiers in what he saw as typical Macedonian equipment. This consisted of a helmet made of raw ox hide, a three-ply linen cuirass, high boots, a round shield, long pike, short spear and a sword. A mosaic from Tunisia showing a mythological scene depicts two soldiers wearing something identical to this description. They are standing alongside a king who looks suspiciously like Septimius Severus. Was the mosaic artist inspired by the soldiers of Caracalla or the other way around? We will also never know how Caracalla's re-created *phalanx* would have performed because ironically, despite his own body armour, his worst fear was realised and he was stabbed to death before the campaign began when he went to relieve himself behind a rock!

According to Plutarch, at the Battle of Tigranocerta in 68 BC when the Armenian king Tigranes fought against a Roman army commanded by Lucullus, he mistook some of the initial Roman manoeuvres for a retreat, until one of the king's aides observed something which probably gave him the shivers!

'O King,' said Taxiles, 'I could wish that some marvellous thing might fall to your good fortune; but when these men are merely on a march, they do not put on shining raiment, nor have they their shields polished and their helmets uncovered, as now that they have stripped the leathern coverings from their armour. Nay, this splendour means that they are going to fight, and are now advancing upon their enemies.' (Lucullus, XXVII)

In a famous passage, the Jewish historian Josephus records that before parading to receive their pay during the siege of Jerusalem in AD 69 the Roman soldiers 'removed the protective coverings from their armour, as was their usual custom'. (BJ, V, 346–369). Furthermore the second century historian Fronto also writes that an officer called Laelianus regarded as a 'disciplinarian of the old school' ripped up soldiers' body armour during a parade with his fingers because it was too soft (Letter to Lucius Verus, xix). This would be very difficult to achieve if the passage referred to mail, scale, or plate armour, but not if Fronto meant a hide covering or leather armour as suggested by D'Amato. Alternatively this is perhaps even more evidence for quilted armour of some sort.

There is no doubt that Frontinus is indicating some type of cover when he describes an action that took place when Pompey the Great was conducting a campaign in what is now modern day Albania. Pompey hid his infantry in a defile, and so that their helmets would not reflect the sun and reveal their position, he ordered his men to cover them (*Strat*, II. 14).

Whether they used purpose-made covers is not clear and perhaps even scarfs could have been used for the task.

A final piece of evidence for protective coverings is supplied by Plutarch, who describes a trick employed by the Parthians before the Battle of Carrhae in 53 BC. The Romans, previously unimpressed at the first sight of the Parthian army, were completely demoralised when at the last moment the Parthians removed the leather and cloth covers from their armour for both man and horse, which then gleamed in the bright sunlight (Crassus, 23–24). The shocking effect is somewhat surprising, as Plutarch's earlier description of the army of Lucullus indicates that the Romans themselves had on occasions employed the very same trick.

THE SCARF

O, what a time have you chose out, brave Caius, to wear a kerchief! Would you were not sick!
(Shakespeare, *Julius Caesar*, Act II. I. 315)

Early Roman writers such as Catullus and Valerius Maximus (Val Max., IX, 12,7) refer to a scarf which they call a *sudarium*, perhaps the ancestor of the later *focale*, which is the name given to the scarf by Martial and by which the scarf is more generally known today (*Epigr.*, VI, 41). However a graffito from Dura Europos mentions a *sudarion* so presumably the earlier term persisted into later times. Wearing a scarf around the neck is seen by modern re-enactors as obligatory when wearing close-fitting body armour. Not only does it protect the neck from chafing, both by all the various recreated types of armour used during the Roman period, but also from the leather thong which fastens the helmet cheek pieces.

There are those who might say that this is simply a case of modern people not being tough enough to endure what the Romans could, but it does seem that Roman soldiers at times also wore scarves, perhaps for the reasons that re-enactors today have discovered. Unfortunately, as scarves in various sculptures are almost invariably depicted tucked beneath either the armour or clothing, it is uncertain what shape they were originally. Two types seem likely and possibly both were used. The first would be a square shaped folded into a triangle, the second would be longer and thinner – the same shape as scarves today. Most re-enactors favour a triangular design as this fits neatly and comfortably beneath the armour. However, some sculptures of civilians feature scarves which appear quite voluminous.

On the Columns of Trajan and Marcus Aurelius all the soldiers wear scarves, either tucked beneath their armour or worn outside the armour and tied in front. Usually it is worn inside the laminated *lorica*, and outside the mail and leather armours. This may be due to the possibility that the scarf helped to hold the position of the *segmentata* armour around the neck, so it needed to be tucked inside, whereas with the other armour its protective function could be just realised by wrapping it around the neck. Very often it is worn in combination with the *paenula* or the cloak, but is not so common with just the tunic alone. Based purely on sculptural evidence the scarves shown on Trajan's Column would appear to be the smaller square type folded in half diagonally.

Antonucci – after observing the scarf worn by the possible praetorian of the Domus Aurea – suggested that the scarf, much more than the tunic, could be used like a badge to identify individual units through its colour. The same theory was proposed by Fuentes who suggested for example that legions of naval origin might have traditionally retained a blue *focale*. A white knotted scarf is visible on some funerary Fayoum portraits and in a mosaic scene from Apamea.

The scarf could also have a very practical purpose, as demonstrated by the para-military troops of provincial governors, such as the *Diogmitai* in Smyrna. St Peonis was captured by a policeman who put his scarf or *maphorion* (or *maphortes*) around the neck of the saint and tightened it until he almost choked (*Acta Martyria Peonii*, XV, 5). This implies that in this case these scarves were rather long and could be used like a lasso to arrest prisoners and to drag them '*obtorto colla*', i.e. by the neck!

116 Detail of Trajan's Column showing
an interesting view of an auxiliary with a
scarf!

117 Tombstone of Apinosus a workman
from Nievre, France, which gives us a
rare glimpse of a scarf from the Roman
period. Wild estimated that this scarf was
approximately 1.70m in length.

A modern affectation amongst Roman re-enactors is to fasten the scarf with a brooch. An Iron Age scarf from Huldre Moss was fastened with a bird bone pin so it is conceivable that the Romans fastened theirs with more sophisticated metallic versions or even small brooches which in some cases were ornamented with white pearls, especially those belonging to officers. It would certainly be safer to keep valuables close to hand rather than leaving them in camp, and perhaps this practice grew out of keeping cloak brooches on one's person when the cloak was not in use.

TROUSERS, SOCKS, LEGGINGS, LEG WRAPPINGS AND BINDINGS

Trousers

Trousers make their appearance in the classical world as early as the fifth century BC when the Greeks encountered nomadic tribes such as the Scythians. Both trousers and boots appear to have been inventions of the warrior horsemen from the steppes. The main types of trousers

118 Statuette of a Roman Auxiliary in the British Museum, wearing a mail shirt over a short tunic with *bracae* underneath. *Photograph by the author.*

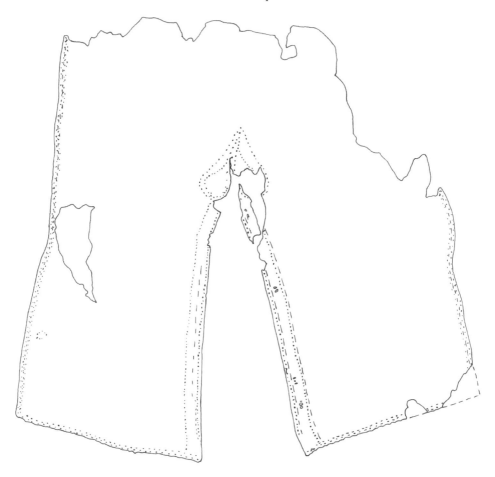

119 Plan of the leather *bracae* found at Valkenburg in the Netherlands. *After Hoevenburg.*

used by the steppe people were a close fitting version that could be made of leather, and a second type that were much looser and wider and were tucked into short riding boots.

While Greek soldiers do not appear to have ever worn trousers, these garments ultimately became a feature of late Roman military equipment. Initially the Roman reaction was that trousers were both barbarian and effeminate. Writers like Cicero referred with contempt to the '*bracatae nationes*' – 'the trouser-clad peoples' (*Epistulae ad Familiares*, IX, 15, 2, 6). Roman soldiers probably began wearing trousers of some sort during the northern campaigns in Gaul and Germany. Both Gauls and Germans are frequently represented in Roman art wearing trousers, for example a statuette of a dead warrior found at Alesia.

Other sculptures reveal that there were alternative versions. Figures of deities in the Dijon Museum and the Musee des Antiquites Nationales wear trousers that reach to just below the knee. These are the type of trousers, more commonly referred to today as breeches or *bracae*. They are also the type of trouser that appear on Trajan's Column. On this monument *bracae* are worn by all the regular auxiliary troops and perhaps more surprisingly by the senior Roman officers too, including the Emperor Trajan himself. The legionaries do not wear them, but the contemporary monument known as the Tropaeum Trajani at Adamklissi in Romania shows the citizen soldiers in *bracae*.

The introduction of trousers into the Roman army was no doubt largely because of the widespread use of Celtic, German and Eastern auxiliary troops who were recruited into the army in increasing numbers after the civil wars at the end of the Republic. It is accepted by

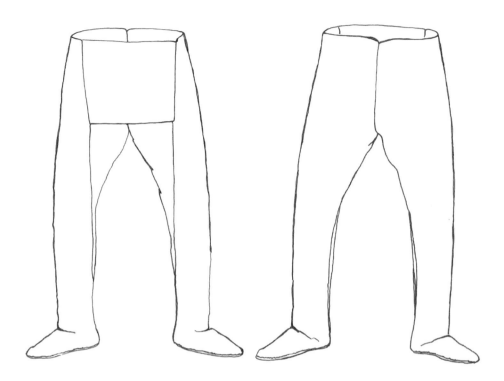

120 Plan of the Thorsberg trousers. *After Schlabow.*

modern scholars that the word *bracae* was Germanic in origin. No doubt the Roman soldiers still mainly recruited from the Mediterranean region found trousers far more practical in the northern climates as an addition to their simple tunics. But it is perhaps not surprising that it is on the tombstones of auxiliary soldiers – especially cavalrymen – that they first appear officially as part of the Roman uniform. The Rhineland tombstone of the Thracian trooper T. Flavius Bassus of the Ala Noricorum is one example and he also wears a long-sleeved tunic. The tombstones give little indication as to what these *bracae* were made of. Wool seems the most likely but a pair of leather *bracae* has been found at Valkenburg in the Netherlands dating to the second or third century AD. Leather *bracae* might have appealed to cavalry as they offered better protection to the exposed leg both from the elements and in combat. Agathias provides further information and says *bracae* could not only be in leather but in linen as well (*Hist.* ii.5).

A pair of wool diamond twill trousers found at Thorsberg in Schleswig-Holstein, Germany, which dated to the third century AD had attached 'feet' like medieval footed hose or a modern baby's romper suit! Their length and waist size was just over a metre and had a leg width of around 0.3m. Unlike early Roman garments they are neatly tailored which ironically somewhat belies their so-called barbarian nature. They are fitted with a separate waist band to which are attached six belt-loops and once a belt was fitted, it is possible the trouser waist was rolled down over the belt giving a sash like appearance. This feature was accurately observed by Roman artists and can be seen on both the Columns of Trajan and Marcus Aurelius. Other trousers from Dammendorf are missing the lower parts of the leg but were clearly longer than those from Thorsberg as they are already 1.15m long. Otherwise they show a similar method of tailoring.

These fairly tight-fitting trousers appear very similar to those illustrated in the fresco showing members of the Roman garrison of Dura Europos and in the mosaics from Piazza Armerina. A fresco from Silistra in Bulgaria shows a pair of trousers identical to those from Thorsberg being carried by a servant. It was probably trousers of this type that the Emperor Honorius tried to ban from being worn within the city of Rome as late as AD 397.

On some sculptures from the third century onwards it is not always easy to decide if soldiers went bare-legged or wore very tight-fitting trousers. The coloured paints on most sculptures have long since worn off so the lines that are visible around the legs can be interpreted in a variety of ways. Tombstones like that of Aries the weapons keeper, now in the British Museum, show lines just below the tunic, lines above and below the knee and lines around the ankle. This could be seen as an under-tunic, *bracae* and leg wrappings or alternatively just an under-tunic and leg wrappings. Other sculptures such as those showing members of the Imperial Horse Guards in Rome indicate that tight-fitting trousers were now an established feature of Roman uniforms. Mosaics and wall paintings from Africa and the Middle East, like those from Dura Europos, show soldiers stationed there wearing long tight-fitting trousers tucked into boots, although occasionally we do see some soldiers just wearing leg wrappings or bindings on the legs. The trousers in these paintings are generally painted in dark colours including a greyish shade or a chocolate brown. Even emperors now wore trousers because according to the *Scriptores Historiae Augustae* the Emperor Alexander Severus had white trousers instead of the scarlet ones which it had been the custom to wear before (SHA, *Sev. Alex.*, XL, 5–11).

Trousers, the Later Empire

In the late empire trousers were an integral part of military uniform although they were still considered 'barbarian' even at the end of the fourth century, because Imperial decrees of AD 397 and 399 tried to ban their use in Rome, even though soldiers had been wearing them for hundreds of years (*Cod. Theod.* XIV, 10, 2–3).

The older styles of trouser that covered the whole leg including the foot, or the Celtic model that was looser and secured by a waist belt were still worn. However the Grue mosaic from Carthage dating to the Honorian period, shows army officers wearing a new type of trouser that is wider than the other kinds and look more like modern flared trousers. They have recognisable pleats, parallel-sides and the lower parts are cut obliquely from the instep to the heel. On the Carrand Diptych three soldiers wear the same type. It is difficult to say if this so-called 'elephant's foot' fashion was adopted from the Easterners, as Parthian and Sassanian models suggest. It passed from the Romans to the Vandals and through them to the sixth century Eastern army.

Straight-legged trousers open in the lower part and decorated with a wide band at the bottom, are worn by barbarian kings in the Barberini Diptych, probably representing the triumph of Justinian and Belisarius over the Africans, Vandals and Persians. Some sixth century ivories from Alexandria – probably representing *milites* of the *officium* and soldiers of the *numeri* under the Dux Thebaidae – show the transformation as complete: very wide trousers ending in a flounce of different cloth. This was the general fashion for sixth and seventh century eastern troops in Egypt and the Near East. Sometimes they are decorated with a broad lozenge-pattern.

The charging Roman armoured cavalryman on the sixth century Isola Rizza silver dish wears tubular trousers, though more fitted to the leg (see MM 150, p.6). His Germanic opponents are wearing highly decorated 'elephant's foot' trousers; they are probably Gothic warriors, wearing the prototype of the trousers later widely distributed in the Roman army. The Souda describes this costume as Persian, referring to the trousers, like the rest of the costume, as *sarabara* (Persian = *sarafan*, *sciarvan*). In the East, trousers and especially 'tights' were called *anaxyrides*; they were of various colours, as attested in the second century in the *scholis* of Dio Chrisostomus:

> the anaxyrides as the superior brakia of various colours are called, began to becalled this from the
> highly decorated leg bands … the anaxyrides [are] called in the popular language toubia.

In the fifth century they were also called *fiminalia* by Hesychios, and defined as 'barbaric dress of the feet'.

Hesychios (*Lexicon* I. 19-190-896) also calls the wide trousers derived from Parthia and Persia *sarabara*, though Procopius does sometimes use the term *anaxyrides*. They could be made of

121 A wall painting from Silistra in Bulgaria shows this servant carrying a pair of Thorsberg-like trousers with attached feet and a belt with belt loop.

different cloth depending on the season, of different colours and variously ornamented with chequered, rhomboidal, flowered or circular patterns, often in a band running down to the feet. Trousers could be more or less loose, extending to the instep or tucked inside the footwear. In the latter cases it is difficult to tell if they are tights or trousers, but normally vertical pleats indicate true trousers folded to fit into the boots.

From the fifth century, trousers became more fitted to the leg, and were laced below the stomach and secured at the sides by a strap (Procopius, *Historia Arcana*, 1,20: 'the strap … which fastened the *anaxyrides*'). But they could also be simple tubes; Gayet found a body with 'voluminous linen trousers, which consisted of two single, unconnected tubes'. At the bottom these trousers were covered by gaiters, but reached to the ankle and were tied there by a string. We can assume that the *anaxyrides* were normally worn with the *campagus* (see below), as in the Ravenna mosaics, while the wider trousers were worn over boots and shoes, covering the instep (even though, towards the end of the sixth century they were worn inside short boots).

A third type of garment still in use were the so-called *femoralia*, short trousers used in combination with leg wrappings or *tibialia* (Jerome, Ep. LXIV). In the Western army they were used particularly by infantrymen. In the Sta Maria Maggiore mosaic a soldier of Herod is shown wearing short white breeches, dark blue leg wrappings and *caligae* or *campagri eticulati* on his feet. This seems to be a fashion that survived in the west, as shown in the Ashburnham Pentateuch, probably produced in Africa or Roman Spain at the beginning of the seventh century. Similar trousers covering the leg to the knee, but of Persian type, are called *skeleai* in the Hesychios Lexicon. A specimen from Panopolis was actually preserved in Düsseldorf before World War II: they were knee-length *bracae* of linen interwoven with red wool. The Column of Arcadius provides evidence for the use by officers and infantrymen of *femoralia* in combination with *tibialia*, and an interesting figure of a mounted official is seen in the Renaissance 'Freshfield' drawing n.37 of the Column of Theodosius.

Leg Wrappings and Bindings

Another form of leg protection which may have been adopted by soldiers are the leg wrappings or bindings that frequently appear in various Roman art forms. They are worn by huntsmen and other outdoor labourers as illustrated by a bronze statuette of a ploughman found at Piercebridge in England. One huntsman on a late mosaic from Apamea in Syria wears both short *bracae* to just above the knee and leg wrappings below the knee, a feature that is seen on several military tombstones. It would be surprising if soldiers in the field did not wear what was seen as a commonplace garment elsewhere for outdoor activities.

Two first century pay receipts for soldiers from Egypt and Masada, Israel, may provide evidence that leg wrappings were in fact included in the basic kit. Among the list of compulsory deductions for clothing and food for Gaius Messius (possibly a legionary cavalryman) found at Masada, and a similar list relating to Quintus Julius Proclus, a cavalryman based in Alexandria, are items described as *lorum fasciari(um)* in the account of Messius and *fascias* in that of Proclus, *fascia* being the term used for a wrapping. In both cases they are listed next to the soldiers' boots, which suggests that they were a leg wrapping of some sort.

Leg wrappings were rectangular and probably made from either wool or felt. There are a number of sculptural renditions which portray the strings which fastened them below the knee and above the ankle, as found on the Arch of Constantine. The soldier in the Via Maria catacomb fresco in Syracuse has blue leg wrappings, as does a soldier in one of the Sta Maria Maggiore mosaics in Rome. A medieval manuscript now in the Bibliotheque Nationale in Paris – which appears to be an accurate copy of a late Roman original – illustrating the *thoracomachus,* also shows black leg wrappings with orange–red ties worn by a soldier. Leg wrappings may also have been called *ocreae* – the term also applied to the metal greaves. This has caused some confusion in translated texts but it could also mean that the leg wrappings might also have had a protective quality in their own right. Some leg wrappings are portrayed as very rigid, as if they could have been made from thick felt or had a stiff lining inside, the Roman equivalent of shin pads worn inside footballer's socks today.

Actual examples of surviving leg wrappings have even been recovered from German and Danish bogs. In one example found at Sogaards Mose in Denmark the remains of a human leg was still wrapped inside the material, graphically proving that wrappings did not cover the feet! Another bog body possibly dating from the Roman period was discovered on Grewelthorpe Moor in northern England in the mid-nineteenth century, may have had leg wrappings that when first discovered were still yellow in colour. A curse tablet found a Caistor near Norwich, England recorded the theft of a list of goods including some pewter vessels, bracelets, a mirror, a cap and some leg wrappings. The victim asked Neptune for the return of the property and that the blood of the thief should be taken from them. If Neptune did this the victim would offer the leg wrappings in return!

Leg bindings are made from long strips of material wound around the leg in a manner reminiscent of the World War I military puttees. These were probably called *fascia crurales*, and a Latin translation of Galen, the physician to Marcus Aurelius, describes hunters wearing them.

122 Leg Wrappings, worn by soldiers, Ares in the British Museum, detail from a tombstone from Barcelona.

123 One of the leg wrappings from Sogaards Mose,
Denmark dating to the Roman period. They correspond
to those seen on Roman monuments and one of them still
preserved the owner's leg, which was found inside!

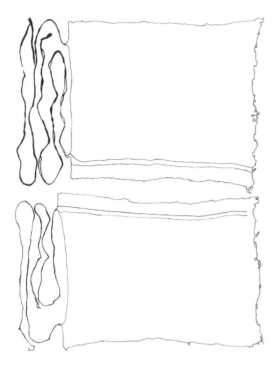

124 The Sogaards Mose leg
wrappings, unwrapped.

125 The early medieval copy of *De
Rebus Bellicis*, as well as illustrating
the *Thoracomachus*, also illustrates this
soldier in a *pileus pannonicus* and black
leg wrappings tied with red laces.

126 A scene from the Arch of Constantine showing a column of soldiers on the march. Many can be seen wearing leg wrappings.

Some of the bandage-like textiles found at Vindolanda and dating to the late first century AD could also fall into this category, suggesting that this type of leg binding was worn even earlier. Like many Roman garments they began inauspiciously. Cicero – self proclaimed guardian of conservative fashion – as usual criticised a certain Clodius for wearing *fasciae* on his feet (*ap. Non. Marc.* xiv.2). However white *fasciae* later became a sign of good taste (Val.Max. *l.c.*; Phaed.V.7.37).

The biographer Suetonius informs us that as protection against the cold Augustus often wore leg bindings (*Aug.*, lxxxii). Another first century writer, Quintillianus says at that time they were only considered suitable for invalids (xi. 3, 144). Nevertheless in spite of this prejudice, by the third century we find that the Emperor Alexander Severus is described as always wearing them (SHA, *Sev. Alex*, XL5–11). Early Christian artists also saw no reason not to depict Christ wearing leg bindings.

Leggings

Leggings are one of the oldest forms of garment; something similar was being worn by the 'Ice man' found close to the Italian border and dated to 3300 BC. However the Romans seem to have adopted the use of leggings via contact with Eastern steppe people. They soon became an established and distinctive part of Roman military dress. In English this type of garment are also called gaiters and are often confused with the *bracae* that are also frequently called leggings in modern works. In Roman times leggings also had different names. They were called *toubia* in the East and *tibialia* or *ocreae* in the West. Isidorus explains, '*ocreae*' are the leggings called '*tibialia*', which cover the legs' (*Orig.* XIX, 34, 5). They were used by Roman cavalry and infantrymen, a fact which can be attested in a number of pictorial sources and confirmed by archaeological finds from Antinoopolis.

The fabric leggings were sewn to form a tube like a trouser leg; in vulgar Latin the term *tubrugi birrei* indicated red cloth leggings, and they were ultimately copied much later by the Lombards (Paulus Diaconus, IV, 22). John of Ephesus (III, 28) describes an official from Edessa wearing leggings with low shoes, called *calcei viatorii* – travel shoes. It is noteworthy that these *tibialia* are furthermore described as *pelliccea*, that is made of fur.

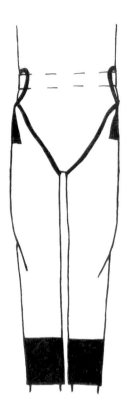

127 Diagram showing how the leggings or gaiters associated with the riding costumes found in Egypt were worn. *Charles W. Evans-Gunther, after K. Mälck.*

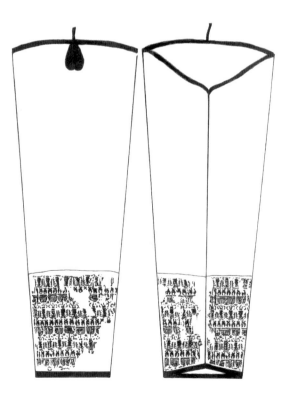

128 Plan of a pair of late Roman Persian-style leggings found in Antinoe (Antinoopolis) Egypt. *Charles W. Evans-Gunther after P. Dal Prà.*

The specimens that survive from Antinoopolis conform more or less to Palmyrene and Sassanian styles visible on their monuments. Two different types are preserved in the Louvre and Berlin Museum of Byzantine Art which both reached above the knee. One of these was of coloured wool with the lower decorated portion imitating silk. Another specimen is decorated with a battle scene that may be Sassanian. The second type was in wool but the lower half of the leg was ornamented with a broad sewn-on silk band also with Sassanian motifs and figurative sources show some leggings highly decorated with human figures, animals both real and mythological and battle scenes that matched the rest of the costume. Leggings made completely from silk were probably the preserve of senior officers.

Examples of these decorated leggings are visible on some carved Coptic panels which represent Roman guards with the Virgin Mary. The surviving specimens allowed German scholars to reconstruct the method of fastening them to the leg; the upper strap was attached to a waist belt or cord under the tunic by means of a loop which was basically the same method used by the 'Ice man' thousands of years earlier. Sometimes the leggings were worn in combination with a form of low footwear or *kampagia*, thus forming the so called *kampotouba* (*De Ger*, 1, 423).

Socks (Udones)
The very idea that Romans wore socks was only brought to popular attention by the mention in one of the first translated writing tablets from Vindolanda of a pair of socks sent as a gift.

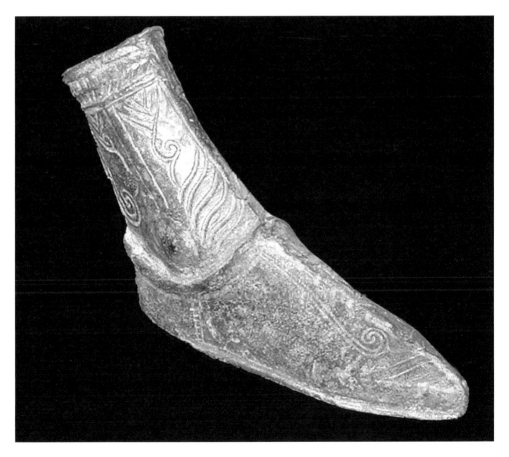

129 A number of miniature bronzes exist which show feet with various types of footwear including socks. This one is from an unprovenanced site spotted by the author in an antique shop in York, which shows a decorated shoe and sock. © *The author.*

130 Part of the first writing tablet discovered at Vindolanda (TV II 346) which mentioned both *subligaria* and *udones*. © *Vindolanda Museum.*

However, the existence in Roman contexts had long been known from a number of other sources. Nevertheless a close examination of the Cancelleria relief reveals at least one of the praetorians wearing socks that were open at the toes and heels. These socks are visible between the straps on his leather boots, and in all probability were a contrasting colour, like those worn by fashionable civilians.

By wearing socks a degree of protection was provided from chafing caused by the straps of the leather boots. However, the open sandal–like design of the early marching boot allowed not only air to circulate but was also was free-draining. Therefore if the feet did get wet they would actually dry quicker if the soldier was not wearing any socks at all. Perhaps then under normal campaign conditions they would have been dispensed with and during the early empire might only have been worn as part of the undress uniform.

The examples of surviving socks from either end of the empire show different methods of manufacture. The rough wool sock from Vindolanda in the North of England is made from two separate pieces of medium weight diamond twill roughly tacked together. The sock is frayed and shows visible signs of wear. Were it not so small – it is 16cm long and 7cm wide – one might have been tempted to say it was the sort of thing a soldier might have put together as a rough and ready replacement. However it seems much more likely that the sock originally belonged to a child.

At first glance the socks that have survived from Roman Egypt seem to be early examples of knitting. In fact the terminology to describe their method of manufacture has been the subject of some discussion. After some experiments Dorothy Burnham concluded that they could be produced by using a length of wool and a large eyed needle. This she concluded was an extension of other existing skills such as basketry or netting. Therefore she suggested that the technique could be called looped needle knitting, knotless knitting, needle coiling, cross knit looping, naalebinding or vatsom. Nevertheless she herself settled for single-needle knitting.

However the term nalbinding is preferred by Richard Rutt, although given that this is a name of Norwegian origin this could have the same effect on this corpus of material as the equally misleading term Coptic has done with tunics and cloaks. Ideally something which clearly defines their origin in the Roman period needs to be decided upon. The socks from Egypt often reach above the ankle and have a gap between the large and other toes to allow a thong from the sandal to pass between it. The socks themselves are constructed from the toe upwards and are frequently decorated with different coloured bands.

The best examples come from the excavations at Antinoopolis and Achmim-Panopolis, which recovered socks for both military and civilian use. From Antinoopolis, a fine rough wool specimen was in bands of green, red, blue and orange. From Panopolis other preserved specimens are calf length, with a string around the upper edge for fastening. Stockings of

131 A roughly made wool sock, probably for a child, found at Vindolanda. © *Vindolanda Museum.*

woven material were found on a body at Antinoopolis, under linen trousers and gaiters: they are quite rare, as socks made by single-needle knitting are more common. Schmidt found black and green socks for cavalrymen; and in the 'horsemen's graves' Gayet recovered calf-length examples of wool, of linen with a green wool sole, and of green wool with a yellow tip.

GLOVES

It is easy to picture a Roman sentry patrolling a rampart in a camp somewhere in Northern Europe on a winter's night wrapped up in his cloak and wearing gloves or mittens on his hands. It seems entirely logical but unfortunately the specific evidence for soldiers wearing anything on their hands is completely missing. Perhaps on occasions such as the scene described above, strips of fabric wrapped around the hands might have been sufficient.

Nonetheless some indirect evidence might be of interest here. Varro for instance mentions that when performing some manual duties *digitalia* could be worn (*de Re Rust.* i.55). Pliny the Younger records *manicae*, which could be used in winter to protect the hands from the cold (*Epist.* iii.5.15). This however is sometimes seen as referring to long sleeves on a tunic rather than gloves, and the Persian-style riding coats seen in late Roman Egypt certainly had long sleeves which extended well beyond the hands and could be used as gloves when the occasion demanded. A more specialist type of glove is shown on a late Roman mosaic from Argos Greece, which shows a hunter with a bird of prey sitting on his gloved left hand. Finally a curse tablet found in Bath records the theft of a pair of mittens (*manicilia*) and damns whoever has stolen them to lose both their mind and their eyes!

UNDERGARMENTS

As well as the socks, (*udones*), mentioned on a Vindolanda writing tablet, the same document records the gift of two pairs of underpants, more correctly loincloths, (*subligariorum*). As well as highlighting the little known subject of Roman underwear, this draft letter reminds us that soldiers were able to receive items of clothing from home. Otherwise there is very little evidence that survives to suggest that Roman soldiers wore any underwear other than under-tunics (*subuclae*).

Even clues to what might have been worn are few and far between. A well known graffito of a quarryman from Kruft in Germany shows him dressed in a loincloth with two straps hanging from the waist ending in a fringe which curiously echoes the 'apron' on first century soldiers' belts. Croom describes another loincloth worn by a fisherman in a mosaic from Leptis Magna in Lybia as being more like a short sarong or kilt hitched up at the sides rather than being true

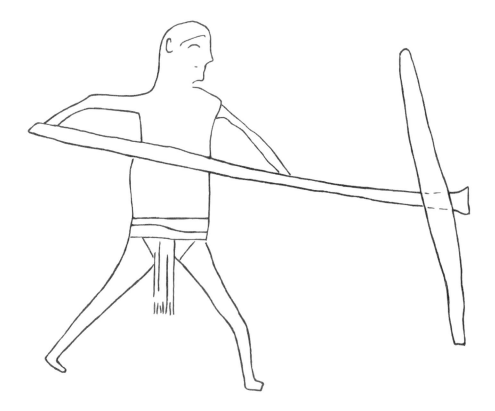

132 A graffito of a quarry man from Grube Idylle, Kruft in Germany. The underwear he is wearing is a curious echo of the soldier's belt and 'apron'. *Charles W. Evans-Gunther, after Wild.*

briefs. Croom also describes two examples of hunters who either do or do not wear underwear. In the first instance an unfortunate man is shown lying dead or wounded in an animal hunt mosaic from Rome. His tunic has hitched up revealing his white, thong-like loincloth beneath. In the second case however another hunter – this time in a mosaic from Antioch – has raised his tunic up around his waist proudly displaying the fact that he is not wearing any underwear.

In earlier times of course many warriors in Italy had fought naked and even when tunics were worn they were extremely short and the genitals must have been frequently exposed. However as time went on tunics became longer. Certainly it was considered indecent to expose oneself by the time of the fifth century Christian writer Sulpicius Severus, who relates how a man was reprimanded for warming himself in front of a fire sat with his feet apart so that his groin was exposed (3.14).

By that date most Roman soldiers were wearing trousers, but at other times those wearing the short tunics worn above the knee must have been at constant risk of exposing themselves. In the military camp this may not have been a problem but at other times this might not have been fashionable or desirable. During the first century AD the elaborate 'apron' suspended from the belt would have gone some way to alleviating any embarrassment because when sitting with the feet apart it hangs between the legs. While at other times as indicated by the the *Scriptores Historiae Augustae* (SHA, Saturninus, XXIV, 10) even showing the legs while reclining at the dinner couch was deemed unacceptable.

FOOTWEAR

Vestiti honeste calciati etiam ad decorum armati nobiliter, equis etiam instructi et ephippiis ac frenis decentibus, prorsus ut Romanam rem publicam intellegeret quicumque Alexandri vidisset exercitum.

for they were respectably clad, well shod, even to the point of elegance, excellently armed, and even provided with horses and suitable saddles and bridles, so that all who saw the army of Alexander immediately realised the power of Rome. (SHA. Sev. Alex. L.3–4.)

In keeping with many contemporary societies the first Roman warriors often fought barefoot. Nevertheless, while archaeological evidence for the early Republic is practically non-existent, literary and artistic sources indicate a number of different types of footwear were worn. These early examples of Roman footwear were influenced if not directly copied from Greek and Etruscan styles, and they include leather and even wooden footwear reinforced with bronze.

Calcei

One of the earliest designs is an enclosed boot with pointed toes called *calcei ripandii*. By the late Republic Cicero says these pointed shoes were reserved for depictions of the goddess Juno Sospita but the term *calcei* continued to be used both then and now to describe the many types of enclosed Roman footwear. The most famous type of enclosed boot were those worn by the patricians and senators; the *calcei patricii* and *calcei senatorii*. In keeping with their taste for red-purple garments some of these boots seem to have been red in colour as they are additionally called the *mulleus* after the highly prized red mullet fish. According to Dio Cassius, Caesar wore high red boots of this fashion in his triumphal parade (43.43.2). Another colour used appears to have been black, which according to Pliny the Elder had a bluish shade (*HN*, XXXV, 25). The boots were fastened not by thin laces but rather four broad straps or *quattor corrigiae* (Seneca. *De Tranq. An.* X,9).

A number of literary sources also suggest that these boots were further decorated with a small crescent shaped decoration called a *luna* made of either bone or metal (e.g. Juvenal, *Satires* 7.192). Such devices were important to the status conscious Romans as they helped to distinguish the upper classes from the rising importance of the equestrian class as they were entitled to wear an enclosed boot of their own, the *calcei equestres*. In Roman sculpture this boot

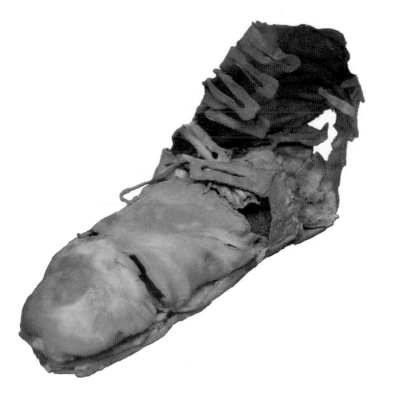

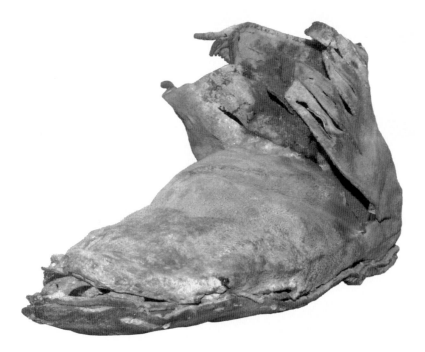

133 Enclosed boots from the isolated desert fort of Qasr Ibrim in Egypt now displayed in the British Museum. © *The author.*

134 Enclosed boot from Mainz, Germany. *Elaine Norbury after Göpfrich..*

appears almost identical to those worn by the upper classes. By the end of the Republic both senatorial and equestrian officers were to be found in the army and both classes would have worn their distinctive footwear on duty.

A tombstone from Padua in Italy shows Centurion Minucius apparently wearing another type of *calceus* which is naturally much less elaborate than those of the senior officers. Sculptures like this also show this type of boot as having a clearly defined separate sole. Therefore a number of sewn boot soles found on military sites of the first century AD have been identified as the remains of *calcei*. Better examples from roughly this period that are virtually complete have been found at remote desert sites like Qasr Ibrim in Egypt.

Caligae

Isidore of Seville states that the term *caliga* derived from the word *callus* which literally meant 'hard leather'; furthermore he accurately describes how the soles were nailed all around (*Origines* 9,34). Due to lack of evidence it is impossible to say with any certainty when the 'classic' military boot, or *caliga*, first appeared, but they were evidently in common usage by the German campaigns of Augustus and his successor Tiberius because of the story of Gaius, the future emperor. Although it is well known it is worth repeating as it demonstrates how closely *caligae* were associated with the military by this date.

As a small boy Gaius was taken by his father Germanicus, the adopted son of Tiberius, on campaign in Germany. Gaius commonly wore miniature versions of the soldiers' dress and boots, and the troops therefore affectionately gave him the nickname 'Little Boots' by which he is infamously better known to posterity – Caligula (Suetonius. *Gaius* 9). Suetonius adds later that when Caligula was emperor he used to wear eccentric dress unbecoming for a man, including silk clothes normally forbidden at that date to men but nevertheless he seems to have retained a fondness for the military boots and occasionally still wore them (*Gaius* 52).

Nevertheless the military association for this type of footwear can certainly be taken back a little further into the late Republic. Cicero for instance said he was suspicious of Pompey on

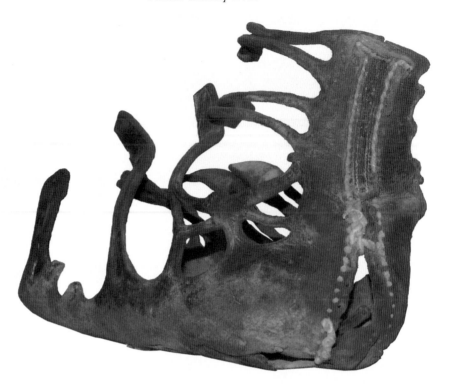

135 *Caliga* from Qasr Ibrim now in the British Museum. It can be noted how the stitching has worn away at the heel, something that many re-enactors would find familiar. © *The author.*

one occasion because he didn't like his 'military' boots and leg bindings '*etenim mihi caligae eius et fasciae cretatae non placebant*' (*Ad Att* ii. 3). The word *caliga* could therefore be used in both as a sign of oppression and in derogatory terms in much the same way as 'foot slogger' or 'under the jackboot' were used in recent times. For example Suetonius refers to the common soldiers as '*caligati*' (*Aug.* 25). While Marius rose to the consulship he did so '*a caliga*' – from out of the ranks (Sen. *De Benef.*V.16).

The identification of *caligae* with the military is further supported by an episode in *The Satyricon* by Petronius. At one point the hero Encolpius tries to pass himself off as a soldier. Unfortunately for Encolpius he is stopped in the street by a real soldier who immediately sees through the deception because of the soft white slippers Encolpius is wearing.

In spite of their sandal-like appearance *caligae* are in fact boots. Typically they were made from cow or ox leather that had been prepared by a vegetable tanning process that took almost two years to complete. Each boot was comprised of three layers: an insole, an outer sole, and an upper, with its distinctive latticework cut-outs. The layers of the sole were clenched together by iron nails. When these were hammered into a boot placed on an anvil or last, they re-curved into the leather and held the soles securely in place.

The open latticework upper provided excellent ventilation reducing the possibility of sweaty feet and blisters, as well as being free-draining. In addition the flexible straps could be adjusted to adapt to the wearer's foot and allow for the expansion of the foot in high temperatures. Van Driel-Murray who has made an extensive study of military boots describes the first century *caliga* as 'ideally suited to its purpose … and its construction is perfectly adapted to the needs of a marching army'. She calculated that a single Legion would require around 36,000 boots a year.

Practical experiments with reconstructions show that if correctly made, abrasions to the feet are minimal because of the absence of pressure on toe joints, the big toe and the ankle.

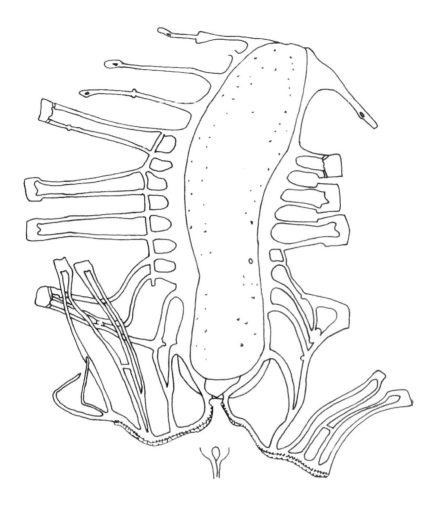

136 Caliga pattern from Castleford, England. *Elaine Norbury after van Driel-Murray.*

Bindings or socks could also be worn for additional comfort or in cold weather. The *caligae* were laced together with thongs that were tied through the openwork strap ends. This method causes a ridge effect along the front of the foot which is clearly depicted on several tombstones. In fact it is often the only feature the sculptors used to indicate a boot is being worn at all and the other more complicated details were obviously added in paint.

Apart from minor variations, surviving *caligae* are extremely standardised, which suggests that patterns were issued for soldiers to copy, perhaps under the supervision of a unit boot maker. In the duty roster *P. Gen. lat. Verso V* some soldiers from either Legio III Cyrenaica or Legio XXII Deiotariana based in Egypt have the word *calcem* marked as their task for a particular day which could mean they are making boots. One other soldier in the same document appears to be away on detachment for at least four days to do with something related to boots, perhaps collecting ready made pairs or maybe the leather to make them. On another day one soldier's duty is marked as '*cal hel*' or simply 'Helius' boots'. Helius is mentioned elsewhere in the roster as being a centurion so maybe the soldier had been detailed to clean his boots!

Except in extreme cases there is little evidence to suggest that boots were constantly repaired. This implies it was quicker and easier to replace worn out boots rather than attempt to make repairs. *P. Gen. Lat 1 recto I* – another document from Egypt – records how two soldiers were

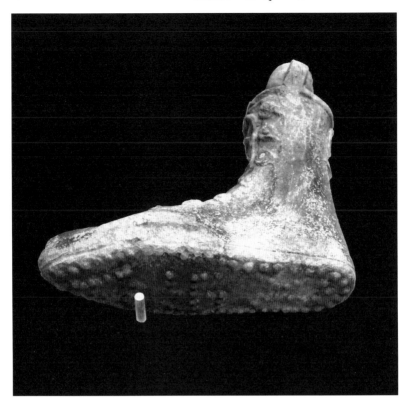

137 Miniature
bronze of a
hobnailed boot
now in the
British Museum.
© *The author.*

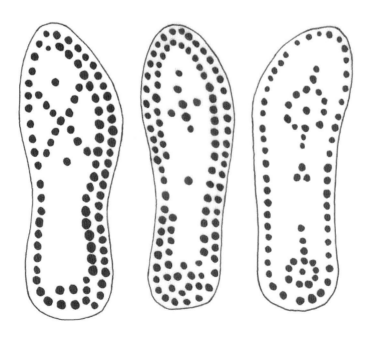

138 Nailing patterns
from boots discovered
at Vindolanda dating
to the first century
AD. *After van
Driel-Murray.*

issued with three pairs of boots per year, which gives a rough lifespan for *caligae* that experiments with reconstructed examples appears to corroborate. However, as we have already seen in one of the letters from Claudius Terentianus to his father, some boots were clearly unsuitable. He describes a particular style of boot perhaps with some form of button fastening as worthless. However his own choice of substitute footwear seemed equally useless as he then goes on to complain that he was forced to obtain replacements twice in a single month! Therefore he begged his father to send him low leather boots with felt socks instead (*Inv.* 5390).

Inevitably what wore out the boots most were the long periods of marching. However as van Driel-Murray has observed it was not the fragile looking straps that broke; either the insoles wore down so the bumps caused by the nails underneath became uncomfortable or the nails themselves wore away. Tacitus records how during the civil war of AD 69 troops of the Danubian army demanded 'nail money' *clavarium,* because of the long forced marches (*Hist* III. 50). Soon after the war the sailors (*classiarii*) who regularly marched from either Ostia or Puteoli to Rome applied for a special boot allowance *calciarium* from the new emperor (*Vesp.* 8, 3). Unfortunately this was Vespasian, who was renowned for being both a strict disciplinarian and notoriously tight with money. He not only rejected their application but said that if they wanted to prevent the wear and tear on their boots then in future they should march barefoot! Suetonius says that this unit of *classiarii* still marched without boots when he was writing his

139 A badly worn hobnailed boot from Vindolanda. © *Vindolanda Museum.*

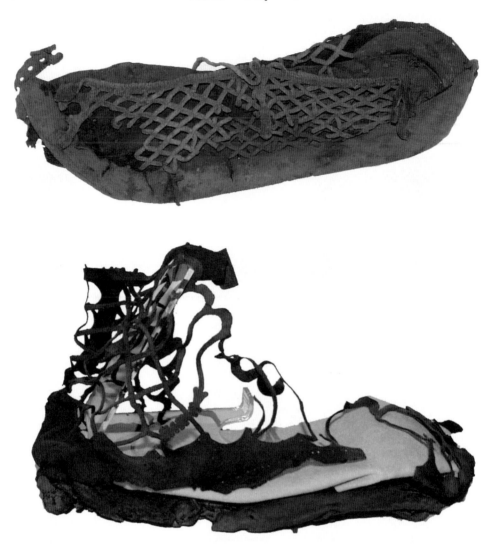

140 Shoes from Vindolanda which are fine examples of the strong and yet delicate work Roman shoemakers could achieve. The open lattice work boot was probably designed originally to display a colourful sock worn beneath. © *Vindolanda Museum.*

Imperial biography of Vespasian and that was almost fifty years later. One can imagine that by then it was a matter of jealously guarded unit pride.

It has been noted that the sound of thousands of men in nailed boots marching in step on metalled roads would have provided an audible reminder of the power of Rome. For example Jews had from long bitter experience learned to equate the sound of hobnailed boots with Romans and therefore trouble. The Mishnah, the Jewish collection of oral laws and traditions, even records that consequently local footwear had no hobnails so they always knew when Romans were approaching (Shabat 6.2). Juvenal also warned pedestrians about encountering a soldier in the street and getting their toes trodden on. He advises not to provoke soldiers, who might kick their shins in retaliation (*Sat.* iii, 232 7 xvi, 25).

While the nails themselves provided an excellent grip on the rough terrain one would expect on a battlefield, they could cause fatal results on smooth surfaces. During the battle for the Temple of Jerusalem in AD 70 one centurion leading a charge slipped on the temple

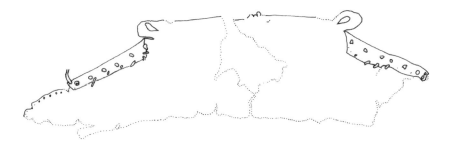

141 Pattern and reconstruction, not to scale, of a closed shoe boot from Mons Claudianus. (*Elaine Norbury after Winterbottom.*)

flagstones and fell on his back, whereupon he was promptly surrounded by the enemy and killed (Josephus. *BJ* VI, 1, 8, 85). Josephus quotes Homer to describe the military boots '*ta hupodemata peparmena puknois*' – 'shoes thickly studded with nails.'

Although the use of nailed soles continued for centuries afterwards it comes as something of a surprise to discover that the classic military *caliga* does not appear to have survived in use beyond the first century AD. This is illustrated in dramatic fashion at the late first century site of Vindolanda where hundreds of examples of footwear survive but the traditional *caligae* are completely absent. The reasons for this are open to speculation. It might simply reflect some difficulty of supply to this particular site, indeed one writing tablet from Vindolanda complains about the poor state of the roads!

Perhaps further evidence of this difficulty in obtaining footwear is that many of the boots from this early phase at Vindolanda had been repaired many times. In some extreme cases boots

had even been worn until all the nails had fallen out and the soles were worn completely flat!
However, later documents from Vindolanda record in minute detail soldiers buying individual
nails for their boots, as few as six in one case but as many as 350 in another! An alternative theory
is that as the army became more and more static and began to settle in permanent bases, the
manufacture of equipment largely passed into the hands of civilian contractors rather than unit
craftsmen on the spot. This might have resulted in uncertainties over delivery and soldiers might
even have been sent away from their fort to collect footwear, as suggested by *P. Gen. lat. Verso V*

Other Styles of Footwear

Evidence of a change in supply policy might be supported by the new style of boots adopted
by the army, which rapidly replaced the old style *caligae*, but this could also be explained simply
by a change in fashion. At Vindolanda various forms of *calcei* exist proving that type at least had
persisted, including a version with the uppers cut into elaborate patterns that were probably meant
to show off the coloured wool socks underneath. The evidence from Vindolanda also suggests that

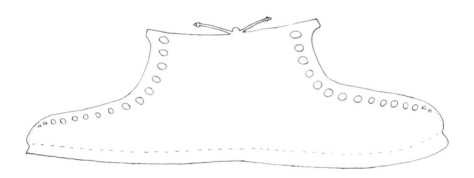

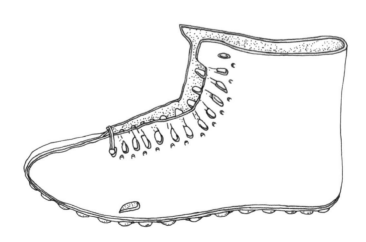

142 Pattern and reconstruction, not to scale, of a 'Fell boot' from Vindolanda. *Elaine Norbury after van
Driel-Murray and Brouwenstein.*

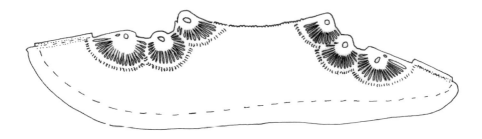

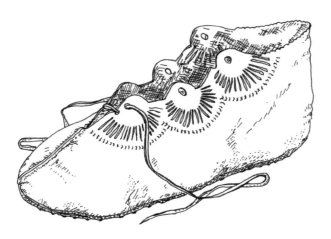

143 Pattern and reconstruction, not to scale, of a shoe boot from Newstead in Scotland. *Elaine Norbury after van Driel-Murray and Goubitz.*

a new type of boot had appeared that had fully enclosed sides and toes giving it a more rugged appearance and something even the modern viewer would recognise as a military boot. Indeed van Driel-Murray has labelled them the 'Fell boot', doubtless due to their similarity to modern climbing boots. In Roman times they were probably classed as *calcei* and when the Emperor Avidius Cassius is described as inspecting his soldiers' clothes, boots, and leg bindings the term *calciamenta* is used and it may well be boots like the Vindolanda type which are referred to (SHA.VI.2).

Compared with earlier *caligae* these new *calcei* would be far easier to mass produce, probably being no different from the type already worn by civilians engaged in any heavy duty occupation. They were made from a single piece of leather which was sewn up at the front. Therefore from the second century AD onwards it is not so easy for archaeologists to identify the presence of soldiers simply by the surviving traces of their boots alone; even male footwear is often only recognisable from those worn by females and children by relative size. Nevertheless the term *caligae* still appears in Roman literature with reference to military boots and sculptures – most famously Trajan's Column and the Adamklissi Tropaeum – continue to show soldiers wearing traditional *caligae*. Furthermore in the third century anyone tall, lanky and awkward apparently earned the nickname 'Maximinus boot' '*caliga Maximini*' after the famously large Emperor Maximinus (SHA *The Two Maximini* XXVIII.9).

It is not known how common it was to wear socks with *caligae*. As Driel-Murray has observed, many surviving insoles preserve the outline of the wearer's foot and toes indicating that socks in these cases were not worn. However with the introduction of the enclosed marching boot

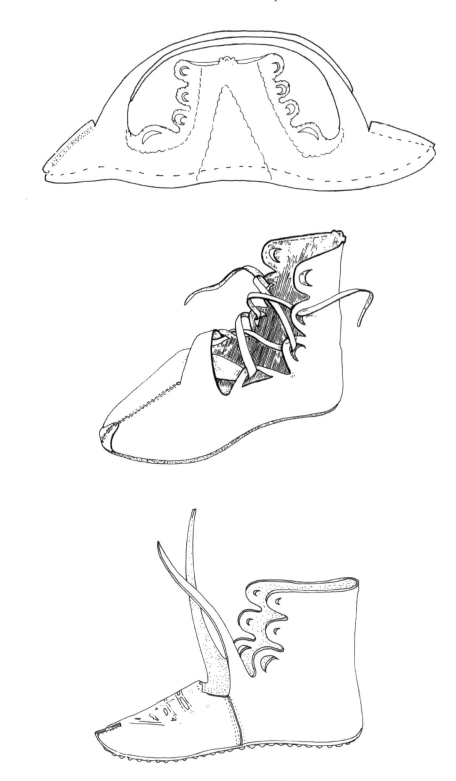

144 Pattern and reconstruction, not to scale, of an early third century integrally laced boot from Zwammerdam, in the Netherlands and below a reconstruction of a similar boot from Vindolanda. *Elaine Norbury after van Driel-Murray, Brouwenstein and Goubitz.*

from the second century onwards soldiers may have worn socks or bindings as a matter of course. One third century tombstone from Apamea appears to show a soldier wearing socks that have been rolled down over the top of his ankle boots, but this is conjectural. However, socks would actually be unnecessary if the soldier was wearing trousers that had integral feet as in the Thorsberg find and the frescoes from Silistra in Bulgaria, which suggests this type of trouser was worn in the Roman Empire too.

An extremely widespread form of footwear in the third century which is attested by both archaeological finds and sculpture is a front-fastening boot that had integrally cut laces. A triangular piece of leather was added at the front for reinforcement and a separate sole was then hobnailed on. From the evidence we have it is tempting to suggest that this was a standard pattern mass produced empire-wide by contractors, since examples of them have been found as far apart as Usk in South Wales and Dura Europos in Syria, both in military and civilian contexts. Vindolanda has revealed its own variant of the integrally laced boot.

However, it was by no means the only type of boot in common usage and indeed, the third century has been described by van Driel-Murray as an age of experimentation and innovation. She also has remarked on how certain styles could be popular at certain times throughout the entire empire and how a number of other features introduced elsewhere display many of the characteristics one normally associates with medieval shoes. These include their sewn construction, the butted side seams and single-layer soles. Older techniques remained in use although boots that retained the openwork cut-outs and strap designs were now made from a single piece of leather rather than the triple-layered construction of earlier times.

The fourth century *Edict of Diocletian* lists two types of *caligae*. Firstly '*caligae primae formae mulionicae sibe rusticae, par sine clavis*' a version for farmers and mule drivers without hobnails selling for 120 denarii and a '*caligae militares sine clabo*' – that is a soldier's boot surprisingly without nails selling for 100 denarii. The Edict also lists a *campagi militares* selling for 75 denarii which Goldman suggests was the boot that totally enclosed the soldier's foot and was the type of footwear that the archaeological evidence from the Northern provinces implies superseded the old style *caligae* as the main type of military footwear.

Carbatinae

A single piece leather shoe frequently found on military sites is the *carbatina*. This has horizontal slits around the upper edge for the insertion of a leather lace. It would appear too delicate to act as a military boot and its presence in and around military sites could easily be explained by the soldiers' families and servants. It is also of course conceivable that the soldiers themselves wore such footwear when they were off duty.

Crepidae

Crepidae were more delicate versions of the *caligae* and was a type of footwear adopted from the Greeks. They were more suited for leisure wear and when Suetonius describes the Emperor Tiberius wearing *crepidae* with a *pallium* cloak instead of exercising in Roman dress on the parade ground he conjures up an image of the retired modern gentleman with his dressing gown, pipe and slippers (*Tiberius* 13). Nevertheless the fact that on occasion soldiers wore this type of footwear too is dramatically brought to light by an incident which took place in Egypt. On one occasion a slave of the Governor of Alexandria was killed by a soldier for saying that he had better sandals (*crepidas*) than he had (SHA *Aemilanus* XXII 3).

Sculponae

One non-military type of footwear that soldiers would nevertheless use on a regular basis were the wooden clogs that are sometimes found on northern sites such as Vindolanda on Hadrian's Wall. Further examples of almost identical design come from the Saalburg fort and other sites in Germany and Holland. They have a thick wooden soles and a carved heel, with some further re-enforced with nails. It would appear that it was the element of carving (*sculpere*) involved in their manufacture which gave rise to their name.

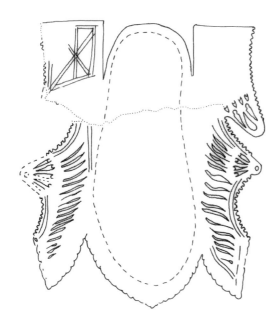

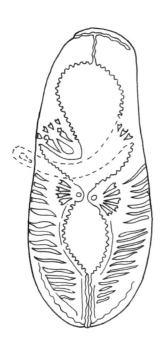

145 Hybrid pattern and reconstruction of
one of the Deurne shoes. *Elaine Norbury
after van Driel-Murray.*

They would have slipped on over the foot like modern slippers and been held in place by a broad leather strap which was sometimes decorated and was fastened at the sides by metal nails. The raised soles and heels would protect the wearer from damp while the wood provided better insulation than a leather boot against heat. Both these conditions would of course be found when the soldier went to the fort bath-house, making *sculponae* the ideal footwear to wear on those occasions.

Nonetheless just to confuse matters a Vindolanda tablet refers to *balnearia* 'shoes for bathing'. Perhaps these are the versions with the more decorative leather bands. Others by comparison have simple crude strips of leather and clogs fitted with these may have been for workers such as stable hands and those in the fulling and dyeing workshops.

Late Military Footwear

Nailed footwear was still much in evidence until at least the end of the fourth century, although there are cases where examples of shoes come in nailed and un-nailed versions. After the third century there are few noticeable changes; open and closed types of boots continue to be represented in the pictorial record, and shoe styles from this period are still around in the early Byzantine era.

Three pairs of shoes each of a different style were found in a peat bog at Deurne in the Netherlands along with other Roman items including a superb gilded helmet. One shoe still retained a spur indicating it had been used by a cavalryman. They had all been made from a single piece of thick cow hide sewn with a plain seam.

Closed *calcei* were still used throughout the fifth and sixth centuries. Pointed, nailed *calcei* can be linked with Germanic *Equites Batavi* levies stationed in the Theodosian barracks at Arras during the fourth and fifth centuries because almost 40 specimens were discovered there. A similar specimen comes from Aquileia in Italy while others from Panopolis in Egypt show a highly decorated surface, often with incised lines. Some pictorial sources similar show boots with lacing across both the open instep and ankle.

The *Strategikon* provides evidence for the use of Gothic shoes.

> They (the infantry) should have Gothic shoes with thick soles, broad toes, plain stitching, and fastened with no more than two clasps; the soles should be studded with a few small nails for greater durability. Boots or greaves are not required, for they are unsuitable for marching and if worn slow one down.

The Roman soldier had marched a long way!

BELTS

Compared with boots the evidence for belts archaeologically is practically negligible. This is at first very surprising considering every soldier would have owned at least one belt as well as a pair of boots. Bishop and Coulston suggest that this lack of evidence might have been because belts were oiled or alum-tawed whereas boots were tanned and that they have a better chance of survival. Another possibility is that many broken belts were simply recycled. Two belts made of goat leather did survive in a fourth century context at Augst in Switzerland and a more elaborate belt with incised decoration including a dolphin motif and a metal disc was part of the material found in a waterlogged deposit at Vimose in Denmark. Although outside Roman territory this was evidently a Roman belt and this is a rare glimpse of this piece of equipment expected elsewhere but sadly for the most part lost.

A belt was used to help hitch up the tunic above the knee to allow freedom of movement. This was one of the most visible aspects of soldiers' dress when not in armour and helped to distinguish soldiers from civilians who generally wore their tunics below the knee or loose to ankle length. Depriving a soldier of his belt, so that his tunic hung loose like a civilian's was in fact a minor punishment. The offending soldier was then made to stand in the camp for all to see. Frontinus tells us that Gaius Titius a cohort commander, who had retreated before an army of slaves, had to endure this form of humiliation (*Strat.*, IV, 1.26). This practice continued into the late empire (*Cod Just.* XII, 7).

The Emperor Julian added an interesting twist to this form of punishment after a squadron of cavalry broke ranks and fled at the battle of Strasbourg. Julian dressed the offenders in womens' clothing (Zozimus, *HN.* 3.3. 4–5). A similar fate befell the military martyrs Sergius and Bacchus who were accused of being Christians (BHL 7599). They were stripped of their cloaks and other military garments and forced to parade in female dress.

Until recently it was thought the popular term for the military belt was the *cingulum militare* or *militiae*. However Bishop and Coulston point out that the term *cingulum* was largely unknown before the third century and in fact Varro states that a *cingillum* was worn by women (*De ling. Lat.*V, 114)! Instead they suggest that numerous papyri and literary sources indicate that the more appropriate term would simply be *balteus*.

One unexpected function of the belt was discovered by the early re-enactors of the Ermine Street Guard was that it helped to take some of the weight of the mail shirts off the shoulders and dispersed it on to the hips. Plain belts are clearly illustrated in Republican pictorial sources including the Altar of Domitius Ahenobarbus and the Aemillius Paullus monument which both appear to illustrate soldiers wearing mail shirts.

By the late Republic archaeological evidence suggests belts were decorated with elaborate metal plates and so even if the belts themselves do not survive it is possible to estimate their size which can also be compared with the various depictions in Roman art. Examples of plates from the site of Numantia in Spain feature openwork or interlaced designs. Over the following centuries belt designs followed a variety of fashions and methods of attaching the sword and dagger. The single belt apparently gave way at the beginning of the Imperial era to two narrow belts which were worn crossed, popularly described as 'cowboy fashion'. Shortly afterwards this method was abandoned and a single but wider belt was introduced.

In the first century AD a popular fashion widely seen on many tombstones was to have a suspended 'apron', in reality a number of strips hanging from the belt in front of the groin. Like the main belt itself these apron strips were decorated with metal fittings, usually studs, furthermore each strap had elaborate terminals in the form of lunate or teardrop pendants. The various forms of belt decoration have been discussed at length by Bishop and Coulston, while Bishop himself has also documented the different types of apron and their own distinctive decoration.

Modern experiments have indicated that the aprons had little practical defensive value. There purpose may have been for modesty as suggested earlier but equally likely explanations are that they both highlighted the visual importance and status of the belt and therefore the wearer and moreover that they also had a psychological effect. Any form of movement would cause the various apron components to clash together and make a noise. An analogy with a western gun slingers spurs is probably not too far off the mark. The sound of thousands of moving, jingling parts combined with the crunch of the hobnailed boots must have advertised the approach of any Roman army from miles away, rather like the famous sequence in the film *Zulu* when the sound of an advancing Zulu army is likened to that of an approaching train.

Whatever its purpose the apron gradually declined in size and does not appear to have lasted beyond the Hadrianic period. Swords appear more and more to be suspended from a baldric crossing over the shoulder. At first these are narrow and both sculptures and the Fayum portraits illustrate that they were decorated with metal discs. As discussed previously the Chatsworth relief also suggests that at some point in the Hadrianic period a secondary belt may also have been worn over the shoulder. Like the baldric which suspended the sword it too may have been decorated with metal discs. In the early Imperial period by and large ordinary soldiers appear to wear their swords on their right side while centurions wore theirs on the more familiar left side.

By the third century the sword baldric became wider and was worn over the right shoulder by all ranks. One of the examples discovered at Vimose was 80mm wide and around 1.185m long. In keeping with examples shown on tombstones it was decorated with a disc *phalera* but the lower end was straight while many sculptural examples appear to show the end cut into an ivy leaf shaped terminal. The sword was attached by a slide to thin straps, part of the baldric itself. Compared with earlier examples the waist belt appears less elaborate. It was often fastened by a ring shaped buckle and straps passing through the buckle from behind were secured at the front either side of the buckle by a stud.

In some cases the strap end on the wearer's right continued, passing in a curved loop back under and over the belt to hang down on the right hip. Before the end it was split into two and like the earlier apron straps, each end was finished off with a metal terminal. As well as being decorative the terminals probably had the same function as before, to produce a noise and make a soldier's presence felt. Also, like the earlier aprons, some tombstones show the soldier fondling the straps and terminals between his fingers, perhaps as an artistic device to draw attention to the belt. Belts continue to be decorated with a variety of metal fittings and plates, sometimes much cruder and simpler than before. James has gone into more detail on mid-third century belts with special reference to the finds from Dura Europos.

Ring buckle belts and broad baldrics are no longer apparent by the reigns of Diocletian and Constantine. Some waist belts are now at their broadest with a width of about 140mm which can be accurately estimated by the surviving decoration and some of the decorative elements are probably at their most ostentatious. This is often seen as evidence of the growing influence of the non-Roman troops serving at all levels within the Imperial armies but this is far from clear. As we have seen from other aspects of military dress the empire and the frontier areas around it had become a huge melting pot of ideas, fashions and influences so it becomes unclear who is copying who.

Many of the decorative elements of these belt designs feature geometric patterns or swirls. Others however incorporate more classical elements including possible Imperial portraits. Others would not look out of place amongst the very earliest belt plates found at Numantia! One of the most easily recognisable forms is the type known affectionately today as the 'propeller' type. Their appearance on the belts worn by soldiers depicted on the Arch of Constantine also helps to identify figures in the Piazza Armerina mosaic as soldiers. Other decorations consist of 'chip-carved' plates and strap ends.

According to D'Amato, from the second quarter of the sixth century Roman soldiers were equipped with composite belts that appear to incorporate fittings and pendants of silver, gold, bronze and gilded bronze. Vandal warriors illustrated in mosaics from North Africa dating from the beginning of the century have pendant belts and Procopius describes Belisarius distributing gold belts as booty to his troops after their victorious campaign against the Vandals (BV, IV, 9). D'Amato suggests that the silver-furnished belt sets from the Crimea and the western Black Sea coast may confirm their earlier use in that region by Roman soldiers stationed in the Bosphorus area.

THE LEATHER INDUSTRY

Forbes lists the specialist leather workers that already existed by the Imperial period. These include the thong-maker (*loriarius*), saddler (*capistarius*), tent-maker (*tabernacularius*), shield-maker (*scutarius*), maker of leather armour (*loricarius*), wine-skin maker (*utricularius*) and the maker of leather water-skins (*ampullarius*). As we know from Vindolanda that there was a unit brewer, all of the above occupations could conceivably have been carried out in any of the fort workshops, (*Fabricae*) by soldiers, and Tarruntenus includes tanners in his list of *immunes,* that is, specialist soldiers exempt from general duties (*Digest* 50.6.7.6).

The army was undoubtedly the single largest consumer of leather and leather goods in the Roman world and we have already seen that a single legion probably required around 36,000 boots in a single year. However, there is little evidence for leather clothing in a military context.

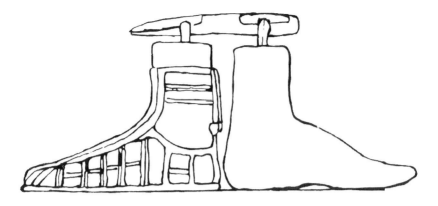

146 Detail of a tombstone of a Roman shoemaker from the Capitoline Museum in Rome. It shows the left and right lasts (*formae*) and illustrates a *caliga* on the left one. The *caliga* also has a tail coming from the back of the ankle, like a boot from Vindolanda. *Elaine Norbury after Goldman.*

This might be because it was not used very often but equally the evidence might not have survived for the same reasons that belts do not. This equally applies to the contentious issue of leather armour. While it is clear that some form of Roman leather armour did exist, such as the pieces from Dura Europos which might account for the existence of a *loricarius* mentioned by Forbes, the very idea that regular soldiers in the Imperial armies could be equipped with leather armour is generally treated by modern scholars with scorn. In fact there is no practical reason for this viewpoint as there are several documented cases of leather being used as body armour even up to the age of gunpowder.

According to Cicero, L. Calpurnius Piso was sent to Macedonia to requisition all the cattle needed to provide equipment for the army (*In Pis.* 36.870). Although Forbes suggested some of the hides obtained by this expedition was to be shaped into armour and shields there is little to support this statement but the passage still illustrates the army's insatiable demand for leather. It has been estimated that 46,000 goats alone would be needed to equip one legion with tents!

Makers of the nailed military boots were called *caligarii* (C.I.L.VI.9225) and in keeping with other tradesmen, leather workers formed guilds and the leather guild was one of the earliest established in Rome. The practice of forming guilds spread to other Roman cities but naturally leatherworkers may have settled closer to the large army camps. Shoemakers used a number of special tools that changed little over the centuries. These included knives, awls, wooden lasts, and a small anvil which was required when hobnailing the soles. Metal circular and semicircular punches were used to make the lace holes. Only a half moon shaped knife and foot shaped last were distinctive tools of the shoemaker and therefore it is these items which appear on a shoemaker's cinerary urn from Altino, Italy.

The main stages of turning hides into leather are firstly the preservation then the preparation of the hide for tanning. The skin has to be cleaned and washed. Then liming takes place so the skin will then accept any of a number of tanning agents of which there are three main types. Vegetable tanning involves using the natural tannic acid which is found in barks, leaves, wood, nuts and fruit. Mineral tanning uses certain mineral salts and alum, and oil tanning using oxygenated fish or animal oils. There is certainly evidence that the Romans used the first two of these processes.

Remains of a Roman tannery were discovered at Pompeii. Like the laundry described earlier it had been converted from a house and the once grand atrium was used for the treatment of hides. In another room were 15 pits in which vegetable tanning took place.

147 Tombstones from Reims
and Bourges in France show
shoemakers at work. *Elaine
Norbury after van Driel-Murray.*

Other pits were used for mineral tanning. At the back of the house the fermenting solutions and tanning infusions were prepared. Pliny quoting Cato says that boiled lees of olive oil was used to grease not only the axles of wheels but also all leather articles and shoes (Cato *R.R.* CXXX, XCI ff.) Tanning was a smelly occupation and tanners were probably not popular neighbours!

In the rubbish dump outside the legionary fortress at Vindonissa near Basle in Switzerland a large collection of leather was found. This was mostly of goat skin but soles of boots were made from cow hide. Footwear was often stamped or inscribed, sometimes incised but at other times impressed with a dye. Some footwear is marked with numerals but sadly Driel-Murray points out that this is unlikely to represent the shoe size! Other markings are clearly a form of decoration. Military boots from the first and early second century have a simple tail with a decorated end hanging from the centre back.

Colour rarely survives on leather shoes but many were probably left their natural colour. Colour paintings show red and black coloured footwear and some examples of boots dyed with purple from the murex have been found. Black leather could be obtained by using melentaria which is a copper-vitriol containing iron, then painting the leather with tar. Driel-Murray also believes coloured twine could have been another inexpensive form of decoration.

ACKNOWLEDGEMENTS

This book could not have been completed without the help and assistance of numerous individuals and institutions over the years, whose contributions great and small have all made this current work possible.

Firstly I am indebted to John Peter Wild who not only wrote the foreword to this book but who also generously found the time to read through the text in its many stages and formats. The works by him listed in the bibliography provided the starting point for much of the text and also the inspiration for some of the artworks in this study. Nevertheless they are only a small fraction of the immeasurable contribution he has made to the study of Roman textiles.

Raffaele D'Amato also made many suggestions to both text and illustrations. He not only provided numerous sources for both but also kindly allowed access to his own concurrent research for our joint project on Roman arms and armour. His assistance throughout has added greatly to this book and I owe him a great debt.

I would also like to thank Ross Cowan for his many valuable comments. In addition he kindly supplied a number of pictures from his own collection. At short notice both Elaine Norbury and Charles W. Evans-Gunther stepped in to help out with both text and black and white illustrations. Paul Holder has also been on hand many times to answer difficult questions and to find some awkward sources.

For almost twenty years I was a member of The Ermine Street Guard, the world's first Roman military re-enactment society. The group has earned many accolades since it was founded in 1972 and it was fitting that its chairman Chris Haines was honoured in 2008 with the MBE for his services to Roman military research and education. It was due in no small part to my membership of the re-enactment community that I began my quest to learn more about the clothing of the Roman soldier, not least because I nearly froze to death on several occasions dressed in a flimsy tunic and cloak! Former Guard colleagues in particular Martin White, Tony Segalini, Chris Jowett, Pete Johnson, John Hindle, Derek Forrest, Clive Constable and Chris Haines himself, cheerfully posed on several occasions for countless paintings.

Thanks to Derek Forrest I discovered the Roman Army Talk Forum and since joining I have had numerous debates and discussions on military clothing and its practical aspects and uses, with many of its members including Robert Vermaat, John Conyard, Travis Lee Clerk, Jim Bowers, Paul Geddes, Ivan Perelló, Cesar Pocinya, Carme Rodriguez, Aitor Iriarte, Dan Diffendale, Martin Moser, John Mc Dermott and Adrian Wink. Special thanks must also go to Jasper Oorthuys, Jenny Cline, Luca Bonacina and Florian Himmler who all supplied some of their own photographs for use in this volume. I would recommend the forum to anyone wishing to learn more about the Roman army and re-enactment in general. Another invaluable starting point for study of the Romans and clothing in particular is the Lacus Curtius website run by Bill Thayer.

There would be nothing to discuss at all without the unstinting efforts of the archaeologists who find the evidence in the first place, which in the case of Roman period textiles often means spending long periods of time in some very inhospitable parts of the world, and also the specialists who then analyse their findings. Lise Bender Jørgensen, Penelope Walton-Rogers, Carol van Driel-Murray, Mike Bishop, Simon James, Cäcilia Fluck, Susan Moller-Wiering, Petra Linscheid, Fiona Handley, Hero Granger-Taylor, Dominique Cardon, Frances Pritchard and Annette Paetz gen Schieck have all assisted in one way or the other at various stages of my research. Most have supplied me with photographs, kindly sent me copies of their own work or just pointed me in the right direction. Most importantly of all, none of them have ever said to me 'just stick to painting!'

Many others have offered continued support or words of encouragement for my work over the years while others have also supplied photographs for this volume. They include Robin and Pat Birley of the Vindolanda Museum, Tim Strickland, Michael Speidel, Peter Connolly, Andrea Bußmann of the Rheinisches LandesMuseum Bonn, Malcolm Chapman and Phyllis Stoddart of the Manchester Museum, Thomas Zühmer of the Rheinisches Landesmuseum Trier, Megan Doyon of the Yale University Art Gallery, Russell Hartman of the California Academy of Sciences, Tom Hardwick of the Bolton Museum and Art Gallery, Alan Jeffrey Spencer and Ivor Kerslake of the The British Museum, Sarah Williams of the Museum of London and Robert B. Partridge, editor of Ancient Egypt magazine.

Finally I would like to thank Peter Kemmis-Betty of The History Press who commissioned the work, to Wendy Logue who took over as editor and who patiently awaited the manuscript and illustrations and to Miranda Embleton-Smith for bringing the book to completion. My apologies to anyone who has been left out and for any errors or omissions which may have crept in and which are entirely my responsibility.

Graham Sumner MAAI&S
Flint 2008.

BIBLIOGRAPHY

ABBREVIATIONS AND TRANSLATIONS OF PRIMARY SOURCES

Apuleius. (*Met*) *Metamorphoses*. The Golden Ass English Translation by R. Graves. Penguin Classics, Harmondsworth 1950.

Arrian. (*Tact*) *Techne Takitika*, or (*Ars Tact*) *Ars Tacitica*. English Translation A.G. Roos revised G.W. Wirth, in Hyland A. 1993.

Isidorus of Seville (Is.) *Etymologiae* (Et.). Latin text in Isidori Hispanensis Episcopi Etymologiarum sive Originum Libri xx, ed. W.M. Lindsay i-ii, Oxford, 1911. Translations courtesy of Raffaele D'Amato.

Lactantius (*Lact*.), *De Mortibus Persecutorum* - Of the Manner in Which the Persecutors Died (*Mort. Pers.*). Latin and English in *De Mortibus Persecutorum*, edited and translated by J.L. Creed, Oxford, 1984, 'Oxford Early Christian Texts' series.

Lydus. (*De Mag*) *De Magistratibus Reipublicae Romanae* - On the Magistrates.

Maurice. (*Strat*) *Strategikon*. Translated by G.T. Dennis UPP, 1984

Palladius, *Historia Lausiaca*;

DOM CUTHBERT BUTLER, *Palladius, The Lausiac History; I. A critical discussion; II. The Greek text* in *Texts and Studies*, VI (Cambridge, 1898, 1904)

Paulinus. (*EP*)

Pontius Meropius Paulinus: *Epistulae/Briefe*. translatae a Matthias Skeb. Herder-Verlag, Friburgi, Basiliae, Vindobonae anno 1998 (Series Fontes Christiani, vol. 25, 1–3).

Servius. (*In Aen*) *In Aeneadem* – Commentary on the Aeneid.

Synesius of Cyrene . *(De Reg) De Regno*

English translation in http://www.livius.org/su-sz/synesius/synesius_monarchy_00.html

Tertullian. *De Corona*. On the crown of the soldier.

Terullian. *De Pallio*. On the Pallium.

Varro. *(De Re Rust) De Re Rustica* – On Agriculture.

Varro. *(DLL) De lingua Latina* – on the latin language.

Vegetius. *(Epit Rei Mil) Epitoma Rei Militaris* – Epitome of Military Science.

Translated by N.P. Milner. Liverpool University Press 1993.

All the following are Loeb Classical Library available from Harvard University Press. www. hup.harvard.edu/loeb/author.html

Ammianus Marcellinus. (Amm. Marc.) *Res Gestae*. Translated by J.C. Rolfe.

Appian. Roman History. The Civil Wars. Translated by H. White.

Aulus Gellius. *(Noct Act)* Attic Nights. Translated by J.C. Rolfe. .

Caesar. (*BC*) *Bello Civilis*. Civil War. Translated by A.G. Peskett.

Caesar. (*BG*) *Bello Gallico*. Gallic War. Translated by H.J. Edwards.

Caesar. (*BA*) (*BH*) (*BAL*) *De Bello Africano, De Bello Hispaniensi, De Bello Alexandrino*. African War, Spanish War, Alexandrian War. Translated by A.G. Way.

Cassus Dio. *Romaika*. Roman History. Translated by E. Clary.

Cato. *(De Agri)* On Agriculture. Translated by W.D. Hooper revised H.B. Ash.

Catullus. *(Carm) Carmina*. Poems. Translated By F.W. Cornish.

Cicero. *(Ad Att)* *Epistulae ad atticum.* Letters to Atticus. Translted by E.O. Windstedt.

Cicero. *(Pro Ses)* *Pro Sestio* . On behalf of Sestius. Translated by R. Gardner.

Columella. *(de Re Rust)* *De Re Rustica.* On Agriculture. Vol. 1 translated by H.B. Ash.

Dionysius of Halicarnassus. *(Rom)* *Roman Antiquities.* Translated by E. Clary.

Frontinus. *(strat)* *Stratagemata.* Translated by C.E. Bennett.

Herodian. *(Rom. Hist.)* History of the Empire from the time of Marcus Aurelius.

Horace. *(EP)* *Epistulae – Epistles.* Translated by H. R. Fairclough.

Horace. *Odes.* Translated by C.E. Bennett.

Jerome. *(EP)* *Epistulae. Letters.* Translated by F.A. Wright.

Josephus. *(AJ)* *Antiquitates Judaicae.* Jewish Antiquities 9. vols. Translated by H. St. J. Thackery, R. Marcus, A Wikgren & L.H. Feldman.

Josephus. *(BJ)* *Bellum Judaicum – Jewish War.* Translated by H. St. J. Thackery.

Livy. History of Rome from the founding of the city. Translations by B.O. Foster F.G. Moore, E.T. Sage and A.C. Schlesinger.

Lucanus. *Pharsalia* – The Battle of Pharsalus. Translated by J.D. Duff.

Martial. *(EP)* *Epigrammata.* Epigrams. Translated by D.R. Shackleton.

Ovid. *(Ars Amat)* *Ars Amatoria.* Translated by J.H. Mozley.

Ovid. *(Fasti)* – The Calendar. Translated by J.G. Frazer, rev G.P. Goold.

Ovid. *(meta)* *Metamorphoses.* Translated by F.J. Miller.

Petronius. *(Sat)* *Satyricon.* Translated by M. Heseltine & W.H.D. Rouse.

Plautus. *(MG)* *Miles Gloriosus.* Translated by P. Nixon.

Pliny the Elder. *(HN)* *Historia Naturalis.* Natural History. Translated by H. Rackman.

Plutarch. Lives. Translated by B. Perrin.

Polybius. Histories. Translated by W.R. Paton.

Procopius. History of the Wars. Translated by B.H. Dewing.

Propertius. *(EL)* *Elegliae* – Elegies. Translated by G.P. Goold.

Quintilian. *(Inst Or)* *Institutio Oratoria.* Translated by D.A. Russell.

Scriptores Historiae Augustae (SHA). Translated by D. Magie.

Seneca. *(Q. Nat)* *Quaestones Naturales* – Natural questions. Translated by T.H. Corcoran.

Silius Italicus. *(Pun)* *Punica* – Carthaginian War. Translated by J.D. Duff.

Strabo. *(Geogr)* *Geographica.* Translated by H.L. Jones.

Suetonius. The Twelve Caesars. Translated by J.C. Rolfe.

Tacitus. *(Ann)* *Annales.* Translated by C.H. Moore & J. Jackson.

Tacitus. *(Hist)* *Histores.* Translated by C.H. Moore & J. Jackson.

Valerius Flaccus. *Argonautica.* Translated by J.H. Mozley.

Valerius Maximus *(Mem).* Nine Books of Memorable Deeds and Sayings. Tranlated by J.H. Mozely.

Vergil. *(Aen)* *Aeneid.* Translated by H.R. Fairclough.

MODERN WORKS

JRMES Journal of Roman Military Equipment Studies.

OTHER MODERN SOURCES

Alexander, J.J.G. 1979: 'The Illustrations of the de Rebus Bellicis' in Hassale and Ireland, 1979, 11–15.

Alfaro, C., Wild, J.P., and Costa, B. (eds.) 2004: *Purpureae Vestes,* Universitat de València.

Anderson, A.S. 1984: *Roman Military Tombstones,* Princes Risborough.

Antolini, L. 1995: *L'Ipogeo di Santa Maria in Stelle,* Verona.

Antonucci, C. 1994: 'The Praetorians: The Bodyguard of the Emperor Trajan, second century AD' in *Ancient Warrior* Vol. 1. 94/95, Stockport.

Antonucci, C. 1996: *L'Esercito di Cesare 54–44 AC,* Milan.

Argüín, A.R.M. 2006: *Pretorianos: La Guardia Imperial de la Antigua Roma,* Madrid.

Baatz, D. 1986: 'Carbatina – Ein lateinischer Schuhname?', *Saalburg-Jaarbuch* 42, 64–7.

Badaway, A. 1978: *Coptic Art and Archaeology: The Art of the Christian Egyptians from the Late Antique to the Middle Ages,* Cambridge, Mass.

Bagnall, R.S. and Rathbone, D.W. 2004: *Egypt from Alexander to the Copts,* British Museum.

Baldassarre, I and Pugliesse Carratelli, G. 1993: *Pitture E Mosaici,* Rome.

Balty, J. 1969: *La Grande Mosaique de Chasse du Triclinos,* Brussells.

Banck, A. 1966: *Byzantine Art in the collections of the USSR,* Leningrad & Moscow.

Bandinelli, R. 1970: *Rome, the Centre of Power: Roman Art to AD 200,* London.

Bandinelli, R. 1971: *Rome, the Late Empire: Roman Art AD 200–400,* London.

Becatti, G. 1968: *The Art of Ancient Greece and Rome,* London.

Bèjaoui, F. et al, 1994: *I mosaici Romani di Tunisia,* Paris.

Bellinger, A., et al, 1956: *The Excavations at Dura-Europos Final Report VIII part I: The Synagogue,* Yale.

Bender Jorgensen, L. 1979: 'Cloth of the Roman Iron Age in Denmark' *Acta Archaeologica* 50, 1–60.

Bender Jorgensen, L. 1986: *Forhistoriske Textiler i Skandinavien,* Copenhagen.

Bender Jørgensen, L.1991:'Textiles from Mons Claudianus: a preliminary report', *Acta Hyperborea* 3, 83–95.

Bender Jørgensen, L.1992: *North European Textiles until AD 1000*, Aarhus.

Bender Jørgensen, L. 2000:'The Mons Claudianus Textile Project' in Cardon, D., and Feugère, M. 2000, 253–263.

Bender Jørgensen, L. and Mannering, U. 2001:'Mons Claudianus: investigating Roman textiles in the desert' in Walton-Rogers, P. Bender Jørgensen, L. and Rast-Eicher, A. 2001, 1–11.

Bender Jørgensen, L. 2003:'Kriegdragten i folkevandringstiden in Snartemofunnene i nytt lys', in Rolfsen, P., and Stylegar F., (ed.), Oslo.

Bender Jørgensen, L. 2004a:'A matter of material: changes in textiles from Roman sites in Egypt's Eastern Desert', *Antiquité Tardive 12*, 87–99.

Bender Jørgensen, L. 2004b:'Teamwork on Roman Textiles: The Mons Claudianus Textile Project' in Alfaro, C., Wild, J.P., and Costa, B., (eds.) 2004, 69–75.

Bender Jørgensen, L. 2006:'The late Roman Fort at Abū Shaār, Egypt: Textiles in their Archaeological context' in Schrenk, S., (ed.): Textiles in situ, Riggisberger Berichte, 2006, 161–173.

Bielajev, N.M. 1926:'Decoration of Late Roman and Early Byzantine Tunica', *Seminarium Kondakovianum*, Prague.

Bierbrier, M.L. (ed.), 1997: *Portraits and Masks: Burial Customs in Roman Egypt*, London.

Birley R. 1977: *Vindolanda: A Roman Frontier Post on Hadrian's Wall*, London.

Bisconti, F., and Mazzei, B. 2002: *Il restauro delle pitture nelle Catacombe Romane*, Vatican City.

Bisconti, F. 2000: *Mestieri nelle catacombe romane*, Vatican City.

Bishop, M.C. 1981: *The Development of Roman Military Equipment in the First Century AD and its Relevance to the Army and Society*, Sheffield.

Bishop, M.C.1983:'The Camomile Street Soldier reconsidered', *Trans LAMAS* 34, 31–48.

Bishop, M.C. 1992:'The Early Imperial Apron', *JRMES* 10, 27–43.

Bishop, M.C. and Coulston, J.C.N. 1993 revised ed 2006: *Roman Military Equipment*, Oxford.

Bishop, M.C.1995:'Aketon, Thoracomachus, and Lorica Segmentata', *Exercitus* Vol. 3, No.1.

Björklund, E. *et al*, 1996: *Roman Reflections in Scandinavia*, Rome.

Björklund, E. 1996: *Romerska Speglinger*, Malmö Museer.

Blas de Roblès, J.M., and Sintes, C. 2003: *Sites et monuments antiques de l'Algerie*, Aix-en-Provence.

Blazquez, J.M. 1982:'Mosaicos Romanos de la Real Acacemia de la Historia, Ciudad Real, Toledo, Madrid Y Cuenca', *Corpus de Mosaicos de Espana*, Fasc.V, Madrid.

Boak, A. and Youtie, H.C.1960: *The Archive of Aurelius Isidorus*, Ann Arbor.

Böhme-Schönberger, A.1997: *Kleidung und Schmuck in Rom und den Provinzen*, Stuttgart.

Borg, B. 1996, *Mumienporträts*, Mainz.

Borgard, P. and Puybaret, M.P. 2004:'Le Travail de la laine au début de l'Empire: L'Apport du Modèle Pompéien. Quels Artisans? Quels Equipments? Quelles Techniques?' in Alfaro, C., Wild, J.P., and Costa, B., (eds.) 2004, 47–59.

Borger, H., et al, 1974: *Römer Illustrierte*, Cologne.

Boschung, D.1997: *Die Antiken Skulpturen in Chatsworth*, Mainz.

Bou, F.T. *Centcelles,* Museu Nacional Archeològic de Tarragona.

Bowman. A.K. 1994: *Life and Letters on the Roman Frontier.* London.

Bowman, A. K. and Thomas J.D. 1996:'New writing tablets from Vindolanda', *Britannia* 27: 299–328.

Bowman, A.K.1986: *Egypt After the Pharaohs*, British Museum.

Bowman, A.K. and Thomas, J.D. 1994: *The Vindolanda Writing Tablets* (Tab Vind II), London.

Bowman, A.K. and Thomas, J.D. 2003: *The Vindolanda Writing Tablets* (Tab Vind III), London.

Breccia, E. 1926: *Monuments de L'Egypte Gréco-Romaine*, Bergamo.

Brogiolo, G.P. and Chavarria Arnau, A. 2007: *I Longobardi, dalla caduta dell'Impero all'alba dell'Italia,* Cinisello Balsamo.

Bruwier, M.C. (ed.), 1997: *Egyptiennes Étoffes Coptes du Nil*, Mariemont.

Burnham, D. 1972:'Coptic Knitting: An Ancient Technique', *Textile History* 3, 116–124.

Bussoni, M. 2004:'Libia, meraviglie tra mare e deserto', in *Archeo*, anno XX, nr. IV (230), April 2004.

Campbell, B.1994: *The Roman Army 31 BC–AD 337 A Sourcebook*, London.

Carandini, A., *et al*, 1982: *Filosfiana La Villa di Piazza Armerina*, Palermo.

Cardon, D. and Feugère, M. 2000: *Archéologie des Textiles des Origines au Ve Siècle*, Actes du Colloque des Lattes, *Octobre 1999*, Montagnac.

Cardon, D. 2002:'Chiffons dans le désert: textiles des *praesidia* de Maximianon, Krokodilô et Didymoi (fin du Ier-fin du IIIe siècle ap. J.-C.)', in Durand, M. and F. Saragoza (ed) 2002, *Egypte, la Trame de l'Histoire*. Paris: Somogy, p.42, fig. 2..

Cardon, D., et al, 2004:'Dye analyses of selected textiles from Maximianon, Krokodilô and Didymoi (Egypt)' in Alfaro, C., Wild, J.P., and Costa, B., (eds.), 145–154.

Cardon, D., H. Granger-Taylor and W. Nowik (forthcoming) 'What did they look like? Clothing textiles from Didymoi: case studies' in Cuvigny, H. (ed.) *Didymoi – Une garrison romaine dans le désert Oriental d'Égypte*. Cairo: IFAO.

Charlesworth, D. and Thornton, J.H. 1973:'Leather found in Mediobogdum, the Roman Fort of Hardknott', *Britannia* 4, 141–152.

Catullo, L. 2000: *L'antica Villa Romana del Casale di Piazza Armerina*, Messina.

Cichorius, C. 1896 and 1900: *Die Reliefs der Trajansäule*, Berlin.

Clarke, D.V., Breeze, D.J. and Mackay, G. 1980: *The Romans in Scotland*, Edinburgh.

Cledat, J. 1904:'Le Monastère et la Nécropole de Baouit' in *MIFAO* XII, Cairo.

Cleland, L. (ed.), *et al*, 2005: *The Clothed Body in the Ancient World*, Oxford.

Close-Brooks, J. 1981:'The Bridgeness Distance Slab', *PSAS* 111.

Connolly, P. 2006: *Greece and Rome at War*, London.

Cotton, H.M., and Geiger, R., 1989: *The Latin and Greek Documents: Masada II, The Yigael Yadin Excavations 1963–1965, Final Reports*, Jerusalem.

Cowan, R. 2003: *Imperial Roman Legionary*, Oxford.

Cowan, R. 2003: *Roman Legionaries 58 BC – AD 69*, Oxford.

Crawford, D.S. (ed.), 1955: *Papyri Michaelidae*, Aberdeen.

Croom, A.T. 2000: *Roman Clothing and Fashion*, Stroud.

Cumont, F. 1926,'Fouilles de Doura-Europos 1922–23', Geuthner, Paris.

D'Amato, R. and Sumner, G. 2005: *Roman Military Clothing 3*, Oxford.

D'Amato, R. 2007: *The Eastern Romans 330–1461 AD*, Hong Kong.

D'Amato, R. 2009: From Herculaneum's Ashes: A *Faber Navalis* of AD 79. In *Ancient Warfare* Vol III Issue 2.

D'Amato. R. & Sumner. G. 2009: *The Arms and Armour of the Imperial Roman Soldier*, London..

Daniels, C. 1989: *Mithras and his Temples on the Wall*, Gateshead.

Davies. R. 1989: *Service in the Roman Army*, (ed.) Breeze, D & Maxfield,V..

De Haas, P. 1991:'The Fascia Ventralis: A follow up', *Arma* Vol. 3, No.1, 6–9.

de Heredia Bercero J.B., Bonnet, C., Alaix, C.M., and López, G. R., 1997: *The Archaeological Remains of Plaça del Rei*, Barcelona.

de Heredia Bercero, J.B. 1997:'Fullonica and Tinctoria, Fabrics, Dyes and Laundry in the Ancient Roman Colony' in de Heredia Bercero J.B., Bonnet, C., Alaix, C.M., and López, G. R., de Llanza I.R. 48–57.

de la Bédòyere, G. 2001: *Eagles over Britannia: The Roman Army in Britain*, Stroud.

De Moor, A.G., and Fluck, C. (eds.), 2007: *Methods of dating Ancient Textiles of the 1st Millenium AD from Egypt and Neighbouring Countries*, Tielt, Belgium.

Dersin, D. (ed.), 1997: *What life was like when Rome ruled the world*, Time Life.

Dorigo, W. 1971: *Late Roman Painting*, London.

Doro, L. 1971: *Antioch Mosaic Pavements*, Rome.

Doxiadis, E. 1995: *The Mysterious Fayoum Portraits*, London.

Driel-Murray, C. van 1985:'The production and supply of military leatherwork in the first and second centuries AD: A review of the archaeological evidence', in Bishop. M.C. (ed.), *The Production and Distribution of Roman Military Equipment: Proceedings of the Second Roman Military Equipment Research Seminar*, Oxford, BAR Int. Ser 275, 43–81.

Driel-Murray, C. van 1986a:'Leatherwork in the Roman Army, part one', *Exercitus* 2, 1. 1–6.

Driel-Murray, C.van 1986b: Leatherwork in the Roman Army, part two', *Exercitus* 2, 2, 23–7.

Driel-Murray, C. van 1987:'Roman footwear: A mirror of fashion and society', in *Recent Research in Archaeological Footwear*. Association of Archaeological Illustrators and Surveyors Technical Paper 8, 32–41.

Driel-Murray, C.van 1989(ed.): *Roman Military Equipment: The Sources of Evidence, Proceedings of the Fifth Roman Military Equipment Conference*, BAR Int. Ser. 476, Oxford.

Driel-Murray, C. van, Wild, J.P., Seaward, M. and Hillam, J., 1993: *Vindolanda Research Reports: Volume III The Early Wooden Forts, Preliminary reports on the Leather, Textiles, Environmental Evidence and Dendrochronology*, Bardon Mill, Hexham..

Driel-Murray, C. van 1995:'Gender in Question', *TRAC2*, Aldershot.

Driel-Murray, C. van 1998:'The leatherwork from the fort', in Cool. H.E.M., Philo. C. (eds.) *Roman Castleford Excavations 1974–85, I: Small Finds*, Yorkshire Archaeology 4, West Yorkshire Archaeology Service, 285–334.

Driel-Murray, C. van 2000:'A late Roman assemblage from Deurne, (Netherlands)', *Bonner Jahrbücher* 200, 293–308.

Driel-Murray, C. van 2001a:'Vindolanda and the dating of Roman Footwear', *Britannia* 32, 185–197.

Driel-Murray, C. van 2001b:'Footwear in the North-Western Provinces of the Roman Empire' in Goubitz, O., Driel-Murray, C. van & Waateringe, W.G-van. 2001: *Stepping Through Time: Archaeological Footwear from Prehistoric Times until 1800*, SPA Zwolle, 337–376.

Dunbabin, K.M.D. 1978: *The Mosaics of Roman North Africa*, Oxford.

Eastwood, G. 1983:'A Dirty Piece of Rag', *Popular Archaeology*, Jan 1983, 45–46.

Edge, D. and Paddock, J.M. 1988: *Arms and Armour of the Medieval Knight*, London.

El-Saghir, M., Golvin, J.C., Reddé, M., El-Sayed, H., and Wagner, G. 1986: *Le Camp Romain De Lougsor*, Cairo.

Embleton, G. 2000: *Medieval Military Costume Recreated in Colour Photographs*, Marlborough.

Emery, W.B. 1938: *The Royal Tombs of Ballana and Qustul*, Cairo.

Englehardt, C. 1863: *Thorsbjerg Mosefund*, Copenhagen.

Erikson, M. 1997: *Textiles in Egypt 200–1500 AD*. Gothenburg.

Feder, T.H. 1978: *Great Treasures of Pompeii and Herculaneum*, New York.

Fedri, M. 1965–1966:'Un Vêtement Islamique Ancien au Musée de Bardo' in *Africa* II.

Ferrua, A. 1990: *The Unknown Catacomb*, Florence.

Feugère, M. 2002: *Weapons of the Romans*, Stroud.

Fink, R.O. 1971: *Roman Military Records on Papyrus*, Case Western Reserve University.

Flower, H. 2001: 'A Tale of Two Monuments: Domitian, Trajan and some Praetorians at Puteoli', *AJA* 105, 625–48.

Fluck, C. and Vogelsang-Eastwood, G. (eds.), 2004, *Riding Costume in Egypt*, Leiden.

Forbes, R.J. 1966: *Studies in Ancient Technology*, Vol. V, Leiden.

Forbes, R.J. 1987: *Studies in Ancient Technology*, Vol. IV, Leiden.

Forrer, R. 1891: *Achmim-Panopolis, Die Gräber und Textilfunde*, Strassburg.

Forrestier, A. 1928: *The Roman Soldier*, London.

Fortes, J.B. and Arguin, A.R.M., 1999: 'New Evidence on the use of Armour by Roman Soldiers of the Fourth Century AD', *JRMES* 10, 21–26.

Fradier, G. and Martin, A. 1989: *Mosaïques Romaines de Tunise*, Tunis.

Frank, T. 1940: *An Economic Survey of Ancient Rome*, Baltimore.

Frauburg-Forrer, 1898: *Die Antiken und Frühmittelalterlichen, Bekleidungen aus Achmim-Panopolis*, Strassburg.

Frayn, J.M. 1984: *Sheep Rearing and the Wool Trade in Italy during the Roman Period*, Liverpool.

Fuentes, A. 1997: 'Le ville tardoromane in Hispania', in various, *Hispania Romana, da terre di conquista a Provincia dell'Impero,* Martellago.

Fuentes, N. 1987: 'The Roman Military Tunic', in Dawson, M. (ed.), *Roman Military Equipment: The Accoutrements of War, Proceedings of the Third Military Research Seminar; British Archaeological Report*, Int Ser 336, Oxford. p. 41–75

Garlick, M. 1980: 'The reconstruction and use of a *lorica hamata*', *Exercitus* 1, 6–8.

Gawlikowski, M. 2005: 'Palmyra', *Current World Archaeology* Vol. 1, No. 12, 26–32.

Gayet, A. 1905: 'L'Exploration des Nécropoles Gréco – Byzantines d'Antinoe' in Fouilles d'Antinoe, 1904–1905 Catalogue, Paris.

Gebühr, M. 2001: *Nydam and Thorsberg: Iron Age Places*, Schleswig.

Gelba, M. 2004: 'Linen production in pre-Roman and Roman Italy' in Alfaro, C., Wild, J.P., and Costa, B. (eds.) 2004, 29–37.

Gervers, V. 1983: 'Medieval Garments in the Mediterranean World', in Harte, N.B. and Ponting, K.G. (eds) 1983: *Cloth and Clothing in Medieval Europe: Essays in Memory of Professor E.M. Carus-Wilson*, Aldershot, 279–315.

Goette, H.R. 1988: 'Mulleus-Embas-Calceus', *Jahrbüch des Deutschen Archäologischen Instituts* 103, 401–464.

Goldman, N. 1994: 'Roman Footwear', in Sebesta and Bonfante 1994, 101–29.

Goldsworthy, A. 2000: *Roman Warfare*, London.

Göpfrich, J. 1986: 'Römische Lederunde aus Mainz'. *Saalburg Jahrbuch* 42, 1986, 5–65.

Graber, A. 1966: *L Età d'oro di Giustiniano*, Milan.

Grabar, A. 1967: *L'arte Paleocristiana*, Milan.

Granger-Taylor, H. 1982: 'Weaving Clothes to shape in the Ancient World: The Tunic and Toga of the Arringatore, *Textile History* 13, 3–25.

Granger-Taylor, H. 2007: 'Weaving clothes to shape in the Ancient World 25 years on: Corrections and further details with particular reference to the cloaks from Lahun', *ATN* 45, 26–35.

Granger-Taylor, H. 2008: 'A fragmentary Roman Cloak probably of the 1st CE and off cuts from other semicircular cloaks', *ATN* 46, 6–16.

Grilli, A. 1990: 'Civiltà delle lettere, in various, *Roma e L'Italia, radices imperii*, Milan.

Grimal, P. 1963: *The Civilisation of Rome*, London.

Guilbert, F. 2004: *Le Soldat Romain à la Fin de la République et sous le Haut-Empire*. Paris.

Guilbert, F. 2006: *Légionnaries et Auxiliaires sous le Haut-Empire Romain*, Paris.

Hack, B. 1967: *I mosaici di Santa Maria Maggiore in Roma*, Baden.

Hadas, M. 1966: *Imperial Rome*, Time Life Books, Amsterdam.

Haines, T., Sumner G. and Naylor, J. 2000: 'Recreating the World of the Roman Soldier: The work of the Ermine Street Guard', *JRMES* 11, 119–27.

Handley, F.J.L. 2004: 'Quseir-Al- Qadim 2003: The Textiles', *ATN* 38, 27–30.

Harlow, M., 2005, 'Dress in the Historia Augusta: The role of Dress in Historical Narrative', in Cleland, L. (ed.) 2005, 143–153.

Hartley, E. *et al* (eds.), 2006: *Constantine The Great: York's Roman Emperor*, York.

Haseloff, A. 1898: *Codex Purpureus Rossanensis*, Berlin-Leipzig.

Hassal, M.W.C., and Ireland, R., 1979, *De Rebus Bellicis*' BAR Int. Ser. 63, Oxford.

Hoddinott, R. F. 1963: *Early Byzantine churches in Macedonia and South Serbia*, London.

Hoevenburg, J. 1993: 'Leather Artefacts' in Van Dierendonck, R.M., Hallewas, D.P., and Waugh, K.E. *The Valkenburg Excavations 1985–1988*, Amersfoort.

Hoskins, N.A. 2004: *The Coptic Tapestry Albums and the Archaeologist of Antinoé, Albert Gayet*, Seattle.

Houston, M.G. 1947: *Ancient Greek Roman and Byzantine Costume and Decoration*, London.

Hubert, J., Porcher, J. and Volbach, W.F. 1968: *L'Europa delle invasioni barbariche*, Milan.

Iacovidis, S.E. 1988: *Micene, Epidauruo, Argo, Tiranto, Nauplia.* Athens.

Ilan, Z., and Damati, I. 1984: 'Notes and News. Kh. Marus, 1983 and 1983', *Israel Exploration Journal.* 34.

James, S.P. 1999: 'The community of the soldiers: A major identity and centre of power in the Roman Empire', *TRAC* 98, Oxford, 14–25.

James, S.P. 2004: *Excavations at Dura-Europos 1928–1937, Final Report VII: The Arms and Armour and other Military Equipment*, British Museum.

Jobst, W. and Behçet, E. 1997: *The Great Palace Mosaic*, Istanbul.

Johnson, J, De M. (ed.), 1915: *Catalogue of the Greek Papyri in The John Rylands Library Manchester Vol. II,* Manchester.

Jones, A.H.M. 1973: *The Later Roman Empire,* Oxford.

Jørgensen, L., Storgaard, B., and Thomsen, L.G. (eds.) 2003: *The Spoils of Victory – The North in the Shadow of the Roman Empire,* National Museum, Copenhagen.

Junkelmann, M. 1990: *Die Reiter Roms, Teil I,* Mainz.

Junkelmann, M. 1991: *Die Reiter Roms, Teil II,* Mainz.

Junkelmann, M. 1992: *Die Reiter Roms, Teil III,* Mainz.

Junkelmann, M. 1996: *Reiter Wie Statuen aus Erz,* Mainz.

Kalavrezou-Maxeiner, I. 1975: 'The Imperial Chamber at Luxor', *D.O.P.* 29, Washington, 227–251.

Keppie, L.J.F. 1979: *Roman Distance Slabs from the Antonine Wall,* Glasgow.

Keppie, L.J.F. and Arnold, B.J. 1984: *Corpus Signorum Imperii Romani, Gt Britain, Vol. 1, FASC 4: Scotland,* Oxford.

King, A. 1982: *Archaeology of Ancient Rome,* Connecticut.

King, D. 1996: 'Roman and Byzantine Dress in Egypt', *Costume* 30. 1–15.

Kiss, Z. 1996: 'Harpocrate-Héron: A propos d'une figurine en terre cuite du Musée National de Varsoie', in Bailey, D.M. (ed.), *'Archaeological Research' in Roman Egypt',* Ann Arbor.

Kybalová, L. 1967: *Coptic Textiles,* Prague.

La Rocca, E. 1990: 'Linguaggio artistico e ideologia politica a Roma in età Repubblicana' in Various, *Roma e L'Italia, radices imperii,* Milan, 287–495; 299, fig. 112.

Leguilleoux, M. 2004: *Le Cuir et la Pelleterie á l'Epoque romaine,* Paris.

Lenzen, V.F. 1960: *The Triumph of Dionysos on Textiles of late Antique Egypt,* University of California Press, Vol. 5, No. 1.

Leroy, J. 1964: *Les Manuscripts Syriaques à Peintures,* Paris.

Lewis, N. 1983: *Life in Egypt under Roman Rule,* Oxford.

Liberati, A.M. 1997: 'Navigare con gli antichi', *Archeo* 8.

Lindenschmit, L., 1882: *Tracht und Bewaffnung des römischen Heeres während der Kaiserzeit,* Braunschweig.

López, G.R. 1997: 'Items of personal clothing in *Barceno* (4th to 7th Centuries)', in de Heredia Bercero J.B., Bonnet, C., Alaix, C.M., López, G. R. and de Llanza I.R. 1997.

Maiuri, A.1953: *The Great Centuries of Painting: Roman Painting,* Cleveland.

MacConnoran, P. 1986: 'Footwear', in Millar, L., Schofield, J & Rhodes, M. (eds.) 'The Roman Quay at St Magnus House, London. Excavations at New Fresh Wharf, Lower Thames Street, London, 1974–78, *L&MAS.* Special Paper 8 London, 218–226.

Mannering, U. 2000: 'Roman Garments from Mans Claudianus', in Cardon, D., and Feugère, M. 2000, 283–290.

Mannering, U. 2006: 'Questions and answers on textiles and their find spots: The Mons Claudianus Textile Project', in S.Schrenk (ed.), *Textiles in Situ: their Find Spots in Egypt and Neighbouring Countries in the First Millenium CE',* Riggisberg 2006, 149–159.

Mano-Zisi, D. 1955: 'Le Castrum de Gamzigrad et ses Mosaiques', *Archaeologica Iugoslavia,* VI.

Maxfield, V.A & Peacock, D.P.S. 2001: *Survey and Excavation at Mons Claudianus 1987–1993* II, Excavations: Part 1. Institut Français d'Archéologie Orientale.

Mc Dowall, S. 2001: *Adrianople AD 378,* Oxford.

Mc Whirr, A. 1982: *Roman Crafts and Industries,* Princes Risborough.

Meyboom, P.G.P. 1995: *The Nile Mosaic of Palestrina,* New York.

Moeller, W.O. 1973: 'Infectores and Offectores at Pompeii', *Latomus* 32, 368–9.

Moeller, W.O. 1976: *The Wool Trade of Ancient Pompeii,* Leiden.

Moller-Wiering, S. 2006: 'The Bog Body from Obenaltendorf', *ATN* 43, 9–12.

Moller-Wiering, S., Andraschko, F.M., Kraus, B., and Meller, B., (eds.), 2007: 'Italienische Mode im Stader Moor?' in *Archäologie Zwischen Befund und Rekonstruktion,* Hamburg, 247–263.

Monneret De Villard, U. 1953: 'The Temple of the Imperial Cult at Luxor', *Archaeologia* 95, 85–105.

Moreno, P. 1997, 'Le forche caudine', *Archeo,* Anno Xiii, n.6 (148), Giugno.

Moscati, S. 1982: 'L'italia riscoperta 7', in *Storia Illustrata,* n. 291, February 1982.

Mould, Q. 1997: 'Leather', in Wilmott, T. *Birdoswald. Excavations of a Roman Fort on Hadrian's Wall and its Successor Settlements: 1987–92,* English Heritage Archaeological Reports 14, 326–41.

Neal, D.S. and Cosh, S.R. 2002: *The Roman Mosaics of Britain: vol 1. Northern Britain,* London.

Nicole, D. 1992: *Romano-Byzantine Armies 4th – 9th Centuries,* London.

Norkert, M. 1991: *The Högum Find and other Migration Period Textiles and Costumes in Scandinavia,* Umeå.

Olson, K. 2003: 'Roman Underwear Revisited', *Classical World* 96.2, 201–310.

Padre Carmelo Capizzi, S.J. and Galati, F. *Piazza Armerina, The Mosaics and Morgantina,* Italcards, Bologna.

Parlasca, K. 1977–1980: 'Ritratti di Mummie', in Adriani (ed.), *Repertorio d'Arte dell'Egitto Greco-Romano,* 2 ser. I (Palermo 1969), II, III, Rome.

Pausch, M. 2003: *Die Römische Tunika,* Wißner-Verlag.

Pavia, C. 1999: *Mitrei di Roma Antica,* Rome.

Pavo, C. 1999: *Guido dei Mitrei di Roma Antica,* Gangerni Editore, Rome.

Perkins, A. 1973: *The Art of Dura Europos,* Oxford.

Peterson, D. 1992: *The Roman Legions Recreated in Colour Photographs,* London.

Pfister, R. and Bellinger, L. 1945: *The Excavations at Dura-Europos, Final Report IV.2 The Textiles,* New Haven.

Piccirillo, M. 1993: *I Mosaici di Giordania,* Amman.

Polidori, R. 1999: *Libya: The Lost Cities of the Roman Empire*, Cologne.

Pritchard, F., 2006: *Clothing Culture: Dress in Egypt in the First Millennium AD*, University of Manchester.

Rankov, B. 1994: *The Praetorian Guard*, London.

Rankov, B. 'Now you see it, now you don't, The British Fleet in Vegetius N.37', Limes XVIII.

Rassart-Debergh, M. 1993: 'Quelques saints militaries dans la peinture copte et leur antécédents' in Vallet, F. and Kazanski, M. *L'Armée Romaine et les barbares, du IIIe au VII eme siècle*, St Germain en Layes.

Rausing, G. 1987: 'Barbarian Mercenaries or Roman Citizens?' *Fornvännen* 82, 126–131.

Ravegnani, G. 1989a: *La Corte di Giustinianea*, Rome.

Ravegnani, G. 1989b: *Soldati di Bysanzio in età Giustinianea*, Rome.

Robertson, A., 1975, Scott, M. & Keppie, L., *Bar Hill, a Roman Fort and its Finds*. BAR 16 Oxford.

Roche-Bernard, G. and Ferdiere, A. 1993: *Costumes et Textiles en Gaul Romaine*, Paris.

Rouveret, A. 1997, 'Chefs d'oeuvre de la lucanienne', in *L'Archeologue*, 31, August/September, 10–19.

Russell Robinson, H. 1975: *The Armour of Imperial Rome*, London.

Rutschowscaya, M.H. 1990: *Tissus Coptes*, Paris.

Rutschowscaya, M.H. 1992: *La peinture copte*, Paris.

Rutt, R., 1987, *A History of Hand Knitting*, London.

Sander, E. 1963: 'Die Kleidung des Römischen Soldaten', *Historia* 12, 144–166.

Santrot, J., 2001: *Au Fil du Nil*, Musée Dobrée, Nantes.

Schlabow, K. 1976: *Textilfunde der Eisenzeit in Norddeutschland*, Neumünster.

Schug-Wille, C. 1970: *L'arte bizantina*, Milan.

Seagroatt, M. 1965: *Coptic Weaves*, Merseyside County Museums, Liverpool.

Sebesta, J.L. and Bonfante, L. 1994: *The World of Roman Costume*, Wisconsin.

Sekunda, N., 1995: *The Ptolemaic Army*, Stockport.

Sekunda, N., 1996: *Republican Roman Army 200–104 BC*, London.

Sekunda, N. and Northwood, S., 1995: *Early Roman Armies*, London.

Shaw, T. 1982a: 'Roman Cloaks part 1', *Exercitus* 1.4.

Shaw, T. 1982b: 'Roman Cloaks part 2', *Exercitus* 1.5.

Sheffer, A. and Granger-Taylor, H. 1994: 'The Textiles': in E. Netzer (ed.), *Masada IV, Final Reports*, Jerusalem.

Sheridan, J.A. 1998: *Colombia Papyrus IX: The Vestis Militaris Codex*, Atalanta.

Shore, A.F. 1972: *Portrait Painting from Roman Egypt*, London.

Simkins, M. 1984: *The Roman Army from Caesar to Trajan* (Revised Ed.), London.

Simonsen, J. 1996: *Daubjergmanden*, Skive Museum.

Southern, P and Dixon, K.R., 1996: *The Late Roman Army*, London.

Speidel, M.P. 1994: *Riding for Caesar, The Roman Emperor's Horse Guard*, London.

Speidel, M.P. 1996: 'Late Roman Military Decorations I: Neck and Wristbands', *Ant Tard* 4, 235–243.

Speidel, M.P. 1997: 'Late Roman military Decorations II: gold-embroidered capes and tunic', *Ant Tard* 5, 231–237.

Speidel. M.P. 2007: 'The Missing Weapons at Carlisle' *Britannia* 38 p.237–39..

Stephenson, I.P. 1995: 'Thoracomachus', *Arbeia Journal*, Vol. IV, 35–44.

Stephenson, I.P. 1999: *Roman Infantry Equipment: The Later Empire*, Stroud.

Stephenson, I.P. and Dixon, K.R. 2003: *Roman Cavalry Equipment*, Stroud.

Stephenson, I.P. 2006: *Romano-Byzantine Infantry Equipment*, Stroud.

Stevenson, J. 1978: *The Catacombs*, London.

Strong, D. & Brown, D. (eds.) 1976: *Roman Crafts*. London..

Strong, E., 1923: *La Scultura Romano da Augusto a Constantino*, Florence.

Sumner, G. 1997: *Roman Army: Wars of the Empire*, London.

Sumner, G. 2002: *Roman Military Clothing 1*, Oxford.

Sumner, G. 2003: *Roman Military Clothing 2*, Oxford.

Swift, E. 2003: *Roman Dress Accessories*, Princes Risborough.

Szilagyi, J. 1956: *Aquincum*, Budapest.

Talbot, R. 1958: *The Great Palace of the Byzantine Emperors*, Edinburgh.

Tarradell, N. 1969: *Arte Romano en España*, Barcelona.

Taylor, G.W. 1990: 'Reds and purples: from the classical world to pre-conquest Northern Britain', Walton, P., and Wild, J.P., *Textiles in Archaeology, Nesat III*, London, 37–46.

Thomas, T.K. 2001: *Textiles from Karanis, Egypt, in the Kelsey Museum of Archaeology, Artifacts of Everyday Life*, Ann Arbor.

Thurman C.C.M. and Williams, B. 1979: *Ancient Textiles from Nubia*, Chicago.

Tomlin, R.S.O., 1998: 'Roman Manuscripts from Carlisle: the ink written tablets', *Britannia* 29, 31–84.

Τηεολογου, M. 1995: *The Sanctuary of Saint Demetrios of Thessaloniki*, Thessaloniki.

Torelli, M. 1982: *Typology and Structure of Roman Historical Reliefs*, Michigan.

Torp, H. 1963: *Mosaikene i St Georg-Rotunden i Thessaloniki*, Oslo.

Toynbee, J.M.C. 1962: *Art in Roman Britain*, London.

Turner, R.C., Rhodes, M. and Wild, J.P. 1991: 'The Roman Body Found on Grewelthorpe Moor in 1850: A Reappraisal', *Britannia* 22, 191–201.

Ubl, H.J. 1989: 'Was trug der Römische Soldat unter dem Cingulum?' in van Driel-Murray 1989: 61–74.

Ubl. H.J. 2006:'Was trug der romische Soldat unter dem Panzer', *Bayerische Vorgeschichtbaltter 71*, 261–76.

Vallet-Kazanski, 1993: *L'Armée Romaine et les barbares du IIIe au VIIe siècle*, Paris.

Van Waateringe, G. 1967: *Romeins Lederwerk vit Valkenburg*, Groningen.

Vanags, P., 1983: *The Glory that was Pompeii,* New York.

Vermaseren, M.J. and Van Essen, C.C. 1965: *The Excavations in the Mithraeum of the Church of Santa Prisca in Rome*, Leiden.

Vermaseren, M.J. 1971: *Mithriaca I: The Mithraeum at S. Maria Capua Vetere*, Leiden.

Ville, G., 1965–1966:'Recherches sur le costume dans l'Afrique Romaine – le pantaloon', in *Africa* II, 139–181.

Walker, S. and Bierbrier, M. 1997: *Ancient Faces, Mummy Portraits from Roman Egypt*, London.

Walton, P. and Taylor, G.W. 1991:'The characterisation of dyes in textiles from archaeological excavations', *Chromatography and Analysis*, 17 (June 1991), 5–7.

Walton, P. 1994:'Wools and Dyes in northern Europe in the Roman Iron Age', *Fasciculi Archaeologiae Historicae*, 6, 61–8.

Walton-Rogers, P., Bender Jørgensen, L. and Rast-Eicher, A., (eds.), 2001: *The Roman Textile Industry and its Influence: A birthday tribute to John Peter Wild*, Oxford.

Walton Rogers P. 2007: *Cloth and Clothing in Early Anglo-Saxon England AD 450–700*, York.

Waterer, J.W. 1976:'Leatherwork' in: Strong, D. and Brown, D. (eds.), 179–193.

Watson, G.R., 1985: *The Roman Soldier*, London.

Werner, P., 1977: *Life in Rome in Ancient Times*, Fribourg.

Wickoff, F. 1895: *Die Wiener Genesis*, Vienna.

Wild, J.P. 1963:'The Byrrus Britannicus', *Antiquity* XXXVII, 193–202.

Wild, J.P. 1964:'The Caracallus', *Latomus* XX III, 532–36.

Wild, J.P. 1967:'Römische Textilreste im Saalburgmuseum', *Saalburg – Jahrbuch* XXIV, 77–8.

Wild, J.P. 1967:'The Gynaeceum at Venta and its Context', *Latomus* XXVI, 648–76.

Wild, J.P. 1968:'Clothing in the North-West Provinces of the Roman Empire', *B.J.* 168, 166–240.

Wild, J.P. 1970:'Button and Loop fasteners in the Roman Provinces', *Britannia* 1, 137–155.

Wild, J.P. 1970: *Textile Manufacture in the Northern Roman Provinces*, Cambridge..

Wild, J.P. 1976:'Textiles', in Strong, D. and Brown, D. (eds.), London, 167–177.

Wild, J.P. 1979:'Fourth Century Underwear with special Reference to the Thoracomachus', in Hassale and Ireland (eds.), *De Re Rebus Bellicis*, (BAR S63), 105–10.

Wild, J.P. 1981:'Some new light on Roman Textiles', in Bender Jørgensen, L., and Tidow, K. (eds.), Textilsymposium Neumünster: Archäologische Textilefunde: 6.6 – 8.5, 1981, Neumünster, 10–24.

Wild, J.P. 1982:'Wool Production in Roman Britain', in Miles, D., (eds.), *The Romano-British Countryside,* BAR Brit Ser 103(i), 109–22.

Wild, J.P. 1988:'Clothes from the Roman Empire: Barbarians and Romans', in Bender Jørgensen, L., Magnus, B., and Munksgaard, E., (eds.), *Archaeological Textiles: Report from the 2nd NESAT Symposium 1–4. V*, 1984, Arkaeologiske Skrifte 2, Copenhagen, 65–98.

Wild, J.P. 1985:'The Clothing of Britannia Gallia Belgica and Germania Inferior', *ANRW* II, 12,3 Berlin, 362–422.

Wild, J.P. 1986:'Bath and the Identification of the Caracalla', *Britannia* 17, 352–353.

Wild, J.P. 1988: *Textiles in Archaeology*, Princes Risborough.

Wild, J.P. 1992:'Vindolanda 1985–1989: First thoughts on new finds', in Bender Jørgensen, L. and Munksgaard, E., (eds.), *Archaeological Textiles in Northern Europe: Report from the 4th NESAT Symposium 1–5 May, 1990, in Copenhagen,* Tidens Tand 5, Copenhagen, 66–74.

Wild, J.P. 1993:'The Textiles' in van Driel-Murray (*et al*) 1993, 76–90.

Wild, J.P. 1994:'A hair moss cap from Vindolanda', in G. Jaacks, Tidow, K., (eds.), *Archäologische Textilfunde, Archaeological Textiles: Textilsymposium Neumünster, NESAT V, 4.–7.5*, 1993, Neumünster, 61–8.

Wild, J.P. and Wild, F.C., 1995:'The Textiles' in Sidebotham, S.E., and Wendrich W.Z., Berenike, (eds), *Berenike 1995: Preliminary Report of the 1995 Excavations at Berenike and the Survey of the Eastern Desert*, Research School CNWS, Leiden, 245–256.

Wild, J.P. and Wild, F.C. m1996:'Berenike', *ATN* 22, 20–21.

Wild, J.P. 2002:'The Textile Industries of Roman Britain', *Britannia* 33, 1–42.

Wild, J.P. 2004:'The Roman textile industry: problems but progress', in Alfaro, C., Wild, J.P., and Costa, B., (eds.), 23–27.

Wilpert, J. 1903: *La pittura delle catacombe Romane*, Rome.

Wilson, A. 2004:'Archaeological Evidence for Textile Production and Dyeing in Roman North Africa', in Alfaro, C., Wild, J.P., and Costa, B., (eds.), 155–164.

Wilson, L.M. 1924: *The Roman Toga*, Baltimore.

Wilson, L.M. 1933: *Ancient Textiles from Egypt in the University of Michigan Collection*, Ann Arbor.

Wilson, R.J.A. 1983: *Piazza Armerina*, London.

Wood, R. and Wheeler, M. 1966: *Roman Africa in Colour*, London.

Woods, D. 1998:'Two notes on Late Roman Military Equipment', *JRMES* 9, 31–35.

Xeroutsikou, L. and Despyris, G. 1997: Chios, Oinousses-Psara, *The fragrant island*, Athens.

Yadin, Y. 1963: *The Finds from the Bar Kokhba Period in the Cave of the Letters,* Jerusalem.

Youtie, H.C. and Winter, J.G. (eds.), 1951: *Michigan Papyri, Vol. VIII, Papyri and Ostraca from Karanis*, Ann Arbor.

INDEX